ISRAELI POLITICS
IN THE 1990s

ISRAELI POLITICS
IN THE 1990s

Key Domestic and
Foreign Policy Factors

Edited by
BERNARD REICH
and
GERSHON R. KIEVAL

Contributions in Political Science, Number 285

Bernard K. Johnpoll, Series Editor

Greenwood Press
New York • Westport, Connecticut • London

Library of Congress Cataloging-in-Publication Data

Israeli politics in the 1990s : key domestic and foreign policy
    factors / edited by Bernard Reich and Gershon R. Kieval.
        p.   cm.—(Contributions in political science, ISSN 0147–1066 ;
    no. 285)
    Includes bibliographical references and index.
    ISBN 0–313–27349–9 (alk. paper)
    1. Israel—Politics and government.   I. Reich, Bernard.
    II. Kieval, Gershon R.   III. Series.
    JQ1825.P3I878   1991
    956.9405′4—dc20   91–3935

British Library Cataloguing in Publication Data is available.

Library of Congress Catalog Card Number: 91–3935
ISBN: 0–313–27349–9
ISSN: 0147–1066

First published in 1991

Greenwood Press, 88 Post Road West, Westport, CT 06881
An imprint of Greenwood Publishing Group, Inc.

Printed in the United States of America

The paper used in this book complies with the
Permanent Paper Standard issued by the National
Information Standards Organization (Z39.48–1984).

10 9 8 7 6 5 4 3 2 1

Contents

Tables

Preface

The evolution of political life in Israel introduced two new terms into the Israeli political lexicon in the mid–1980s. One was the concept of rotation, and it was directly linked to the second, that of power-sharing.

From 1948 to 1977, as prior to independence, Labor was the dominant political party in Israel. In 1977 Likud supplanted Labor as the party in power but did not dominate the scene as Labor had done earlier. Over the ensuing years, Likud under Menachem Begin slowly established itself as a major political force while in power. Yitzhak Shamir continued the pattern, albeit briefly, following Begin's sudden resignation in 1983. By the election of 1984 the two major parties seemed to be roughly in equal balance at the center of the political system. The election results therefore required a new variant of the old system. A national unity government (NUG) in which Labor and Likud would share power, based on the general concept utilized during the crisis accompanying the 1967 war, was developed but with the twist of a rotation of Shimon Peres and Yitzhak Shamir in the positions of prime minister and foreign minister. The national unity government with the power-sharing and rotation concepts lasted its full term despite numerous forces attempting to terminate its tenure and more numerous projections of its downfall. The jockeying for power between the left half of the center and the right half of the center continued in the election campaign of 1988. But, the election results were not very much more conclusive than in 1984. The concepts of a coalition government and some form of power-sharing continued, although Likud emerged as the dominant factor in the new government and no rotation was required—Shamir was to remain as prime minister for the duration of the tenure of the government. Peres became finance minister. The fall of that government in the spring of 1990 became something of a test of the centrist parties' strengths. Although Labor, led by Peres, was able to bring down the government and to secure a mandate to form a new one, it was Shamir who ultimately proved able to form a new government. This was not a national unity government composed of the two major parties at the political center but rather a Likud-right-religious coalition in which Likud would be the dominant partner that would have to share only some of the power with a grouping of parties that was close to it in position on the central foreign policy and security issues facing the state.

The Likud-right-religious government established in June 1990 was labelled by many as a government even more to the right and more hard-line than that established in 1977 by Begin. In fact, the new government was an outgrowth of the trends in Israeli politics since the mid-1970s and should not have been seen as a particularly hard-line, right-wing government but rather as one that reflected the sentiments and perspectives of large segments of the Israeli population.

Israel entered the decade of the 1990s as a mature country facing a series of critical issues and problems with a divided body politic. The long-term and central issues facing the Israeli political system were not resolved by the elections of 1988 or by the subsequently established government. The fall of that government in the spring of 1990, due to an unprecedentedly successful motion of no-confidence, pointed to the division within the government and the country on the process by which peace might be achieved. Israelis remain united on the need and desire for peace but disagree vehemently on the best methods and policies to achieve it. In a similar way Israelis agree on the goal, central to Zionist thought and practice, of ingathering the exiles (that is, promoting immigration for distressed Jews everywhere), despite the problems thus created by rapid influx of Soviet Jews (and the questionable religious status of some of them). But there were wide debates on how best to achieve that objective without placing existing Israelis in a disadvantaged position.

The debates over these and other issues raised questions about the nature of politics in Israel in the 1990s. Is there, as some have suggested, an inexorable movement toward the right of center in Israeli politics? Can Labor recapture its dominance? Is Likud the party of the future? Is Israel fated to have a right-of-center or right-religious leadership in the future? What are the dynamics of Likud and its "natural" political allies—the small right-of-center allies—especially as the leadership generation begins to be replaced by a newer cadre. Leadership remains an important and interesting question. As the leadership of the 1970s and

1980s begins to depart the political scene all of the parties will need to identify new leaders and then seek to promote them to national prominence. Already in 1990 this question has emerged with challenges to both Shamir and Peres within their own parties (albeit in Labor primarily by Yitzhak Rabin of his own generation). Peres and Shamir both retained their leadership of the parties and Shamir of the government, but within the early part of the decade shifts to other and younger politicians with different credentials and often different outlooks and different political constraints will take place in the parties and in Israeli national life.

A related matter is the question of political constituencies. What will the demographics of Israel foreordain in terms of the constituencies for and therefore the political successes of the various leaders and parties and policies? The decade of the 1990s promised to be different even before the massive Soviet immigration wave began under the policies of Mikhail Gorbachev in the Soviet Union. Clearly the growing size and influence of the Oriental Jewish community was a factor of considerable importance. But, at the same time, the implications of the retention of the occupied territories for the demographic balance and for the political future of the state also had to be weighed.

The perennial religious issue not only affects religious and political developments on the domestic scene but also raises questions about the relationships between Israeli political parties and groups and prominent Jewish leaders abroad. This cuts two ways: Jewish religious leadership abroad was concerned that as the religious parties gained strength they would seek to alter the religious status quo thus potentially affecting the sizeable numbers of Jews in Israel and abroad who were less religious in orientation and practice. At the same time, there was concern about the roles played by a small number of distinguished rabbis, some residing outside Israel, who could sway (if not command) Israeli political figures and political parties to move in a particular way. Among the religious issues was the question of the religious groups forming a cohesive bloc— or would they, like their secular counterparts, be caught in a cycle of splits and mergers of political groups and parties thereby dissipating their strength? Will the religious parties continue to be central to the formation of government coalitions as they have been in the first four decades of the state and thereby continue to gain disproportionate strength to promote their own political programs? The 1988 election and the 1990 political crisis highlighted the religious factor as a consequence of the special roles played by several distinguished rabbis (*rebbes*) in Israel and abroad.

In the decade of the 1990s the Arab-Israeli conflict—with its *intifada* component and affected by the Iraqi invasion of Kuwait and the resultant "new" Middle East that emerged from the Gulf crisis—and the peace process will remain at the core of Israeli politics and foreign and security policy concerns. At the same time, there will be a growing interaction between domestic politics and foreign policy issues. Many of these are direct outgrowths of past failures to come to grips with central issues; some have developed over time and became central only in the decade of the 1990s. The momentous decisions on these issues may well be made by the electorate in its votes for members of the Knesset, but many of the decisions will be made in the halls of government or in the Knesset. The parties and their leaders will be crucial in developing the positions on the major issues, and they, in turn, will determine the nature and direction of the state's response.

Acknowledgments

As before, Mim Vasan, senior editor for the social and behavioral sciences at Greenwood Press, and Alicia Merritt, our production editor, have been instrumental in ensuring the transformation of our manuscript into the final product presented here. To them goes our gratitude for their invaluable assistance.

We dedicate this book to our dear wives and children who have borne with us throughout the conceptualization and completion of this analysis of contemporary Israeli politics.

1

Introduction: The Changing Center in Israeli Politics

Gershon R. Kieval and Bernard Reich

More than a decade and three elections have passed since the electoral "earthquake" (*hamahapach*) of May 18, 1977—the day Israeli voters ended the Labor party's multidecade dominance of Israeli and Yishuv (the Jewish community in Palestine before independence) politics and put Menachem Begin, the then perennial outsider, and his Likud bloc into power. The nostalgic yearnings of Labor party strategists notwithstanding, the outcome of the 1977 parliamentary election was not an aberration. Indeed, it underscored the fundamental transformation of Israeli politics that was already well under way, which was eroding Labor's decades-long hold on the Israeli political scene and especially its political center.

Subsequent Knesset elections have confirmed the trend that was revealed in 1977. Likud has established its place at the center of Israeli politics, and Labor has been unable to challenge effectively its rival's growing strength. The precise location of the new center of Israeli politics has varied over time. From 1984 to 1990 it was somewhere to the left of where it was during the heyday of Likud rule under Begin (1977–83) and even under Yitzhak Shamir (1983–84). Over time Likud became a less doctrinaire and more pragmatic party, probably as a consequence of assuming power and having to face daily decisions requiring responsible policies. Israeli voting patterns indicate that Likud's hold on the center will not be a short-lived phenomenon. Shamir's success in forming a Likud–right-of-center–religious party coalition in June 1990, after an earlier vote of no-confidence and the failure of Shimon Peres to capitalize on the loss, further illustrates this factor and suggests that the new center of Israeli politics has moved somewhat more to the right than it was previously.

Likud was established in 1973 as a political bloc composed of the GAHAL alliance (Herut and Liberals); the La'am alliance (the State List and the Free Center); Achdut (a one-man faction in the Knesset); and Shlomzion, Ariel Sharon's former political party. By the time of the 1988 Knesset election, Likud was essentially a coalition of four smaller parties that ran together on one list: Herut, Liberals, Ometz, and TAMI (Movement for a Traditional Israel). Likud today is a party rich in young political figures of which a significant number are of Oriental background.

The background of Likud is the Herut party which comprises some 60 percent of the Likud election list. Herut was founded and dominated until his retirement by Menachem Begin and was built around him. It was his personality, as well as his interpretation of Vladimir Zeev Jabotinsky's ideology, that gave the party its shape.

Herut, a nationwide grass-roots political movement, has branches throughout Israel through which the election campaign is run. There are some 2,000 central committee members who select the Herut candidates for the Knesset and decide where they will appear on the election list. Central committee members are chosen because of their involvement in the movement or their allegiance to a particular person or faction in the party. Individuals in these desirable positions decide who will lead the party and who will represent them in the Knesset. Thus, committee members tend to form the constituencies of the Members of the Knesset (MKs).

Within the Herut component there are three major camps: Shamir-Arens, Levy, and Sharon. Both MKs and central committee members generally identify with one of the three camps, although there are exceptions.

The Shamir camp, with from 50 to 60 percent of the membership, is the largest and generally considered to be the most intellectual; it has been described as a group of "pragmatic hawks." The largest number of Knesset members belong to this camp, and among them are the young rising stars, some of whom are referred to as "princes" of the party and some of whom come from distinguished Herut/Irgun families. The Shamir camp includes Moshe Arens, currently minister of defense; Benjamin (Bibi) Netanyahu, deputy foreign minister, former ambassador to the United Nations, and a protegé of Arens; Benjamin (Benny) Begin, an MK, a geologist, and the son of Menachem Begin; Minister of Justice Dan Meridor, the son of Yaacov Meridor; Minister of Health Ehud Olmert; Minister of Police Affairs Ronnie Milo; and Tzachi Hanegbi, the son of Geula Cohen of Tehiya, among others. Arens is seen as

Shamir's successor, and the group looks to Arens to lead them and to resolve internal disputes. Under Shamir this younger generation has been groomed for leadership and given important positions. Well-educated, they tend to be less ideological than the older generation of the party. Nevertheless, some are clearly identified with hard-line positions on the political right.

The Levy camp, led by Deputy Prime Minister and Minister of Foreign Affairs David Levy, is the second largest group with from 30 to 40 percent of the party stalwarts. This camp, which generally represents the Sephardic element in Herut, overall tends to be less educated than the Shamir camp. There is an intense rivalry, characterized by some as "hatred," between Arens' supporters and those of Levy. In the 1984 election, Arens allowed Levy to have the number two spot on the election list for the sake of party unity. Levy has threatened to upset the party if he does not secure his demands. Although Sharon and Levy do not like each other, they share a common antipathy to Arens and periodically, it is alleged, Levy and Sharon have combined efforts against Arens and even against Shamir. Among the MKs who support Levy are Minister of Economics and Planning David Magen, Ruby Rivlin, Yehoshua Matza, Ovadia Eli, and Shaul Amor.

The Sharon camp is the smallest of the three groups and is led by General (Res.) Ariel Sharon, currently minister of construction and housing. This camp probably comprises only several hundred at most (and no MKs), but they are drawn from the party hard-liners and they support Sharon's policies. They tend to be vocal and active.

The Liberal party component of Likud held 12 of Likud's 40 Knesset seats after the 1988 election. The Liberals had their own central committee which selects representatives to the Knesset, who are then placed on the Likud list. There has been constant bickering between Herut and the Liberals regarding how many candidates the Liberals should be allowed, and what positions they should have. To a great extent, because of the control of Herut and Likud by Menachem Begin, the Liberals have always been in a secondary status in the party and have not generated a major figure of national stature, with the exception of Yitzhak Moda'i, currently the minister of finance. The relationship between Herut and Likud has been regulated by the formal rules to which they agreed, but also by practical political accords and compromise.

In August 1988 Herut and the Liberals signed a merger agreement that technically put an end to the bickering and formally established a single party called "Likud—the National Liberal Movement." The idea was that the separate caucuses will cease, and candidates for the Knesset will be elected by a joint central committee of 3,000 members. This could foreshadow a complicated internal election process for party positions and the election list.

The Liberal party is divided into three camps, headed by Yitzhak Moda'i, Moshe Nissim, and Avraham Sharir. The largest camp belongs to party leader Moda'i. Following the 1988 election, Moda'i became minister of economics, and Nissim became minister without portfolio. Sharir was excluded. Both positions were marginal, reflecting limited Liberal power in Likud and in the coalition. This was to play a role after the March 1990 vote of no-confidence and the subsequent efforts to form a coalition government. When the new Shamir government was formed in June 1990, Moda'i became minister of finance, and Nissim became deputy prime minister and minister of industry and trade.

ISRAELIS VOTE: LABOR OUT, LIKUD IN

Israeli national election results since 1977 highlight the Labor party's declining political fortunes and the Likud bloc's growth in voter popularity. As a result, the dominant party system that had characterized Israeli politics prior to 1977 was replaced by that of government-versus-opposition. Labor gained 24.6 percent of the vote in the 1977 election, 15 percentage points less than it won in 1973; its share of Knesset seats declined from 51 to 32. Likud won 33.4 percent of the vote, 3.2 percentage points greater than in 1973, and it gained four more seats in the Knesset. The two major parties increased their combined share of the seats in the Knesset at the expense of the smaller parties, but, like the Labor party, Likud was unable to gain a majority of seats in parliament, and a coalition government was required.

In Israel the 1977 election was seen by many observers as reflecting and foreshadowing substantial change as Menachem Begin and his Likud now formed the government and took control of Israel's bureaucracy. The parties constituting the Likud bloc, especially Begin's Herut party, had been serving as the opposition since independence, with the exception of their joining the "wall-to-wall" coalition government of national unity during the 1967 war crisis and remaining in it until their withdrawal in the summer of 1970, when they vocally opposed the government and criticized its programs, politics, and leadership. As a consequence of the 1977 election, Likud led the ruling coalition responsible for establishing and executing programs and policies for Israel. It sought to implement its own programs within the broad ideology developed decades earlier by Vladimir Zeev Jabotinsky. Once in power as prime minister, Begin found in Jabotinsky a source of inspiration and a guide for concrete policy, and he worked toward the implementation of Jabotinsky's vision.

The 1981 Knesset election was not conclusive in identifying a popular preference for Likud or Labor. Most of the electorate virtually divided its votes between the two blocs but awarded neither a majority of seats in parliament. Likud won 37.1 percent of the vote and 48 Knesset seats;

Labor's share was 36.6 percent of the vote and 47 seats. President Yitzhak Navon's assessment of the political balance led him to grant the mandate to form the new government to Begin, who succeeded in forming another Likud-led coalition. The election highlighted the political dimension of the ethnic issue as Likud secured the majority—probably about 70 percent—of the vote of the Oriental Jewish community, who are generally referred to as Sephardim (Israelis of Asian and African background), following the pattern of the previous election.[1]

Extensive Oriental support for Begin and Likud in 1981 must be seen as a desire to achieve change through support of a party and government perceived as sympathetic to the Oriental agenda. Begin's popularity in the Oriental community was a direct result of previous failures by political parties and movements within the Oriental community, his personal and political courting of the community even as opposition leader, and his responsiveness to their needs and demands during his first administration. This support of Begin and Likud, an apparent identification of a political "home," to a significant degree came instead of an effective independent Oriental political organization, although both TAMI in 1981 and 1984 and SHAS (Sephardi Torah Guardians) in 1984 were able to draw some voters to Oriental-based political movements. Oriental voters saw Likud as the party best able to assist them to emerge from their second-class status, partly because it was clearly in the mainstream of political life.

The second Begin government (1981–83) had only a narrow margin in parliament, but the prime minister was able to maintain that control despite the traumatic events associated with the war in Lebanon and major economic problems. Begin, personally, was a popular politician with strong charismatic appeal to broad sections of the populace, and he was an able and skilled political leader, in much the same manner as David Ben-Gurion[2] and Golda Meir.[3] He remained popular and powerful until his resignation from office in the fall of 1983—a decision he chose and was not forced to make.[4] His foreign minister, Yitzhak Shamir,[5] a relative newcomer to politics and to Likud, replaced him. The short-lived Shamir government was virtually the same as its predecessor in personalities, and Shamir pursued, to the extent possible, a policy of continuity.[6]

The 1984 election results seemed partly to reflect a small but perceptible shift to the right in the electorate as a whole. Fifteen of the twenty-six political parties that contested the election obtained the minimum 1 percent of valid votes cast necessary to obtain a seat in parliament. The two major blocs were relatively close: the Labor Alignment secured 724,074 votes and 44 Knesset seats, and Likud secured 661,302 votes and 41 seats. Labor and its closest parliamentary allies together secured about the same number of seats they had held in the outgoing parliament. Likud lost some of its mandates, but Tehiya, to its right, gained seats. Meir Kahane's Kach party, after failure in previous elections, gained nearly 26,000 votes, the minimum required for one mandate. Kahane had campaigned on a theme of "making Israel Jewish again" by seeking the expulsion of the Arabs from Israel, as well as from the West Bank and Gaza. Initially, the party was banned from participation in the election by the Central Elections Committee, but its ruling was reversed by the supreme court—a move that gained the party additional publicity and probably facilitated its effort to secure a Knesset seat.

The vote of the Oriental Jewish community was once again associated with Likud and its allies to the right. It seemed to play a role in Kahane's victory, as well as in the rightward swing of the soldiers' vote and in the securing of the four seats gained by SHAS. The electoral success of SHAS apparently came at the expense of the more European-dominated "establishment" Agudat Israel (Association of Israel), which lost half of its seats, and TAMI.

The election results also underscored the widening gap between the extreme left and extreme right wings of the Israeli body politic. On the right, Kach advocated the expulsion of Arabs from Israel and the territories Israel occupied in the June 1967 war. On the left, the Arab-Jewish Progressive List for Peace and others accepted the Palestine Liberation Organization (PLO) as the legitimate representative of the Palestinians and advocated a Palestinian state in the West Bank and Gaza Strip alongside Israel. There were other signs of the increasing polarization of Israeli society. On the West Bank, extremists among Jewish settlers carried out a deadly campaign of intimidation against Palestinian Arabs, until the government cracked down in 1984. Meanwhile, in Tel Aviv, thousands of Israeli demonstrators protested Israel's continued presence in Lebanon following the 1982 war.

There were also more subtle signs of extremism, even among factions of the political mainstream, during the election campaign. Some politicians on the right described their challengers not as opponents but as traitors and implied that Labor's policy advocating an exchange of territory for peace was a prescription for the destruction of the state. The tone of the campaign was set by Likud's practice of calling itself the "national camp," with the implication that others were less than wholly patriotic. Likud newspaper advertisements showed a picture of PLO Chairman Yasir Arafat under the headline, "He wants Ma'arach," referring to the Hebrew acronym for the Labor Alignment. The caption under Arafat's picture said that Jordan's King Hussein, Bethlehem Mayor Elias Freij, PLO leader Abu Iyad, and former Austrian Chancellor Bruno Kreisky, an outspoken supporter of the Palestinians, also hoped for a Labor victory.

The results of the 1988 election were similar to the inconclusive outcome of the 1984 balloting. Likud emerged with only a slight edge over Labor, winning 709,305 votes (40 Knesset seats) to Labor's 685,363 votes (39 seats). Likud's showing represented a loss of one seat from 1984 and eight seats from 1981. The Oriental Jewish community continued to vote for Likud in greater numbers than for Labor, although there were some suggestions that Oriental support for Likud was weakening. One Israeli observer suggested that many Orientals no longer regarded Likud as the party most sensitive to their needs and were turning increasingly to SHAS and other orthodox religious parties.[7]

Labor's poor showing in the 1988 election underscored the power of incumbency of Yitzhak Shamir and Likud. As prime minister during the national unity government's first two years, Labor leader Shimon Peres established himself as the dominant figure in Israeli politics, transforming his image from that of a widely disliked, unscrupulous politician to that of a dignified, self-confident political figure and an asset, rather than a liability, to his party, issues that were to become a matter of public discussion once again in the spring and summer of 1990. During the latter half of the NUG's term, however, Foreign Minister Peres struggled to pursue an activist foreign policy to revitalize the Arab-Israeli peace process to keep from being overshadowed by Prime Minister Shamir. Among other actions, Peres travelled widely and sought to promote his own Arab-Israeli peace plan and programs. In the end, however, all of Peres's diplomatic maneuvering did not enable him to escape the relative political obscurity of the foreign ministry. Even within the Labor party, Peres found himself taking a back seat to his long-time rival, Yitzhak Rabin, who benefitted from the importance and high visibility of the defense portfolio, which he retained throughout the government's term, especially after the outbreak of the intifada. The outcome of the balloting in November 1988 highlighted Labor's continuing electoral decline, from 47 Knesset seats in 1981 to 44 in 1984 and to 39 in 1988.

The establishment of a new and different national unity government in December 1988 under the leadership of Yitzhak Shamir was a complicated process. After weeks of maneuvering, Shamir was able to establish a government in which he would remain as prime minister throughout its tenure. Shimon Peres was relegated to minister of finance, an important post, but one with little visibility on the international scene and with little chance to generate popularity or support within Israel. His chief rival, Yitzhak Rabin, retained the post of minister of defense. Despite strong personal and political differences among the members of that government, it survived until the spring of 1990.

The breakdown between the two main elements and the various smaller components of the government in the spring of 1990 provided an interesting if not wholly conclusive view of the balance of political forces and personalities within the Israeli structure on a wide range of matters. The resignation from the government of the Labor members and the subsequent vote of no-confidence in the Knesset that led to the fall of the government tested the various leaders and their political skills. It also gave an indication of the political constituencies of the various players.

The historic vote of no-confidence gave Peres and Labor an opportunity to secure a mandate to form a coalition and to run the government. Despite substantial efforts, including a number of episodes of political maneuvering and promises of patronage that raised serious doubts about Peres as a political leader and that further eroded his image, Peres was unable to construct a government that would secure a vote of confidence from parliament. Upon obtaining the mandate, Shamir engaged in lengthy maneuvering to construct a cabinet and ultimately succeeded in establishing a government supported by Likud and by parties and individuals from the political right and from the religious community. One Labor party defector (Ephraim Gur) also voted for the new government. The government was formally confirmed by the Knesset on June 11, 1990, by a vote of 62 to 57 with one abstention. In presenting the government to the Knesset for its approval, Shamir noted that it included "all the national forces which have fought and worked for the sake of Eretz Yisrael."[8] The newly established government was both relatively narrow and potentially fragile. But it was a further indicator of the difficulties facing Labor in its efforts to achieve the ouster of Likud from power or power-sharing and the problems facing Labor in its efforts to recapture some semblance of its former dominance of the Israeli political system. The center of Israeli politics seemed to have shifted more to the right.

Within the Labor camp, there emerged a second issue—the question of Peres's role as leader. In the wake of the formation of the new Shamir government, increasing voices within Labor, led by Peres's perennial rival Yitzhak Rabin, questioned Peres's record as party leader. It was noted that Peres not only failed to establish a government when given a chance in the spring, but also, during the process of trying to gain coalition support, he tarnished his and Labor's image through a series of widely publicized political "deals." In addition, it was pointed out, the party had never won a national election with Peres as party leader, thus leading the party to diminishing fortunes within the system. Public opinion polls continued to point to Rabin as Israel's most popular politician, and many in the party saw him as a logical replacement for Peres. A test of those views took place within the party hierarchy in July 1990, but Peres succeeded in staving off the onslaught and retaining his position as leader of the party, at least in the short run.

UNDERSTANDING LABOR'S DECLINE AND LIKUD'S ASCENDANCY

The decline of the once dominant Labor party cannot be traced to any one act or failure. Rather, it stemmed from the erosion of its power base, which, in turn, must be understood within the context of the party's maturation, moving from the generation of its founding fathers into the generation of Sabra leadership, the effects of the June War of 1967 and the occupation of Arab territories on the national agenda, and the changing demographic characteristics of the electorate. The Palestinian uprising (intifada) in the West Bank and Gaza Strip that began in 1987 also had a major effect on Labor's electoral prospects insofar as it helped to blur the distinction between Labor's and Likud's approaches to the future of the occupied territories.

The Challenge of the Territories

During the first two decades of Israel's existence and of Labor's preeminence, there was virtual unanimity within Israel concerning both domestic and foreign policy priorities. The primary domestic task involved the ingathering and absorption of Jewish immigrants from wherever they came and economic growth and development. Foreign and security policy was oriented toward survival in the face of an unremitting Arab hostility and accompanying bellicosity. The national agenda was altered by the territorial acquisitions of June 1967. Israel was unprepared to deal with the postwar situation since it had not gone to war to expand its boundaries but to respond to the Arab threat created by the massing of Egyptian forces along Israel's southwestern frontier, as well as by the revival of the Arab military alliance against Israel, and to achieve more narrow objectives, such as relieving the blockade of the port of Eilat. After the war, it was hoped that the military victory and the occupation of substantial Arab territories (the Sinai Peninsula, the Golan Heights, the West Bank, and the Gaza Strip, as well as East Jerusalem) could be used as bargaining chips to achieve a negotiated settlement with Israel's Arab neighbors.

At the same time, however, the extension of Jewish control to territories associated with the historic land of Israel (Eretz Yisrael) revived the traditional attachment to the land and brought to the forefront of political debate long-dormant questions about the fundamental nature of Zionism (Jewish nationalism)—primarily the issue of the relationship between the possession of the land of Israel and the nature and quality of Jewish life on whatever portion of the land was available to the Jewish people. Menachem Begin and the political allies of his Herut party and the Land of Israel Movement (which began its efforts shortly after the

June war) championed the cause of retention of the territories and the establishment of settlements there. This message, which struck a responsive chord in the hearts and minds of many Israelis, was a more readily comprehensible position than the ambiguous declarations of the Labor party and its allies, which maintained that Israel should do nothing to foreclose any options for peace and held out the prospect of exchanging territory for a negotiated settlement. Labor had no precise answers to the fundamental questions of how much territory should be returned, to whom, or under what conditions.

In the period between the June 1967 and October 1973 wars, the debate was not facilitated by the absence in the Arab world of any substantial moderate voice. There was no Arab interlocutor with whom moderate Israeli forces could interact, and this made the policies of Labor even more difficult to sustain and to gain support. From the Arab world came calls for the termination of the Israeli occupation of Arab territory and for the end to the consequences of the aggression of June 1967 and calls for war but not the needed interlocutor to focus on the concept of exchanging land for peace that was being promoted by Labor party programs and personalities. The general euphoria and confidence that prevailed in Israel after the 1967 war helped to foster a mood of relative quiescence that precluded major debate or discussion of the central issues of the peace process and contributed to the lack of general support for some of the compromise concepts of the Labor leadership. Some shifts in this perspective began to develop with the Yom Kippur War of 1973.

The turmoil in the political life of Israel at the time of the Yom Kippur War set in motion forces that subsequently affected the political process and created a new party balance. The change from prewar euphoria to postwar uncertainty accelerated political change and facilitated the replacement of personalities and the alteration of policies. The effect was not obvious in the elections for the Eighth Knesset and local authorities held at the end of December 1973. Indeed, the elections did not mark the turning point in Israeli politics that many observers expected in the wake of the October War. Although about one-third of the members of the Knesset were new and the party composition of the parliament was modified, the profile of the new body was not substantially different from that of its predecessor. Golda Meir was charged with creating a new government and did so in early 1974, but she resigned a month later, primarily because of the dissension within the Labor party that centered on the question of political responsibility for lapses at the outset of the war.

This set the stage for the selection of a new prime minister and the formation of a new coalition. Yitzhak Rabin, the choice of the MAPAI (*Mifleget Poalei Eretz Israel*, or Israel Workers' party) establishment for the post of prime minister, was relatively young (in his fifties) and of a new generation—not one of the group of pioneers who had immigrated to Palestine at the beginning of the twentieth century and who had controlled the situation since then. Rabin's government represented a departure from the past and ushered in the new era in which some of Israel's best-known names and personalities moved from the focus of power. The coalition was constructed initially with a structure different from its predecessors, as the National Religious Party (NRP) was replaced by the Citizens' Rights Movement (CRM), although this was reversed within a matter of months when the NRP joined the government in the fall of 1974 and the CRM withdrew. Leadership had begun to be transferred from the immigrant-founder generation to the native sons. The policy process was altered as Golda Meir's singular role gave way to the representation of diverse views in Israel's three-man shuttle diplomacy negotiating team (Rabin, Yigal Allon, and Shimon Peres) and their coterie of advisers. Although constituting the leadership of the government and the party, they, and especially Rabin and Peres, were constantly seeking to ensure their individual preeminence, and each sought to gain advantage over the other in the struggle to lead the party and the government.

Several protest movements and new political parties resulted from the October War and had varying degrees of success in establishing themselves in the political structure. They developed initially in response to perceived mismanagement during the war and focused on the need for political reform. Among the resultant parties was the Democratic Movement for Change (DMC), which secured sizeable representation in the Knesset in 1977 and joined the Likud-led coalition in the fall of that year. It later split into several smaller groups and had disintegrated by the time of the 1981 Knesset election.

In a more general sense, many of the forces set in motion by the October War and its aftermath seemed to coalesce to affect the situation in a tangible way when Israel's electorate went to the polls in May 1977. Likud, led by Menachem Begin, won the largest number of Knesset seats; Labor lost a substantial number of seats compared to 1973. Many of Labor's lost mandates went to the newly established DMC, but Likud also gained additional seats. This ended Labor's dominance of Israeli politics that had begun in the Yishuv period. Israel thus chose a new regime; and Likud, under Begin's leadership, emerged as the leading political force.

To a substantial degree, the results of the polling suggested that Labor lost more than Likud won. To be sure, Likud's electoral strength had been increasing steadily, but it did not dominate the election results and the system as Labor and MAPAI had done previously. Labor had become entrenched in power, and voters were concerned with the lack of leadership and the weakness of the Labor-led government in dealing with a wide variety of issues ranging from labor unrest to broader social problems. The government's vacillation in response to challenges seemed to confirm general impressions of weakness, and several major scandals prior to the election contributed to the negative image. The emergence of the DMC allowed voters to shift their support from Labor and to choose a somewhat similar and respected new alternative rather than being forced to cast their ballots for Menachem Begin and Likud.

The Impact of the Intifada

The 1967 war set in motion political and other forces which, among other effects, helped to end the dominance of Israel's political system by the Labor party and its cohorts a decade later in the 1977 election. But the war also set in motion other forces that ultimately emerged in the Palestinian uprising or intifada in the West Bank and Gaza Strip in December 1987 and must be seen as a factor affecting the relationship between the political right and the political left in Israel in previously unseen and unanticipated ways. The intifada has emerged as a factor that, at least in the short run, has complicated Israeli politics but has been of primary benefit to Likud and the right of center in terms of generating electoral results and control of national politics. At the same time, and in a somewhat contradictory manner, it has contributed to a growth of those opposing Likud policies and has made the forces of opposition more vocal in their efforts to change Israeli policies on issues of this type.

The intifada erupted on December 9, 1987, in the Gaza Strip and quickly spread to the West Bank. It came as a surprise to Israel, to the Arab states, to the PLO, and to virtually all observers of events in the Middle East. Its continuation since then, although at varying levels of intensity, has become a major feature of the Arab-Israeli conflict and an element in the policy calculations of almost all actors in and dealing with the region. The minimal objective of the intifada remains the termination of Israeli occupation. Beyond that, the objectives appear to vary, but most Palestinians appear to seek self-determination, that is, a Palestinian state at least in the West Bank and in Gaza.

The origins of the uprising can be traced to many factors, but most observers agree that it was deeply rooted in the Palestinians' overwhelming frustration with the continuing Israeli occupation and the inability of the Arab states, the PLO, and other outside powers to obtain for them the self-determination that they sought. The intifada developed at a time when the Arab-Israeli conflict and the Palestinian question were losing much of their international appeal. Many of the Arab states had made the issue one of lower priority as was clear at the Arab summit in Amman in November 1987. The superpowers were increasingly more concerned with their own bilateral relations as a consequence of the new policies of Mikhail Gorbachev and the Soviet Union. At the same time the PLO was not making much progress toward meeting the demands of the population of the occupied territories. Israeli responses in the initial phases of the intifada turned out to be ineffective, and the intifada grew in size and violence. But, it also gained international attention for the plight of the Palestinians in the territories as well as for the Palestinian demands.

Israeli actions eventually were able to limit the activities of Palestinian protesters and were successful in achieving a routinization of the intifada. Still, the intifada proved to be costly to Israel in economic and in political terms. Economic costs included such matters as the costs of military actions; disruption in production; disruption in construction, which utilizes a large Palestinian labor force; disruption and some reduction in tourism; disruption caused by lengthier periods of military reserve service, and other elements. The political costs have been perhaps more problematic and ultimately will have a greater effect. Israel has lost sympathy, and its reputation as a humane and democratic state has been tarnished. The intifada has had practical effects on Israel's relations with a number of states, particularly with the United States, and it has resulted in some harsh and sometimes public criticism of some of Israel's policies, such as deportation and arrest.

The intifada has fundamentally altered the relationship between the Palestinians in the occupied territories and the Israelis. It has reflected a new Palestinian assertiveness in dealing with Israel and is a consequence, in part, of the maturation of a new generation of Palestinians who were born and raised under Israeli occupation and seem to know and better understand Israel and its weaknesses. The indigenous leadership of the intifada seems to have created something of an authentic local leadership, even if it does retain substantial links with the PLO.

The intifada became an issue within Israel and began to affect its political discourse and the fortunes of the political parties and political leadership. Israelis were surprised by the suddenness of the intifada as well as their own inability to bring it to a quick end. The initial effect of the uprising in Israel was to reinforce the sharp cleavages dividing Israelis between those who believe the Palestinian problem must be resolved through territorial compromise and those who believe Israel can have both peace and the territories. To many Israelis, particularly those identified with Labor who argue for territorial compromise, the uprising exposed the folly of their compatriots who insisted that the territorial status quo is tenable and reaffirmed the urgency of withdrawing from the bulk of the territories and returning them to Jordan. To Israelis associated with Likud and its right-wing allies who seek to retain all of

Eretz Yisrael, the uprising underscored the dangers Israel would face if it relinquished control over the territories.

While reinforcing existing attitudes on the desirability of trading land for peace, the intifada appeared to have a subtle effect on the right-of-center parties. Likud's association—by virtue of its partnership with Labor in the national unity government—with Labor Defense Minister Yitzhak Rabin's handling of the uprising and Shimon Peres's maneuverings on the peace process compelled right-wing nationalists to move farther to the right to establish a clearer line of distinction between themselves and Likud. The uprising and the United States–sponsored peace initiative, based on Yitzhak Shamir's plan of the spring of 1989 for Palestinian elections, also affected the religious parties' political agenda. They were forced to place greater emphasis on foreign policy issues and all but ignore domestic religious matters.

THE DEMOGRAPHICS OF ISRAELI VOTING BEHAVIOR

While Labor was grappling with the problems of political maturation in the decade after the June War of 1967, a fundamental demographic change was occurring within Israeli society, which, among other effects, undermined Labor's electoral base of support. It was at this time that the Orientals became a majority of Israel's population, exceeding in number the Ashkenazim (Israelis of European origin), who constituted the overwhelming majority of Labor's power base. Orientals, on the other hand, especially the children of those who immigrated to Israel, were increasingly attracted to Likud.

The Salience of Ethnicity

During Israel's first three decades of statehood when Labor was dominant, it drew support from all groups in society, including the new immigrants from Asian and African countries who came to Israel in the mass immigration of the early 1950s. The new immigrants were dependent on the Labor establishment for all aspects of their day-to-day existence—jobs, education, health, and cultural welfare. Labor sought to translate that dependence into political support, and the new immigrants responded.

Eventually, the Labor establishment atrophied as it became increasingly preoccupied with preserving its dominance in society and with developing a lifestyle that stressed a continuous rise in the standard of living and conspicuous consumption. With the rapid absorption of the relatively disadvantaged Sephardi segment of the population, the Labor elite became distanced from other strata of society, showing evidence of behavior that appeared to be in contradiction to the Labor-Zionist ideology by which they had legitimated themselves. The prevailing socialist democratic ideology subsequently became increasingly identified by broad sectors of the public as a mechanism for preserving the power position of the ruling elite in a changing, more open society.

By the late 1960s, Labor's estrangement from the disadvantaged segments of the population was apparent in the widening ethnic split in Israeli voting preferences as Ashkenazim tended to vote for Labor in greater numbers than Orientals, and Orientals tended to vote more for Likud. Still, in the 1969 election, the majority of support for both Labor and Likud came from Ashkenazim, which undoubtedly reflected their numerical predominance in the electorate. It was only in the 1977 Knesset election that a majority of the Likud vote came from Orientals for the first time. The Labor party continued to be supported overwhelmingly by Ashkenazim. In subsequent Knesset elections, between 60 and 70 percent of Israeli voters of European origin voted for Labor, and about 60 percent of Oriental voters voted for Likud. Labor's support among Ashkenazim fell to about 50 percent in the 1988 election, probably because of the relative success of other left-of-center parties among that ethnic group.[9]

Resenting the treatment they had received under the Labor establishment, the Oriental community found in Menachem Begin a figure of authority to whom they could relate as they sought to manifest their resentments. Despite his European demeanor, Begin was also estranged from the establishment, which had frustrated his political aspirations. Moreover, Begin embodied the Oriental Jews' sense of traditional Jewishness and respect for authority, whereas Labor incorporated secularism, socialism, egalitarianism, and the elimination of power structures—concepts more alien to the Oriental tradition.

Begin's appeal to Israel's Orientals contrasted sharply with that of Labor leader Shimon Peres. Oriental Jews viewed Peres as a symbol of the smooth Labor party politicians of Ashkenazi origin, who they feel patronized their community for years. Oriental Jews also tended to view Likud as offering them greater upward mobility and rapid political advancement. This perception has not always been based on hard political facts insofar as Labor often has had more Oriental members in the Knesset than Likud. In the Twelfth Knesset, elected in November 1988, for example, Labor had 14 Oriental Knesset members while Likud had 12. Still, Likud's Oriental Knesset members generally enjoyed greater popularity than Labor's; Likud's Oriental Knesset members tended to be viewed as genuine representatives of the "second Israel," the underprivileged sector of Israel's population, who emerged from development towns and other deprived areas to assume positions of national prominence.

The young generation of Likud leaders who hail from the Oriental blue-collar class and generally are self-made men are commonly referred to in Israel as the "paupers." Moshe Katzav is one of these paupers, a representative of the "second Israel." Katzav, in his mid-forties, was born in Iran and came to Israel as a child, living first in an immigrant transit camp. He studied at the Ben-Shemen agricultural boarding school and later received a degree in economics from the Hebrew University. Before entering the Knesset, he was active in local politics and served as chairman of the council in Kiryat Malachi in the Negev. His first cabinet post was as minister of labor and social welfare in the 1984–88 national unity government, and he was minister of transport in the 1988–90 national unity government. Other prominent Orientals in the Likud stable include Moroccan-born David Magen, who rose through Likud ranks as a protegé of Ariel Sharon but later shifted to David Levy's camp. Magen is joined by Ovadia Eli, who was born in Iraq, and Jewish Agency treasurer Meir Shitreet.

The other young leaders in Likud are known as the "princes," the sons of prominent Likud (or Herut) figures, who generally are well educated, politically sophisticated, and financially secure. Among Likud's princes are Ehud Olmert, Dan Meridor, Ronnie Milo, Benjamin Netanyahu, Benny Begin, Uzi Landau, and Tzachi Hanegbi.

Labor also can claim representatives of the "second Israel" among its Knesset deputies, although its Orientals are generally seen as lacking authenticity and as having been coopted by the party's Ashkenazi elite. Moreover, as a group, they have not enjoyed independent power bases comparable to those of their Likud rivals. The exceptions include Eli Dayan, born in Morocco, who was the mayor of Ashkelon. Trained as a lawyer, Dayan got his start in politics in TAMI but was recruited to Labor by Shimon Peres prior to the 1988 Knesset election. Amir Peretz, also born in Morocco, was mayor of Sderot. The inclusion of Dayan and Peretz on Labor's ticket in the 1988 election was not sufficient, however, to draw substantial numbers of working-class votes from Likud. Not only has Labor failed to produce attractive paupers, it also has failed to produce its own generation of princes.

The perception that Labor's young Oriental leaders are merely front men for the party's Ashkenazi elite has been reinforced by the treatment Dayan and Peretz received in the wake of the 1988 election. Both men joined the party expecting to be appointed to positions of leadership in the new government. Neither of them—nor any of the other new Oriental faces in the Labor party—was given a position of even minor importance in the 1988 Labor-Likud government. Peretz noted that he was betrayed by party leader Peres, who "broke faith with the people."[10] Dayan complained that, "They [Labor party leaders] said we were going to be the first revolution for the Labor party, but after the elections, the revolution ended. We see that our leaders speak differently before and after the elections."[11]

Soviet Jewry as a Political Factor

At the beginning of the decade of the 1990s, a new factor was introduced into Israeli politics partly as a consequence of the upheavals in the Soviet Union. During much of the first four decades after independence, Israeli policy focused on securing the right of Soviet Jews to exit the USSR and to emigrate freely to Israel. There was some success. The relatively slow pace of emigration typical before 1990, and even in the early months of 1990, had changed dramatically by year end. In 1990 more than 200,000 Soviet Jewish immigrants arrived in Israel, and they continued to arrive at a significant pace in the early months of 1991. This was the largest single group of immigrants from a single country in Israeli history and posed problems of absorption including housing, training, and employment for the new arrivals. The pace of immigration seemed likely to continue with the attendant problems for the Israeli system.

While the absorption process was central and crucial in the short run, the longer term political implications of this massive increase in numbers was not fully foreseen, and the political parties and organizations of Israel were not prepared to deal with the issue. Clearly the success or failure of the authorities in dealing with the problems facing the immigrants—such as language, housing, and jobs—will have political ramifications. The large influx of potential voters can influence the balance of power between the right and left in the political spectrum and particularly in the Knesset. The initial numbers suggest that as many as six to ten seats may be affected by the new Soviet voters. Given the delicate balance in the Knesset and the need for coalition formation to establish a government, this bloc could be an important determinant of the nature and direction of the future government by as early as the projected 1992 election. A central question is whether the right (primarily, but not exclusively, Likud), the left (essentially Labor), or others ("the center") will benefit from the voting potential and power of the new immigrants. An interesting perspective is that, despite all of the factors, in the final analysis, the left will gain some support as the party out of power and therefore will be able to capitalize on any failures of the Likud in the absorption process. On the other hand, there will be a natural tendency of the former communist subjects to turn away from socialism to the right, and their tendency in this direction will be influenced by the fact that their emigration from the Soviet Union and to Israel was facilitated by Likud. Successful integration will likely be rewarded with votes; failure probably will lead to votes for the party out of power. But, when all is said and done, it may well be that the voters will divide along the entire political spectrum with a small advantage to the right of center (even if not all to Likud).

OTHER RIGHT-OF-CENTER ACTORS

The demographic shift that benefitted Likud also aided Likud's potential and actual political allies on its right, including both the secular groupings—Tehiya (Renaissance), Tzomet (Junction/Zionist Renewal), and Moledet (Motherland)—and the religious parties—SHAS, Agudat Israel, Degel HaTorah (Flag of the Torah), and the National Religious Party. Likud's political strength has been increased by the potential for alliances with each of these small parties, which generally draw their support from among the same segments of the population—nationalists, Orientals, and traditional or religious voters—as Likud. The secular parties, which advocate the establishment of Israel's international borders based on the boundaries of the historic Land of Israel, reject Labor because it promotes the partition and relinquishing of that territory. The non-Zionist ultra-Orthodox parties, which have never accepted the secular or political basis of Zionism and which have felt deprived of their fair share of the state's resources, have felt a closer attachment to Likud even though many disagree with Likud's foreign policy. The value of the right-of-center parties to Likud was underscored at the time of the 1984 election, when Labor was unable to form a coalition government from among the parties of the left-of-center and religious camps despite its plurality of 44 seats to Likud's 41.

Secular Parties

Tehiya was created in 1979 by former members of Likud, supporters of the Gush Emunim (Bloc of the Faithful) settlement movement, and secular members of the Greater Israel Movement in response to the Camp David Accords and the Egypt-Israel Peace Treaty. The party's founders saw these agreements as inimical to Israel's interests because they relinquished territories that were seen as important for Israel's security and made other concessions deleterious to Israel's future. As the standard bearer of Israel's nationalist militants, Tehiya demanded the unequivocal annexation of the West Bank and Gaza Strip. It won three Knesset seats in its first electoral campaign in 1981 and gained five seats in 1984, bolstered by the incorporation into the party of former Chief-of-Staff Rafael Eitan and his Tzomet movement. Eitan's subsequent defection from Tehiya contributed to the party's disappointing showing in the 1988 election, when it won only three seats.

Tehiya was a member of the Likud-led coalition from 1981 to 1984, but it refused to join the two subsequent national unity governments. This undoubtedly stemmed from Tehiya's distrust of Labor leader Shimon Peres and the belief that the coalition agreements were deliberately vague on the fate of the occupied territories, leaving open the possibility of trading land for peace.[12] Tehiya supported the government position in the vote of no-confidence in the spring of 1990 and subsequently joined the government coalition led by Yitzhak Shamir in June 1990.

Tzomet did well in the 1988 election, running as an independent list under the leadership of Rafael Eitan and winning nearly 46,000 votes and two seats in the Twelfth Knesset. The party's unyielding position on the status of the occupied territories was highlighted in its election platform, which asserted that Israel's security needs demanded that it not give up parts of the West Bank and Gaza Strip. On the question of the Palestinian intifada, the party maintained that it must be treated with "uncompromising determination" and recommended the expanded use of deportations, economic and other forms of communal punishment, and the formation of territorial defense organizations among the Jewish settlers to share responsibility with the army for maintaining law and order in the territories.[13]

Moledet, a right-wing nationalist party formed by retired Army general Rehavam Ze'evi, won slightly more than 44,000 votes in the 1988 election and two Knesset seats. Ze'evi created the new party in reaction to what he and other right-wing nationalists believed was the Labor-Likud unity coalition's weakness in failing to quash the Palestinian intifada. The party's campaign literature called for the "transfer" of all Arabs out of the West Bank and Gaza Strip.

Moledet benefitted from the decision by the Central Election Commission to ban Rabbi Meir Kahane's Kach party from the election. Kahane's election to the Knesset in 1984 and his subsequent activities under the protection of parliamentary immunity were controversial in Israel, but his message calling for the forced departure of all Palestinians, not only from the occupied territories but also from Israel proper, did not sound so far removed from the political mainstream. This was partly because the right-wing nationalist ideology and rhetoric of the Likud governments of Menachem Begin and Yitzhak Shamir, emphasizing the primacy of Jewish rights over those of the Arabs in the occupied territories, created a favorable environment for the acceptance of Kahane's views. His message was particularly attractive to many younger Israelis born after 1967 who were accustomed to the differences in civil rights enjoyed by those in Israel and those in the territories and who welcomed the simplistic solution offered by Kahane to a problem that Israel's other political leaders seemed too weak to tackle.

Still, Kahane was increasingly seen as an embarrassment to the nation by most Israeli leaders who, as the November 1988 election approached, worked together to remove Kahane and his party from the ballot. In October 1988 the Central Election Commission ruled that Kach would not be allowed to participate in the November election. Kahane appealed the commission's decision to the High Court of Justice but to no avail. The court ruled that Kahane had violated an amendment to the election law of 1985 that banned parties that incited ethnic hatred, did not accept Israel as the state of the Jewish people, or rejected the democratic character of the state. As a result, in the November election, Kahane's supporters were probably dispersed among other right-of-center parties, particularly Moledet, which expressed many of the same goals as Kahane albeit somewhat more respectably.

The parties of the political right share a number of perspectives and goals that make them natural allies with each other as well as with Likud on many foreign and security policy issues. At the same time, they exist as separate entities because of differences in policy and perspective as well as because of personality differences. Nevertheless, they constitute a formidable grouping that can challenge any left-of-center political bloc and can enhance the position of Likud, as well as make it appear to be more at the center of Israeli politics by themselves being to Likud's right on the major foreign policy and security issues facing the system.

Religious Parties

A major unexpected result of the voting in 1988 was the success of the religious parties in capturing 18 seats, 6 more than they had won in 1984. The religious parties' success came despite the fragmentation of the three existing religious parties—NRP, SHAS, and Agudat Israel— so that six religious parties participated in the election.[14] The NRP, SHAS, Agudat Israel, and Degel HaTorah (which broke off from Agudat Israel on the eve of the election) won seats in the Knesset. MEIMAD (the Religious Center Camp), a dovish offshoot of the NRP, fell about 7,000 votes short of the minimum needed to secure a Knesset mandate. The electoral success of the religious parties did not augur well for Labor because, for the most part, they were not among the parties that would back a Labor-led government. The ultra-Orthodox, in particular, continue to see Labor as much more secular than Likud, and some see it as even antireligious in tone and policy.

The religious parties' electoral success meant that they held the political balance of power between Labor and Likud insofar as they could determine who would be able to form a new government. Some—particularly Agudat Israel—overplayed their hand in the coalition bargaining by alternating between the two major parties to see which would offer the better deal in return for their coalition support. As a group, the religious parties provoked widespread dismay among secular Israelis, and especially among American Jews, and protests against changing the Law of Return (and the determination of "Who is a Jew?") which would delegitimatize the Judaism of an overwhelming majority of American Jews, as well as non-Orthodox Israelis. In the end, Labor and Likud undercut the religious parties and their power by agreeing to form another national unity government, thereby rendering those parties unnecessary for the formation of a government and thus relatively impotent politically. It was not until the falling out between Labor and Likud in March 1990 that the religious parties recovered some of their political clout when their votes were crucial both for the vote of no-confidence and for the formation of a successor government. But this time they exercised their leverage more with regard to foreign policy and defense issues than their usual agenda of religious legislation. Most notable by its absence was any talk about changing the Law of Return. When a government formed in June, its guidelines, as presented to the Knesset, represented this factor by talking of retaining the religious status quo rather than promoting major programs for the religious parties. The guidelines state: "The national status quo on religious matters will be scrupulously observed."[15]

The nationalist tendencies of the National Religious Party had been strengthened by 1988 partly as a result of the reintegration of the right-wing MATZAD faction, which had split off from the NRP in 1984 to form the Morasha (Heritage) party. Moreover, the leadership of the NRP had changed, which also contributed to the party's rightward swing. Yosef Burg, the party's moderate elder statesman who had sought to make the NRP a bridge between Israel's Orthodox and secular communities, was no longer influential in party affairs. Burg's successor as party leader, Zvulun Hammer, who held more hawkish views on the future of the occupied territories, was himself replaced by Avner Shaki, a Sephardi, who was an ardent supporter of Gush Emunim and was committed to retention of all the occupied territories. Shaki also took a less conciliatory position on domestic religious issues, particularly the question of changing the Law of Return to recognize only Orthodox conversions. It is notable that Shaki's takeover of the NRP marked the first time in Israel's history that an Oriental controlled the leadership of one of the country's major political parties.

Despite these changes in the NRP, the party did not share in the overall electoral gains made by the religious camp in the 1988 Knesset election. Having lost half of its strength in the 1981 election and then falling to only four Knesset seats in 1984 after the defection of the MATZAD faction, the NRP suffered a small additional percentage loss in the popular vote in the 1988 election notwithstanding the reintegration of MATZAD.

In response to the NRP's rightward swing, party doves split off and formed the MEIMAD party under the leadership of Rabbi Yehudah

Amital, the head of the Hesder yeshivot, which combine religious and military training. The party coopted Yehuda Ben-Meir, who had been a close associate of Zvulun Hammer but was excluded from the NRP's new leadership. MEIMAD fell about 7,000 votes shy of the 1-percent threshold for attaining a seat in the Knesset.

The religious camp's electoral gains in 1988 were limited to the ultra-Orthodox or *haredi* (pious) parties. Indeed, the 1988 election was noteworthy in that, for the first time in Israel's history, non-Zionist religious parties won more seats than did Zionist religious parties. The Oriental ultra-Orthodox party SHAS saw its strength increase from four to six Knesset seats. The party's success was largely the result of its participation in the previous national unity government. SHAS controlled the interior ministry—traditionally the bastion of the NRP—which enabled it to channel funds through the local governments to provide services to its constituency of haredi Sephardi Jews, whose share of the population was growing rapidly. SHAS also exploited the Sephardi-Ashkenazi split, stressing in its platform the restoration of Oriental culture to a position of prominence in Israeli society. The party also benefitted from having as its spiritual mentor former Sephardi Chief Rabbi Ovadia Yosef, who was popular even among non-Orthodox Orientals. SHAS's success among non-Orthodox Orientals in the 1988 election was underscored in survey results that indicated that the party won as much as 16 percent of the vote in Sephardi-dominated development towns, which had previously voted overwhelmingly for Likud.

SHAS has among its leaders one of the most interesting of Israel's young politicians, the Moroccan-born Rabbi Arye Deri. A protegé of Rabbi Yosef, Deri shares Yosef's belief that *pikuach nefesh*, the saving of lives, is more sacred than land so that territorial compromise can be made for the sake of peace. His appointment as minister of interior in 1988 initially caused a stir among secular Israelis, particularly after it became known that he had evaded military service as a young yeshiva student. As minister of interior, however, Deri initially impressed observers and opponents with his sharp mind and native wit, and he won plaudits for his sympathetic and surprisingly liberal approach to many domestic religious issues. His career appeared to suffer at least a temporary setback in mid-1990 when he was investigated for fraud and the misappropriation of government funds.

The Ashkenazi-dominated Agudat Israel entered the 1988 election seemingly in a weakened position as a result of the defection of the wing led by the Lithuanian-born Rabbi Eliezer Schach. Schach had earlier engineered with Rabbi Yosef the breaking off of Agudat Israel's Sephardi elements to form SHAS in 1984. In 1988 he sought to exploit his political strength within Agudat Israel to curb what he saw as the growing influence within the party of the Lubavitch Hassidic sect and its leader, Brooklyn-based Rabbi Menachem M. Schneerson. Schach had little respect for Schneerson's rabbinic scholarship and belittled him for his presumed Messianic aspirations as well. When Schach made his move against Schneerson and his Lubavitch movement, all but one of the other Hassidic sects within Agudat Israel refused to back him, so Schach pulled his followers out of the party to form Degel HaTorah.

The formation of the rival ultra-Orthodox party led Schneerson to mobilize his followers to vote for Agudat Israel in the November 1988 election. The battle between the Lubavitch Hassidim and their Lithuanian opponents was complete with promises of Schneerson's blessings for those who voted for Agudat Israel and threats of his curses for those who were considering shifting allegiances. There were also numerous allegations in the media of ballot-box stuffing by Lubavitch supporters. The stridency of the campaign apparently worked in Agudat Israel's favor, however. It won nearly three times the number of votes it had gained in 1984, from just over 36,000 to roughly 103,000. Its Knesset seats increased from two to five. Degel HaTorah made a respectable first-time showing in the election, winning more than 34,000 votes and two seats.

The continuing rivalry between Rabbis Schneerson and Schach was very much in evidence in the coalition crisis that brought down the national unity government headed by Yitzhak Shamir in March 1990 and the subsequent political maneuvering to form a new coalition. Agudat Israel, which had earlier left the coalition because it felt betrayed by Shamir for breaking written commitments made during the coalition-formation negotiations in 1988, sided with Labor in the vote of no-confidence. It subsequently signed a coalition agreement with Labor leader Shimon Peres despite Rabbi Schneerson's more hawkish position on the issue of retention of the occupied territories.

Somewhat paradoxically, SHAS, whose leadership held more dovish views on territorial issues, was partly responsible for Peres's inability to form a Labor-led government even after it had abstained on the no-confidence vote to give Peres his margin of victory. SHAS refused to support Likud on the no-confidence motion because Rabbi Yosef wanted Shamir to say yes to the U.S. initiative to convene Palestinian-Israeli peace talks in Cairo. Rabbi Schach, who retains considerable influence within SHAS, was not happy with the party's abstention, and subsequently he ordered party leaders not to endorse Peres's efforts to form a new government. One reason for this decision was almost certainly Rabbi Schach's rivalry with the Lubavitcher rebbe, Rabbi Schneerson, who was aligned with Labor.

THE STABILITY OF POLITICAL ATTITUDES

Likud's movement to the center of Israeli politics is underscored in the stable distribution of attitudes in Israel over the past two decades.

One would expect that, as the power of Likud has grown, the distribution of attitudes identified with the right would also have grown. As Asher Arian points out, this has not been the case, particularly with regard to attitudes on key Arab-Israeli issues, which have remained fairly constant since the June War of 1967.[16] Indeed, some public opinion experts maintain that since 1983, and particularly since the beginning of the Palestinian intifada in December 1987, there has been a slight trend toward greater moderation of Israeli attitudes on the question of trading land for peace.[17] The apparent softening of attitudes further suggests that what has happened in Israel has been a process of political change, not ideological change, as Likud has been transformed into the ruling elite replacing Labor.

Likud has emerged as a mainstream and thereby centrist party in Israeli politics as a representative of the majority perspective able, through various political techniques, to control a majority in parliament both with and without the support of the Labor party. It is no longer an extreme party—among other factors, there are others to its right and extreme right, which are, in a sense, its strongest political rivals. It is solidly entrenched in the center of Israeli politics, a place it shares (although increasingly it has the largest share) with the Labor party on the left side of the center. Labor too has more extreme parties to its side, but they are to the left. The religious parties tend to be more rightist (but not always and not solidly) on foreign policy and related security issues, but they are badly split owing to a wide variety of factors. Primarily, though, the religious parties are in concord on religious necessities but not always on the best or appropriate means to achieve them.

The government of June 1990 demonstrates among other things the fact that Shamir is an able and dextrous politician. He has been able to outmaneuver his opponents and challengers both within his own party and the governing coalition as well as his opponents in the Labor party, especially Shimon Peres.

As Israel entered the decade of the 1990s it was demonstrated once again that coalition politics are at the center of the system and that a dramatic and major change in those politics is possible only with substantial electoral reform. Although these ideas are numerous in type and variety and have been promoted before, the extent of popular support for, indeed demand for, such political reform has never been greater. This was clearly evident in the more than 500,000 signatures that were gathered on petitions for electoral reform at the height of efforts by Peres and then Shamir to form a new government after the successful vote of no-confidence that ousted the old Likud-led national unity government. Nevertheless, with the formation of the June 1990 government, the zeal and ardor in support of such reform efforts seemed to dwindle significantly. Barring electoral reform or a major change in the regional situation (a war or an Arab-sponsored peace initiative that was seen by Israel as significant, such as Anwar Sadat's in 1977), the basic balance of power between the major parties is unlikely to change dramatically.

An additional, but as yet unclear in its extent or direction, possibility is the role that might be played by the large-scale Soviet immigration that began to develop in 1990. That immigration had the potential to increase the size of Israel's Jewish electorate by a substantial margin and could ultimately affect the disposition of perhaps 10 percent of the seats in parliament, perhaps more depending on Soviet policy. Much will of course depend on how many new immigrants arrive, how they are socialized into the system, and whether they form a bloc or spread their votes across the political spectrum. All of these questions could only be raised, but not answered, at the beginning of the decade of the 1990s.

Likud's arrival in the mainstream of Israeli political life—viewed as an aberration with the 1977 victory and the establishment of a coalition by Menachem Begin—must now be seen as a political fact of life. With the formation of the Likud-led right-of-center and religious party coalition government in June 1990, Likud has confirmed its role as a major if not the major political force in Israeli politics and has firmly captured at least a part of the political center around which other parties must establish their positions and credentials. As Israel moves into the decade of the 1990s, the political reference point has moved from the leftist Labor party as the center and dominant party to the rightist Likud as the center reference point.

The religious parties of Israel, which hold the key to the political balance between Likud and Labor, have undergone substantial internal and intramural turmoil since the establishment of the state. Although there has been a religious party in virtually every government established in Israel's history, the participating party and its demands for participation have varied over time. In recent years the religious parties have drawn growing attention to themselves because they have been essential for the formation and maintenance of governments. Their price for participation appears to have grown over time, and the demands have become more public, raising additional public concerns for the future of the political scene. The role played by the rabbis who "direct" or guide them and the role they have played in swaying the governments of Israel have also come under increasing scrutiny, to the chagrin and dismay of many within and outside of Israel.

The Likud-right-religious coalition inaugurated in June 1990 was a new configuration in Israeli politics. It was a new departure for the participants and for the opposition. The diverse elements reflected the various strains in Israeli political life and their varied and variable demands for the future of the state.

NOTES

1. See Maurice M. Roumani, "Labor's Expectation and Israeli Reality: Ethnic Voting as a Means Toward Political and Social Change," in *Israel Faces the Future*, ed. Bernard Reich and Gershon R. Kieval (New York: Praeger, 1986), 57–78.

2. See Marver H. Bernstein, "David Ben-Gurion," in *Political Leaders of the Contemporary Middle East and North Africa: A Biographical Dictionary*, ed. Bernard Reich (Westport, Conn.: Greenwood Press, 1990), 97–108.

3. See Marver H. Bernstein, "Golda Meir," in Reich, ed., *Political Leaders of the Contemporary Middle East and North Africa*, 325–32.

4. See Ilan Peleg, "The Foreign Policy of Herut and the Likud," in *Israeli National Security Policy: Political Actors and Perspectives*, ed. Bernard Reich and Gershon R. Kieval (Westport, Conn.: Greenwood Press, 1988), 55–78; and Peleg, "Menachem Begin," in Reich, ed., *Political Leaders of the Contemporary Middle East and North Africa*, 71–78.

5. See Bernard Reich and Joseph Helman, "Yitzhak Shamir," in Reich, ed., *Political Leaders of the Contemporary Middle East and North Africa*, 486–94.

6. For further elaboration on Shamir and his programs and policies, see Bernard Reich, "The Shamir Government: Policy and Prospects," *Middle East Insight* 2, no. 3 (January/February 1984):25–31.

7. See Don Peretz and Sammy Smooha, "Israel's Twelfth Knesset Election: An All-Loser Game," *Middle East Journal* 42, no. 3 (Summer 1989):401.

8. For the text of Shamir's address to the Knesset, see Foreign Broadcast Information Service, Daily Report, *Middle East and North Africa*, June 12, 1990, 24–29.

9. See Asher Arian, *The Choosing People: Voting Behavior in Israel* (Cleveland, Ohio: Press of Case Western Reserve University, 1973); Arian, ed., *The Elections in Israel, 1981* (Tel Aviv: Ramot, 1983); Howard R. Penniman, ed., *Israel at the Polls: The Knesset Elections of 1977* (Washington, D.C.: American Enterprise Institute, 1979); and Howard R. Penniman and Daniel J. Elazar, eds., *Israel at the Polls, 1981: A Study of the Knesset Elections* (Washington, D.C.: American Enterprise Institute and Bloomington: Indiana University Press, 1986).

10. *The New York Times*, December 21, 1989.

11. Ibid.

12. For elaboration, see Aaron D. Rosenbaum, "Tehiya as a Permanent Nationalist Phenomenon," in Reich and Kieval, eds., *Israeli National Security Policy*, 147–68.

13. *Yedi'ot Aharonot*, October 26, 1988.

14. TAMI, the fourth religious party represented in the outgoing Knesset with one seat, was absorbed into Likud prior to the 1988 election. Its leader, Aharon Abuhatzeira, was given a safe seat on the Likud list and was put in charge of seeking religious votes, especially among Oriental Jews of North African origin.

15. The text of the new government's policy guidelines was published in *Ha'aretz*, June 10, 1990.

16. Asher Arian, *Politics in Israel: The Second Generation*, 2d ed. (Chatham, N.J.: Chatham House, 1989), 250–52.

17. See Gloria H. Falk, "Israeli Public Opinion on Peace Issues," in Reich and Kieval, eds., *Israeli National Security Policy*, 169–206; and United States Information Agency, Office of Research, Research Memorandum, *Israeli Public Shows More Flexibility on Palestinian Election, Despite Hard Line on East Jerusalem and Concern About U.S. Pressure*, October 4, 1989.

2

The Balance of Political Power and Israel's Political Future

Daniel J. Elazar

THE LIKUD AS ISRAEL'S CENTRIST PARTY

It is important to emphasize that what most non-Israelis think of as Israel's political right, namely the Likud, has become in reality Israel's political center. It is still common in certain circles in Israel and abroad to describe the Likud as the political right. In fact, in the last fourteen years the Likud has moved well into the political center.[1]

This has always been true in domestic matters with regard to the welfare state where the Herut position was opposed to Histadrut control of key health and welfare institutions because it wished to replace Labor movement control with nationalization, not privatization. It is true with regard to the economy where there are few, if any, differences between the Labor and Likud mainstreams with regard to privatization or, more accurately, the appropriate public-private mixture to stimulate Israel's economic growth, except, again, the Likud's interest in weakening the Histadrut, in contrast to Labor's interest in bringing about the adaptation of that Labor movement institution to new realities. The 1984 national unity government (NUG) lasted partly because, on these issues, there is so little difference between the two major parties, a factor that contributed to the initial strength of the 1988 unity coalition as well.

THE "REAL" POLITICAL RIGHT—HOW RIGHT IS IT?

In regard to the Israeli-Palestinian conflict, there is a political right in Israel, which consists of three parties that are represented in the present

Knesset—Tehiya, Tzomet, and Moledet—and Meir Kahane's Kach party, which was excluded from the ballot in 1988 for being racist under the terms of Israeli law. The political right has seven seats in the Knesset and is united by a view of the Israeli-Palestinian struggle as an uncompromising one in which the Palestinians will never truly recognize Israel's right to exist and cannot be trusted with more than local political power west of the Jordan River, if that. This view flows in part from the three parties' strong commitment to the retention of all of Eretz Yisrael west of the Jordan under Israeli rule by right as the ancient homeland of the Jewish people. They view the Six-Day War as the culmination of the Zionist enterprise in which the remaining territory west of the river was liberated and opened to Jewish settlement and control.

In social and economic matters, which in other countries usually define the right and the left—in other words, on most domestic policy issues— these parties consist of social democrats or new free enterprise progressives. Since most of the leaders and supporters of these three parties had their political beginnings in the Labor camp or in the National Religious Party when it was a religious version of the Labor party, they share most of the social welfare goals of the Labor camp, modified by the experiences of the last thirty years. In fact, they may be even greater supporters of the welfare state than much of the Israeli mainstream today because they believe in the communitarian character of the Jewish state. In other words, their right-wing character is confined to the twin issues of Israel's relationship to its land and to the Palestinians.[2]

THE TWO MAJOR PARTIES AND THE PEACE PROCESS

It is in connection with the future of the territories and the Palestinians that the two parties most differ. Even so, for the past several years, both have moved in the same overall direction, toward recognition of the need to accommodate the Palestinian Arabs in some realistic way. Labor has moved to a position more willing to accept territorial compromise; Likud has also softened its stance in the direction of finding some satisfactory political role and status for the Palestinians.

Yitzhak Shamir's plan for elections in the territories as a first step toward a political settlement is a sign of how far he has moved from his original rejection of the Camp David agreement a decade ago to his reliance on it to start peace negotiations now. Shamir's proposal calls for the election of a Palestinian council which would be responsible for the internal government of the Palestinians in the territories under an autonomy plan and, more important, would also act as the Palestinian negotiating team for talks leading to a permanent solution. Shamir has indicated that, although only Palestinians resident in the territories will be acceptable as candidates, Israel will not question whether they have any PLO connections. In fact, if a single-member district system were utilized, it would ensure that those elected would be connected with the PLO, which is preferable from both the Israeli and PLO standpoints to a system that would allow the far more extremist Muslim fundamentalists, who totally reject Israel's right to exist and represent over one-third of the total population in the territories, to be represented in the negotiating process. This step, which carries very great risks for Israel, has become the rallying point for all who want to pursue a peace settlement realistically and has further strengthened Shamir's position at the center of Israeli politics.

As we have seen, this continues to be true despite the action of the Likud central committee (the party's principal governing body) on July 5, 1989, when Shamir and his supporters felt it necessary to compromise with those opposed to the peace initiative in order to preserve party unity and continue the peace process.[3] That is another reason why the Likud can be described as Israel's centrist party today.

Most of the former liberals in the Likud favor some form of Israeli-Palestinian power-sharing in the territories—a position which, once unknown in Herut, has gained strength even in that party, albeit among only a few. Prime Minister Shamir has combined very hard-line statements with suggestions that he, too, has moved toward some kind of power-sharing arrangement. The opposition to his right on this issue, voiced primarily by Ariel Sharon, David Levy, and Yitzhak Moda'i, is more a matter of internal party politics than deep conviction on the part of at least two of those figures who have on other occasions shown different faces to the public.

People "in the know" in Israel are firmly convinced that, if Sharon were prime minister, anything could happen including significant territorial compromise if he thought it advantageous; Levy and Moda'i traditionally have been more moderate than hawkish. This is even more apparent among Likud voters who, since most are less ideologically bound than their party's leadership, are willing to be more realistic about the changes that have taken place among the Palestinian public. The leadership is well aware of this and will undoubtedly have to take it into consideration as they move the country farther into the current peace process.

SHAMIR OUTMANEUVERS HIS RIVALS

In the meantime, it is important to recall that Yitzhak Shamir has outmaneuvered all of his foes within his own party and outside to consolidate his position in a way that few would have expected. He has now survived two Knesset elections as party leader, internal struggles within his own party, and three difficult bouts at coalition formation; each time he has emerged with a new success. Whereas prior to the 1984 election when his position in his own party was severely threatened, today he has the overwhelming majority of the party behind him and faces no serious opposition, even from two skilled and potentially powerful opponents, namely, Sharon and Levy. This position was demonstrated again in the spring and early summer of 1990.

The Labor party, Shamir's chief rival, is widely perceived to be a "loser," an image that party head Shimon Peres has personally acquired. In the 1985–86 time period Peres was upstaging Shamir at every turn. In the 1988–90 NUG, Peres struggled for his own political life and had to bear the burdens of being finance minister at a time of economic crisis, high unemployment, and the incipient collapse of several major Israeli industrial firms.

Shamir is clearly dominant on the Israeli and world political scenes. At the beginning of the second national unity government, Peres tried to present himself as a competitor as he had in the previous government, but he was unable to carry out any significant measures in that direction. Moreover, Shamir's principal supporter and colleague, Moshe Arens, became foreign minister, so that the prime minister and foreign minister spoke with a single voice. Arens's shift to the position of minister of defense in June 1990 only strengthened this situation. Peres's principal rival in the Labor party, Yitzhak Rabin, served as minister of defense, so that Labor had to bear at least equal responsibility with Likud over the conduct of the war against the intifada, and Rabin pursued policies that were quite congruent with those of Shamir. Up and down the line, Labor's share in the coalition government established in 1988 and terminated at its initiative in 1990 involved a maximum of burden with a minimum of potential benefit.

Labor's effort to bring down the national unity government in the wake of the Likud's reemphasis of its hard-line position definitely demonstrated the party's weakness. Even though a majority in the party supported Peres's effort to bring down the government and replace it with a Labor-led coalition, the result was a disaster. Labor failed to dislodge Shamir and had to take the blame for a prolonged, ugly government crisis. Without elections, Shamir formed a right-leaning government. No doubt the peace initiative would have fallen had external events not killed it. Elections would have led to a further Labor decline. The failure should have led to the replacement of Shimon Peres as party leader, but no leading substitute satisfactory to those seeking change was available. As expected, Peres fought successfully to retain this post.

Shamir's new power is visible in every way. Take the World Jewry Solidarity Conference held in March 1989. Shamir and his close associate, Ehud Olmert, the Likud cochairman of the conference, managed to overcome what were initially strong objections from many diaspora

Jews, as well as from the Labor party, to score a major symbolic victory. The Labor party was co-opted and Mordechai Gur, who sees himself as a strong contender for party leadership, used his role as cochairman to persuade skeptical diaspora Jewish leaders that the conference was not to back the Likud but to back Israel, thereby not only strengthening his own contacts with the diaspora but also bringing Shamir the desired successful outcome. Olmert, by the same token, no doubt under Shamir's direction, clearly defined the conference as one of support for the present Israeli coalition government as a whole, something that is very acceptable to Jews the world over. Thus the conference took place amid predictions of dissension, but when it concluded on a positive note, everyone was more than pleased and Shamir was handed another victory.

Less than a month later, Shamir achieved a similar victory in Washington, D.C., by bringing a plan for Palestinian elections that promised sufficient progress in the short term, foreclosed nothing in the long term (despite his rhetorical disclaimers), and was clearly the best that the U.S. government, or anyone else, could get. The world supported the Shamir plan with more or less enthusiasm. Within Israel, where Shamir was attacked on his right, his plan served as a magnet for most of the center and even the moderate left.

Personally, Shamir no doubt agrees with the strictures adopted in the Likud compromise resolution, namely that whatever peace negotiations are pursued, East Jerusalemites should not be allowed to vote in the elections, Jewish settlement in the territories should continue, no foreign sovereignty should be allowed west of the Jordan, and there should be no negotiations with the PLO. On the other hand, he insists that those strictures represent only his party's stance and do not determine the meaning of the plan adopted by the government as a whole. Moreover, he claims that his party's endorsement of the government plan is more important than the strictures they have attached.

All told, Shamir has shown his mettle in his strongest resources— patience, solidity, and gentlemanly behavior—to secure his position and to advance his policies in the face of more outspoken and frenetic rivals within his party and outside. The real question today, then, is where he stands on the immediate issues of land and of the Palestinians as well as on such critical domestic issues as constitutional and electoral reform.

SHAMIR'S PEACE POSITION

With regard to peace, land, and the Palestinians, Shamir began his new term with a number of leaks that suggested that, under the rubric of "confederation," he was prepared for what might be described as a joint Israeli-Jordanian rule over the administered territories through which an autonomous Palestinian entity would be linked to Jordan for

civil and political purposes, while Israel would retain principal control
of the territory involved. This solution would still be an interim one, but
it could develop into a more formal confederation in the future. Subsequently he seemed to retreat from that position with a series of very
harsh statements, at first delivered within Herut forums but later broadcast publicly and then delivered in other forums as well.

Which is the real Shamir? It is hard to say, but it is at least plausible
that he was prepared for the first option under the right circumstances.
Nevertheless, as he saw Israeli and diaspora Jewish "doves" rushing to
embrace the PLO and to grant the Palestinians an independent state
when even Yasir Arafat was talking about a confederation along the lines
of the Benelux arrangement—although not a true confederation, certainly an interesting opening position for the PLO—he may have felt
that it was necessary to reaffirm and reemphasize that the people in
power in Israel are not about to give away the store. Whatever certain
vocal Israelis and other Jews might be saying at a round of conferences
in Belgium, New York, and Switzerland about a two-state solution,
Shamir made it clear that the decision would be made in the government
center in Jerusalem where he and his supporters rule the roost. At the
same time Shamir has continued to hint that he is prepared to be forthcoming and conciliatory on his terms.

What remains is something of an enigma but has room for intelligent
negotiation and maneuver; however, neither Shamir nor his government
will be a party to any formal surrender of territory west of the Jordan
River in the sense of giving it up completely. In the long run, the possibility seems to be there for a federal solution, probably labelled "confederation," even if it is unconventional and does not follow the strict
definition of a confederation. It will have to be a position that consti-
tutionally preserves a strong, legitimate Israeli presence in those territories. It may be that this will be the great test for the U.S. peacemaking
effort—whether Americans can draw upon their own experience and
that of others to devise such a federal solution.

In an atmosphere of uncertainty over what can or should be done to
achieve peace with the Palestinian Arabs, the Israeli population remains
almost equally divided between those who think there is a possibility of
conceding territory for peace and are willing to do so, and those who
think there is no such possibility and that therefore a hard line is necessary. In fact, Israeli public opinion is more sophisticated than this
summary would suggest. It is just that Israel continues to be faced with
Hobson's choices, a situation exacerbated by Shimon Peres's misplaying
of the Jordanian option which he had so patiently built in his two years
as prime minister and Yitzhak Shamir's refusal or inability to present
himself to his public as more than a standpatter, even when in private
he has made significant proposals for breaking the deadlock. The trag-

edy of these two intelligent and patriotic men, who have done so much for their country in other situations, has very sad public consequences. Most immediately, it seems to be contributing to a perpetuation of the deadlock.

Shamir's patience and his ability to wait matters out gave him two great successes in 1990. The first was his victory over Peres after the latter's effort to replace him as prime minister with the backing of the United States. The second came when the PLO openly resumed its terrorist activities against Israel at the end of May and then aligned itself firmly with Saddam Hussein when the Iraqi dictator invaded Kuwait on August 2.

Subsequently, the events of the second half of 1990 seemed to indicate that Shamir had been right all along, that the PLO had not changed its spots and that negotiations with it would be dangerous for Israel. By late summer the peace camp was in disarray, Peres was well off center stage, and the only Labor party voice heard regularly was that of Rabin as a political commentator as the Gulf crisis unfolded. Many of the doves among the diaspora Jewish leadership were reconsidering their position vis-à-vis Shamir and Israel's stance. More firmly in the saddle than ever, Shamir was now leading an increasingly united people whose support for him was nearly unanimous, this in place of the highly polarized society of only a few months before.

Shamir's ability to keep Israel from retaliating against the Iraqi missile attacks once war broke out added to his stature and to international support of him and Israel. Overnight, Israel went from a wild and violent violator of human rights to a sober and sensible country in the eyes of much of the world. It was clear that Israeli-Palestinian peace would be high on the world agenda after the war was over, with or without formal linkage to Iraq's removal from Kuwait. Israelis were saying that efforts would be made to "pay for part of the war in shekalim." Now, however, Shamir will be better able to press Israel's case as he understands it.

THE PROGNOSIS FOR CONSTITUTIONAL AND ELECTORAL REFORMS

In the wake of the ugly and embarrassing coalition negotiations of November 1988, Shamir seemed, for a while, to have resolved to press for far-reaching constitutional and electoral reforms. Understanding that electoral reform alone, whether in the form of raising the minimum threshold needed to obtain seats in the Knesset under the present proportional representation system or moving to some form of district elections or some combination of both, will not solve the problem of minor parties being decisive in determining which of the two major parties will form a government, the prime minister apparently opted for the direct election of the head of government as a chief executive.

In December 1988 several private draft bills calling for the direct election of the head of government were introduced by Likud members of the Knesset. This led to the appointment of the Interministerial Committee on Electoral Reform, consisting of leading Likud and Labor ministers and Knesset members, to work out a plan combining constitutional and electoral reform agreeable to both parties and capable of being enacted early in the life of the present Knesset. In May 1989 that committee reported a compromise electoral reform proposal that satisfied the political needs of both major parties but was problematic in its ability to build public confidence. At the same time, it backed away from any recommendation of the direct election of the head of government. The Likud had second thoughts after Peres made a public statement that such a change would work in Labor's favor.

By July 1989 the interministerial committee had come to realize the impracticalities of certain aspects of its reform proposal and began to consider revisions to it. Two months later the government experienced another mini-crisis and the big parties scrambled for the support of the small parties once again. Indeed, Agudat Israel seemed to take advantage of the situation, threatening to leave the coalition unless, among other things, they would be guaranteed that there would be no further action on electoral reform. In the end, Shamir conceded to them on this issue.

With the end of the 1990 government crisis, a cross-party coalition— led by MK Uriel Lynn of the Likud, chairman of the Knesset Constitution Committee; MK Amnon Rubenstein of Shinui; MK David Libai of Labor; and MK Yoash Tzidon of Tzomet—introduced bills for the direct election of the prime minister. Initially each man introduced his own bill, and all four bills passed the preliminary reading in the Knesset; the four were instructed to get together and bring in a joint bill for second and third readings. That was done over the summer of 1990: the joint bill was presented to the Knesset and the public on September 11, and by November it attracted the support of approximately one-quarter of the Knesset membership on an individual basis and the endorsement of the Labor party. Likud, on the other hand, made no commitment since Shamir's coalition rested on the ultra-Orthodox parties who were strongly opposed to any change in the electoral system as an effort to weaken their ability to determine who would rule. The Gulf crisis put the entire issue aside as, once again, national security concerns moved to the top of the Israeli agenda.

Needless to say, as time passes, ugly memories of the coalition negotiations fade, and as the stability of the present government decreases, the major parties will become less interested in an electoral reform that would bring them into conflict with the small parties whom they might need for coalition purposes. Thus Israel is currently in a race between feeling it necessary to make constitutional changes and feeling relaxed about making changes as a result of the daily experience of the present government. The smaller parties, left, right, and center, remain opposed to any changes that would weaken them. Even the large parties agree that they do not want any change that would result in a strict two-party system that would deny such permanent minorities as the religious bloc and the Arabs the chance to elect their own representatives to the Knesset, even if it is desirable not to leave either of those two groups in a position of being able to determine which major party will form the government.

At this writing, electoral reform is once again in suspended animation. At the same time, the idea of direct election of the head of government is growing in popularity. Although no action is expected until the security situation stabilizes, direct election will be the first step in any constitutional reform that is undertaken. In truth, it is the only step that would enhance governmental stability, which is one of the purposes of constitutional reform in Israel; at the same time, it would not deny permanent minorities representation in the Knesset, a step contrary to Israeli conceptions of democracy.

THE CONTINUED RISE OF THE LIKUD AS A CENTRIST PARTY

Any doubt over the Likud's position as Israel's leading party should have been dispelled by the results of the municipal elections held on February 28, 1989. The 1989 local elections saw Likud gain control of most of the major cities and almost all of the development towns, a reversal from the previous five years when Labor controlled the cities with a total population of 1,150,000, as compared to 600,000 for the Likud. In addition to retaining Tel Aviv, Herzliya, and Netanya, Likud wrested Holon, Beersheba, Ramat Gan, Petah Tikva, and Ashdod from Labor, and Tiberias from a National Religious Party mayor.

The Likud victory was, in a sense, the completion of what the Likud started in 1977, that is to say, the establishment of the Likud as a full, firmly rooted, equal contender for political power with the Labor party, if not the majority party in the country. It also reflected the movement of the Likud toward the center of Israel's political spectrum, so that, as Asher Arian noted when analyzing the Knesset elections, the Likud has become, for all intents and purposes, the centrist party in Israel today.[4]

Additionally, the election results demonstrated that the Likud has acquired the organizational capacity to take advantage of the demographic trends that are running in its favor: younger people tend to vote Likud more than older, and Sephardim tend to vote Likud more than

Ashkenazim. This time the Likud was able to translate those factors to its advantage in local elections where turnout depends more on organization than it does in Knesset elections. On the other hand, as the tremendous anti-Labor feeling that originally brought people to Likud has faded to some extent, in each election there is a larger percentage of people who decide how to vote based on other considerations. Hence there was a decline in the youth and Sephardi anti-Labor vote per se. Another sign of growing political maturity was a greater tendency toward split-ticket voting; some voters opted for a charismatic local personality of one party for mayor but supported another party for the city or local council.

While Shamir was wrong to claim that those elections were a referendum on his policies toward the PLO and the territories—these were fought out on local issues almost exclusively in each community—he could legitimately claim that the serious drubbing that the Likud administered to Labor in the municipal arena for the first time was strong evidence of Likud's expanded grass-roots support and superior party organization.[5] The municipal elections further stabilized his government and gave him more of the political muscle he needed to lead the country, especially along a path that may well lead to confrontation with the United States and Europe, not to mention the rest of the world.

DECLINE OF THE LABOR PARTY MACHINE

Likud's greatest triumph was to be found in its ability to field a better organization over much of the country. In the past, Labor has been especially known for the strength of its organization. The old MAPAI party, Labor's predecessor and core, was a political machine par excellence. More than that, in addition to the usual organization common to all political machines, it could call upon institutions like the Histadrut, the Histadrut companies, and the kibbutzim for resources, for buses and cars to transport voters to the polls, for people to work at the polls even in communities where Labor itself might not have had enough activists to do so. In 1988–1989, by all accounts, Likud was stronger than Labor in this respect. Many people in the kibbutzim simply refused to work for Labor because of their own problems with the Labor party or problems related to the economic situation of the kibbutzim. Beyond that, Likud had finally built an organization that could turn out its voters on election day.

Forty-eight percent of all eligible voters in the Jewish sector voted in the municipal elections. Throughout the Western world, turnout in local elections is lower than turnout for national or parliamentary elections. This is true in Israel as well. While it is still much higher than in the United States or Canada, it is much lower than in Knesset elections. In the Arab sector, the turnout was extremely high—over 80 percent—and in some localities exceeded 90 percent of eligible voters. No doubt this is because the vast majority of Israeli Arabs live in their own municipalities, making local elections their only opportunity to choose their own leaders. In other words, salience is clearly a major factor affecting voter turnout.

The impact of local issues and candidates was paramount. In a large number of localities, the Likud put up the better candidates in the eyes of a majority of the voters, which is why they did so well. Responsible for conduct of the Likud campaign was Foreign Minister Moshe Arens, Shamir's closest associate, and MK David Magen, once Ariel Sharon's key man but now in the Shamir camp. Both deserve much of the credit for the Likud victory. They prepared the Likud for the local elections by actually intervening in local affairs to promote "good" candidates in place of mediocre local activists. This was accepted by the local branches of the party. According to the new game as played by the Likud, the national party took care of its local branches by putting in the right people, a tactic that succeeded quite well. Unfortunately this is an ominous sign for the local politicians who are getting the message that they are not capable of selecting good candidates and for the local autonomy gained over the past several years. Labor, on the other hand, was internally quite fragmented. In about two dozen localities, Labor people competed on two or even three lists. Hence, at best, their vote was divided.

What was the impact of the election results on the leadership of the Labor party? Under normal circumstances, one would have said that this would have been the last nail in Shimon Peres's political coffin. Instead, he survived that and the still worse debacle that came a year later. While there are never normal circumstances in Israel, the odds are strong, though not overwhelming, that Peres will not lead the party in the next Knesset elections. On the other hand, the future of the Labor party depends upon whether the party can make a change of leadership or whether Peres can somehow rebuild the party while staying in power.

THE RELIGIOUS PARTIES DEAL FOR BENEFITS

With regard to the religious parties, this election witnessed a modest extension of the process begun back in 1981 when Agudat Israel partially joined the Begin coalition, a process which strengthened with the rise of SHAS in 1984, and which really took off last November with the integration of the ultra-Orthodox parties into the political system. Working in local elections is one of the most prominent signs of integration into the political system, and the religious parties achieved significant benefits for themselves as a result.

One example of this could be seen in Ramat Hasharon where, out of

43,000 citizens, there are only about 1,000 religious voters split among four parties. Because, for the first time, they voted as a bloc, they managed to gain a seat on the city council. They also made a deal beforehand with the Labor candidate for mayor; nearly all of the religious voters voted for him because of their advance agreement to receive a number of benefits. In many other localities, the religious parties gave their support to the Likud, which contributed to the success of the Likud in many places where the power of Labor and Likud was almost equal.

Any assessment of the impact of the religious parties in the local elections must consider the specific situation in each community. In many communities there are few conflicts over issues of religion; in some, such as Jerusalem or Petah Tikva, there have been chronic problems. It may be expected that the religious parties in the local arena will gain or at least maintain their power irrespective of what happens on the statewide scene. One party that could have been expected to gain in strength was SHAS, at the expense of Likud, but recent scandals associated with its leadership may change that. It depends on the issues that come up, because a good number of not necessarily religious people would vote for SHAS for ethnic or other traditional attitudes which are prevalent among Sephardim.

THE NEW ZIONIST LEFT—ISRAELI "GREENS"

The Zionist left, which had acquired more cohesiveness as the political voice of the Israeli doves, especially as the Labor party lost power, put on a different and very successful face in the local elections. Locally the parties of the Zionist left—the CRM and MAPAM (*Mifleget Poalim Hameuhedet*, or United Workers party), plus the more centrist Shinui— attract the suburban voters of the upper middle class. These are the people who want more efficient, more effective, and cleaner municipal government. They are environmentalists who see themselves on the progressive side of issues. In some cases, two or three of the parties joined together in a common local front, representing Israel's equivalent of the European "Green" party phenomenon which is finding expression around the world. The curious thing is that, as the CRM and even Shinui become even more leftward oriented in the Knesset elections and have begun to form a more cohesive bloc, they have also gained strength for very different reasons in the local elections.

In the actual campaign, the left and center-left was split, with the CRM and Labor competing in almost every city. In Ramat Hasharon, for example, the wealthiest families voted for the CRM and Shinui. It was not only a matter of local interest but also a sign that they simply are no longer willing to vote for Labor anymore. With the CRM running so strong locally, Labor has a real problem on the local level. This emerged as a trend in the Knesset elections and is being continued in the local arena. At the same time, the parties of the far right did not compete in the local elections this time, allowing the Likud to sweep the entire right, plus the center.

THE RISE OF FUNDAMENTALISM IN THE ARAB SECTOR

In the Arab sector, the big news was the arrival in strength of Islamic fundamentalism. The impact of this phenomenon is not yet clear because part of it was a reaction against the inefficient, unconcerned, oligarchic, entrenched governments of the old elites—the leaders of the notable families—in a situation where there have not been many opportunities even for the circulation (or rotation) of elites. Under such conditions, any movement for change requires cohesion around a party that came out with a very strong message, which the Islamic fundamentalist party could do. On the other hand, there is no question that Islamic fundamentalism is sweeping the entire Arab world. Only the future will tell us to what degree the voting results were a reaction to local conditions and to what degree they were part of the worldwide trend toward the entry of religious fundamentalists into politics.

The first signs of the resulting change came as the intifada turned more violent and Saddam Hussein occupied Kuwait. These events led to anti-Israel stirrings in the Israeli Arab towns and villages comparable to those among the Palestinians in the territories, if not yet as extensive or intense.

In the Knesset elections, Labor received substantial Arab support, though in numbers smaller than in previous elections. This factor was not present in the local elections where most Arabs voted in their own municipalities for their own parties. In fact, the Likud advantage in November 1988 became even greater in the local elections because the Jewish vote was separate and distinct.

THE FUTURE OF THE LIKUD

In the 1984 Knesset elections, a large number of mayors were included in the Likud list. This definitely strengthened the Likud as the party with a younger generation of leaders who were ready to be integrated into state politics and who were given responsible positions in the state government. In the 1988 Knesset elections, there were few additions of this sort in the Likud list, but Labor took the cue and included a number of mayors on its Knesset list, with good results. Many politicians now see local government as a more attractive, vibrant, and politically worthwhile place to invest their efforts, realizing that it can be a springboard to the

Knesset, bypassing the traditional twenty- or thirty-year period of working up through the party ranks.

It is also becoming more attractive to run for local office today because to be a Knesset member is less important now than to be mayor of Jerusalem or Tel Aviv, or even of one of the smaller cities. In terms of recognition, benefits, and power, the position of mayors today compares much more favorably than it used to to that of Knesset members, especially backbenchers.

On the other hand, Likud does not have the internal strength to consolidate its power position beyond a certain point. This was reflected in the Histadrut elections of November 15, 1989. Though given a good chance to seriously threaten Labor's control of the powerful General Workers Federation for the first time in Israel's history, Likud managed to field a lackluster candidate for secretary-general against an attractive incumbent of Yemenite background who appealed to Histadrut's normal constituency. After a campaign that concentrated on criticism of the present Histadrut administration without putting forward a program of its own, the result was a Labor victory.

Since 1977 it has been apparent that Israel's demographics are such that, all other things being equal, the Likud should gain one or two additional seats at every quadrennial election. It is only the Likud's failure at actual governance that has prevented this result. Even so, the demographics have meant that Likud does not lose. This situation is likely to persist, especially if Labor cannot revivify and revitalize itself with new leadership that will be attractive to Israel's floating vote. At present, Likud seems strong, if relatively inflexible, and still not highly competent at governing, while Labor seems flexible but weak, torn apart by internal struggles, and obsolete, with no new leadership visible in the wings. Under such circumstances Likud will continue to constitute the political center and a generally victorious one at that.

NOTES

1. Howard R. Penniman, ed., *Israel at the Polls: The Knesset Elections of 1977* (Washington, D.C.: American Enterprise Institute, 1979); Howard R. Penniman and Daniel J. Elazar, eds., *Israel at the Polls, 1981: A Study of the Knesset Elections* (Washington, D.C.: American Enterprise Institute and Bloomington: Indiana University Press, 1986); Daniel J. Elazar and Shmuel Sandler, eds., *Israel's Odd Couple: The 1984 Knesset Elections and the National Unity Government* (Detroit, Mich.: Wayne State University Press, 1990); Asher Arian, ed., *The Elections in Israel, 1977* (Jerusalem: Academic Press, 1980); and Asher Arian, ed., *The Elections in Israel, 1981* (Tel Aviv: Ramot, 1983).

2. See Ilan Greilsammer, "The Religious Parties," in Elazar and Sandler, eds., *Israel's Odd Couple*; Shmuel Sandler, "The Religious Parties," in Penniman and Elazar, eds., *Israel at the Polls, 1981*, esp. pp. 110–19; Yael Yishai, "Factionalism

in the National Religious Party: The Quiet Revolution," in Arian, ed., *The Elections in Israel, 1977.*

3. Cf. *The Jerusalem Post*, week of July 1, 1989.

4. See Asher Arian, "The 1988 Israeli Elections—Questions of Identity," *Jerusalem Letter/Viewpoints*, 83 (January 15, 1989).

5. See Daniel J. Elazar and Chaim Kalchheim, "The 1989 Local Elections: What Happened?" *Jerusalem Letter/Viewpoints*, 87 (May 1, 1989).

3

Toward the 1990s in
Israeli Politics

Asher Arian

Four simultaneous processes operating at the end of the 1980s presented the observer of Israeli politics with fascinating paradoxes. These processes had to do with the distribution of political attitudes among Jewish Israelis, and with the distribution of political power in the country. The manner in which these paradoxes will—or will not—be resolved will hold the keys to the political future of Israel. The four processes were (1) an almost even *split* between the right and the left, led by Likud and Labor, respectively; (2) a growing *polarization* of attitude and political power between the more conciliatory left and the more hard-line right; (3) a generalized, short-term *hardening* of positions regarding security matters—specifically, the territories—with a concomitant trend toward *moderation* of Israeli public opinion on long-term policy goals; and (4) the emergence of the Likud squarely and exclusively at the *epicenter* of Israeli politics, as Labor continued its decline.

The paradoxes generated by these combinations were obvious: If a split, how could one party emerge? If polarization, how could there be moderation? If moderation, why would a split occur? And, more pointedly, if moderation, why would the Likud be the party of the center, rather than Labor?

Surface action often grabbed the headlines; the future of the country seemed to hang on the latest crisis or proposal. But what counted in the long run was often more low keyed; processes removed from the flow of current events were having their impact.

There was division, but a center was emerging in Israeli politics after a two-decade period of rift. To be sure, that new center was considerably to the right of the one that had previously dominated Israeli politics. Still, it will probably be more useful to think of the Likud of the 1990s as a party of the center rather than as a party of the right. For a historical analogy, the socialist origins of the Labor party were not very relevant in understanding Labor policy of the 1960s and early 1970s; what was of note was that Labor was then a party of the center which tried to retain the loyalty of what it considered to be the central stratum of the electorate. Labor was doomed to relinquish its dominant role and to share power with the Likud because it failed to retain the loyalty of its predominantly Ashkenazi electoral base, and it ignored the changing allegiances of the growing Sephardi electorate. By the end of the 1980s, after consolidating its hold on a sizeable and loyal electoral group, the Likud could stake its claim on the political center by choosing to distance itself from more extreme rightist parties—such as Moledet, Tehiya, and Tzomet—and by displaying alert instincts of coalition formation with parties of the ideological center. Its success was not assured, but of the two big parties, the Likud seemed to have the best chance of success during the next decade.

The trajectory of the system at the beginning of the 1990s seemed to be toward short-term *hardening*, long-term *moderation*, and the control of the political *center* by the Likud.

SPLIT

Political competitiveness was very intense in the 1980s, but, as the decade ended, although the competitiveness continued, both big parties won fewer Knesset seats than they had before. After decades of dominance by the Labor camp, the two biggest parties were still very close, but Likud and Labor each won a smaller share of the vote in 1988 than it had in the other two elections of the 1980s. The share of the two-party vote declined. The number of seats won by the two parties had dropped to 79 in 1988 (Likud 40 seats, Labor 39), from 95 in 1981 (48/47 in Likud's favor), and 85 in 1984 (44/41 in Labor's favor).

In the 1988 elections, the Likud came out one Knesset seat stronger than Labor, but Likud's twenty-year record was much better than was Labor's. The number of people who actually voted increased between 1969 and 1988 by almost 900,000. The difference between the Labor vote of 1988 (685,363) and the Alignment (Labor and MAPAM) vote of 1969 (632,035) was only slightly more than 50,000 votes. (In 1988, MAPAM ran alone and won 56,345 votes). The Likud, on the other hand, added more than 370,000 votes, growing from 338,948 in 1969 to 709,305 in 1988. Three patterns were operating at the end of the 1980s:

(1) intense competition between Likud and Labor, (2) a shrinking of the size of the two-party vote, and (3) a continuing decline for Labor.

POLARIZATION

The polarized nature of the system was clear, as evidenced by the growth of smaller parties of the ideological extremes and the distribution of political attitudes. As the intifada's outbreak passed its second anniversary at the beginning of the decade of the 1990s (it began in December 1987), attitudes were in flux. One clear trend was for attitudes to become more extreme: Many rightists moved further to the right, leftists further to the left. This was evident in the results of the 1988 elections, as the power of the smaller extreme parties was strengthened. These lists played a major role in the coalition calculations of the big parties.

Were it not that the two large parties finally preferred to coalesce with each other, the smaller parties would have been very influential in a "narrow" coalition. Making the assumption that vote choice reflects policy position, one would have to conclude that the system was becoming more and more polarized, as the ideological extremes became more articulated and vocal.

This is seen in the matrix of voter exchanges comparing the 1984 vote and the 1988 decision. Each of the two big parties retained their 1984 voters at about the same rate. Some Alignment voters drifted to the left, but others moved to the Likud and the right. A similar pattern for the Likud voters was evident, but in the opposite direction. Among army voters in 1988, the Likud won 35.1 percent, and the parties to the right of it received an additional 15.1 percent. Labor achieved 29 percent among army voters; the parties to the left of Labor won 11 percent. This pattern of a 50:40 split in favor of the right repeated a familiar pattern among voters in the army. The other 10 percent of the vote went primarily to religious parties.

But there was also evidence of possible change in the future. The pattern among new voters indicated that the political system may be even more fractured in the future. Surveys showed that new voters split evenly between the right and the Likud, on the one hand, and Labor and the left, on the other.

HARDENING AND MODERATION

At the same time, a dual pattern of hardening and moderation was evident in survey results. Israelis remained hawks on short-term issues, but increasingly they were conciliatory regarding long-term outcomes. Israeli public opinion has been and continues to be sensitive to political developments, both internal and external. Willingness to enter into eventual negotiations with the PLO, assuming that the PLO were to recognize Israel and to renounce terrorism, increased.[1] Substantial portions of the Labor party take a more moderate position regarding the PLO, and in the 1988 elections, this seemed to be the party's message. But when Labor tried in the 1988 campaign to present itself as the party of peace and the only one that could lead the country to successful negotiations with the Arabs, it was rejected. Labor gambled and lost. It was able to change its message, but not its image as the tired party of the past.

The results of a study in which 416 adult Jews were interviewed twice—once at the outbreak of the intifada, in December 1987, and then again just before the November 1988 elections—provide evidence for these developments.[2] The percentage that supported territories for peace increased from 34 to 41 percent; those who opposed negotiations with the PLO given the present situation jumped from 37 to 46 percent. Labor support stayed the same within this sample (34%); Likud support jumped from 34 to 41 percent.

The respondents of the panel were asked a series of questions regarding policy issues, among other things. Change took place, but it was neither monotonic nor uniform. The panel on the whole (using a measure that will be presented in the next section) became more militant in the ten months that passed, but the change was a matter of degree, rather than a complete reversal. In fact, change occurred in both a more militant direction and in a more conciliatory direction, at the same time, within the panel.

When respondents' attitudes changed, the change tended to be in the direction in which they were already leaning. This is evident when the perceived effect of the intifada as reported by the respondents is compared with the answers of the respondents to policy questions. Those who said that the intifada had a hardening effect on their attitudes were much more likely to have had hard-line views before the beginning of the uprising. The opposite was also true: Those who reported a softening of their views because of the intifada were much more likely to have begun with dovish views. This is also seen with regard to political party preferences. Those who reported a 1987 vote intention for Labor and the left were much more likely to identify the parties that benefitted from the developments as Labor and the left; those who said that they intended to vote for Likud and the right were much more inclined to see the Likud and the right as gaining from the intifada. Moreover, most respondents who reported in 1988 that the intifada influenced their vote choice in favor of the left and Labor were already left and Labor supporters in 1987; the obverse is true for the right and the Likud.

Four of the nine questions in the policy scale occasioned change in a more dovish direction; four others changed in a more hawkish direction. A ninth was indeterminate. Those who changed in a more dovish direction included agreeing with the principle of exchanging land for peace, the eventual establishment of a Palestinian state, the assessment of the effect of the army's presence in the territories on its fighting ethic, and attitudes toward encouraging Arabs to leave the country.

Questions that generated a hawkish change concerned the forced choice the respondents were given between peace negotiations and increasing Israel's military power, and of whether security interests were more important than the rule of law when these two values were in conflict. These two questions displayed the highest rate of change among all policy questions. Change in a more hawkish direction also included the idea of an international peace conference and negotiations with the PLO. It is likely that some opposed negotiations during ongoing violence, and not necessarily because they had come to far-reaching decisions about the Palestinian cause. This is probably an example of the panel members "rallying around the flag" especially because the two large parties steadfastly opposed negotiations with the PLO.

An uncertain direction of change regarded the question of the civil rights of Arabs were the territories to be annexed. This hints at a reluctance to change under pressure. During this period of crisis, many opted for retaining familiar patterns rather than for experimenting with new solutions.

Polarization was highlighted by the same analysis when it was applied to the vote decision of the respondents. The only group for which no statistically significant change occurred between the two time periods was the group who responded in 1987 that they would vote for Labor if elections were to be held at that time. By 1988, those individuals had shifted slightly to the right but at levels below statistical significance. The 1987 Likud voters switched to the right at an extensive rate.

The change among those who declared that they would vote for the Likud just before the 1988 elections was significant. The Likud benefitted from this general shift in public opinion in the direction of its stated policies. By extension, Labor was hurt by the flow of opinion away from its platform. Those who communicated their intention to vote Labor on the eve of the 1988 elections identified with the conciliatory ideas that Labor put forward. These voters generated the only instance in the study of a voting group that had a statistically significant change in a dovish direction. This underscores the impossible mission faced by Labor in the 1988 elections: to win a majority for its positions when all social categories were distancing themselves from those positions. It is little wonder that the election results appeared to be so glum for Labor.

THE NEW CENTER

Israeli democracy has dealt successfully with threats from the political extremes throughout its history. David Ben-Gurion was successful in excluding the communists and Herut from his coalition calculations; in so doing, he stigmatized these groups in popular thought for decades. No less important, Ben-Gurion successfully staved off his more ardent socialist colleagues and marched the country to the center. On his watch, Ben-Gurion initiated the status quo arrangements that allow the religious parties to participate in the establishment while struggling against it.

Menachem Begin's failure to annex the territories and the peace treaty he signed with Egypt, which entailed withdrawal from the Sinai, are evidence of his centrist drift. A 1988 example of the battle of the center against the extremes is the joint effort by Likud and Labor to disallow from the election race Rabbi Meir Kahane's Kach list, on the one hand, and nationalist Arab lists that supported a Palestinian state alongside Israel, on the other.

Centrifugal forces working to tear a system apart prosper on more, not less, polarization, and they pull adjacent parties from the center toward their extreme pole.[3] Rabbi Kahane's Kach party and the Tehiya party had that kind of influence on the Likud, and Labor was affected, but to a much lower degree, by the Arab parties, MAPAM, and the Citizens' Rights Movement. These processes enfeeble the center.[4] In the Israeli case, the reaction has been for the center (Likud and Labor) to counter with attempts to outlaw the extreme parties and to fashion a centripetal political mechanism—the national unity government. But having the government on hold does not prevent change in Israel. By forging a minimal common denominator, the unity government defined the consensus of the middle. The army withdrew from Lebanon, inflation was controlled, and the Lavi project was abandoned—all by joint agreement. Beyond that, however, the symmetry broke down in favor of the right. By agreeing to some settlement—albeit less than before— and by avoiding a definite answer to the Shultz proposals in 1988, the 1984–88 national unity government in essence accepted a mild version of the Likud platform.

The political and military frustration which accompanied the intifada was an additional push in the direction of the right. Regardless of wish or fantasy, in the absence of a moderate interlocutor, the only realistic policy in the minds of many Israelis was a policy of holding on. The inability of the Labor party to rejuvenate its leadership, to penetrate the growing ranks of the Israeli-born middle class of Sephardi background, and to convince voters that its vision of the peace process was realistic all made greater the likelihood that the Likud would emerge as representing the national consensus.

Parties in office become coopted by the center; before long they are champions of the middle and they do their best to coopt others into their position. The Likud—and even Yitzhak Shamir—have progressed a long way on this path. Images notwithstanding, the Likud and Shamir must be seen as centrist in the Israeli context of the 1990s. What is more, Shamir is in the center position of the intraparty skirmishes in the Likud: Ariel Sharon is to his right, and David Levy . . . somewhere else. The political constellation in Israel at the beginning of the 1990s saw Shamir emerge as an extremely powerful prime minister of Israel. This did not result from his charismatic personality (most observers agree that he does not have one) but from the kinds of structural factors described above. Shamir's successors are likely to inherit these structures, and, unless they badly miscalculate or perform very poorly, these structures will work in their favor as well.

The Likud is not only forging its place in the center, Labor is failing to react in a credible manner. There is absolutely no doubt of the long-term decline of the Labor party. From almost 50 percent of the vote in the 1960s, Labor has sunk to 30 percent in 1988. The list of reasons why Labor did not regain its earlier dominance is long: bitter internal fights between Shimon Peres and Yitzhak Rabin, the slow rate of elite circulation, its estrangement from the growing Sephardi electorate, and the leadership's inability or lack of desire to recruit a younger generation of leaders.

At the beginning of the 1990s, the party seemed to be dealing with many of those problems. Peres and Rabin had coordinated the 1988 Labor campaign together, and they were generally united regarding the handling of the intifada and the continuance of the peace process. Peres's continued leadership was challenged a number of times in the year after the 1988 debacle but never successfully.

The Labor party appeared to be undergoing a quiet revolution even as the elections of 1988 took place. Processes were unfolding which would likely affect the cast of characters in Israeli politics for years to come. These processes included the introduction of a large number of new legislators and a growing degree of democratization in the choosing of candidates. Change was happening in other parties as well, but it was especially obvious in Labor, mainly because these processes had emerged in some of the other parties but had long been stymied in Labor.

In 1988, many of the candidates elected by both Labor and the Likud were new to the Knesset. A third of the thirty-nine elected from Labor, and eight of the forty elected from Likud had never served in the Knesset before. The Labor party delegation's average age was a year younger than was the Likud's: 51 for Labor, 52 for Likud. But Labor's Knesset members tended to be older the higher on the list they were. A throwback to the good old days, it clearly indicated that the oligarchical tendencies of the party have persisted. When studied in groups of ten, the average age of the first Labor group was 60.7, the second 50.7, and then 46.7 and 44.1. For the Likud, the first group of ten elected was the oldest (56.8), but the second group was youngest (47.7); the other two

groups were 51 and 52.5 years of age. The introduction of younger
members did not affect the one-sided gender distribution of Knesset
members. Only seven women were elected to the Knesset in 1988; four
of them came from the Alignment.

Both Labor and Likud, as well as many of the smaller lists, placed
Sephardi candidates in prominent places on the lists. Labor elected two
new members of the Knesset who were Sephardi mayors—Amir Peretz
of Sderot and Eli Dayan of Ashkelon—although there was no evidence
that their place on the list improved Labor's success among Sephardim.
In a major revision, compared with past lists, Labor in 1988 fielded
eleven candidates born in Asia or Africa among the first forty on its list.
The parallel number for the Likud was six. Twenty of Labor's first forty,
and twenty-nine of the Likud's first forty, were born in Israel. The
leaders of the parties (Peres and Shamir) were both born in Poland, but
the composition of the Knesset delegations was coming more in line with
the demographic changes taking place in society, especially the growing
numbers of Sephardim in the electorate.

Important structural and procedural developments occurred as well.
In 1988, both Labor and Likud ran as parties which fielded a single list
each. In the past (as recently as 1984), the Labor and MAPAM parties
jointly set up a single list called the Alignment, and the Likud list was
made up of two autonomous parties, Herut and the Liberals. But by
1988, Labor and MAPAM ran separate lists, and Herut and the Liberals
merged their parties into a single one, retaining the name Likud for the
new party.

In 1988, Herut's center selected its candidates for the Knesset list
separately, and the Liberals selected their own. The parties agreed to
place the leader of Herut, Shamir, in the first place. Shamir, like Begin
before him, was exempted from the rigors of competition; he was selected by acclamation. Herut selected its candidates in a relatively open
and democratic manner; the complete Likud list was made up of the
choices of Herut and the Liberal party, and others, as well. By previous
arrangement, Yigael Hurewitz, Zalman Shoval, and Aharon Abuhatzeira
were added to the choices of Herut and the Liberals. The merger agreement between Herut and the Liberal party provided for a united center
selecting the Likud's candidates in the future.

Labor attempted to introduce a greater degree of democratization in
1988. In the past, a nominating committee controlled by the party leadership presented a list which was approved by the center. In 1988, a
complex system decentralized the system somewhat. The democratic
nature of the exercise was immediately tarnished by the fact that the
important leaders were granted the luxury of being nominated to the
list without facing election within the party. Those who made the head
of the list without election included Peres, Rabin, Yitzhak Navon, Knesset

speaker Shlomo Hillel, party secretary general Uzi Baram, and Histadrut head Yisrael Kessar. In addition, in the agreement that brought Ezer Weizman's Yahad list into the Labor party, it was understood that Weizman would automatically be put in one of the top ten positions. At least a partial success, Labor followed Herut into an era of greater—if not perfect—democracy in the selection process.

Perhaps these changes need time to set in; in 1988, mending these ills did not seem to help Labor penetrate the Sephardi electorate. Until this happens, the decline of Labor will continue. The dominant group in Israel's future will be the native born. Already in 1992, a majority of the Jewish voters will be Israeli born. As the importance of the ethnic background of the parents and the grandparents recedes, and as Israelis become more educated—and hopefully better educated as well—this Israeli-born group will become more and more important. It will be a salaried and middle class group on the whole. As a group, it is likely to opt for middle-of-the-road political positions, as long as its social and economic status can be maintained. The headlines will be grabbed by the religious fundamentalists and the supernationalists, and the opponents of each, but the elections will be won by the party that is most successful in attracting the votes of the center. At this time, that party appears to be the Likud.

To repeat: The trajectory of the system today seems to be toward an emerging *moderation* and toward the control of the political *center* by the Likud, Shamir, and his successors. Labor might head the government in the near future as a result of a crisis or a shift in political allegiance on the part of smaller parties. But, in a more fundamental sense, the structures seem to be in place for Likud dominance through the decade of the 1990s.

This is likely to be a Likud that is more pragmatic than ideological, more middle class than working class, and more attuned to the growing native-born segment of the population. That growing and key part of the electorate is likely to express nativist sentiments, and it is likely to demand security, prosperity, and peace—in that order. There undoubtedly will be very serious crises in the Likud in the near future over issues of succession and policy, but, if there are no serious defections from within the ranks of the party leadership and if most of the crucial decisions are supported by the key leadership, its chances seem to be good in the decade of the 1990s.

NOTES

1. Hanoch Smith's time series reports the acceptability of negotiation with the PLO, if it officially recognizes Israel and ceases terrorist activity, moving from 43 percent in April 1987, through 53 percent in August 1988, to 58 percent in

March 1989. See *The New York Times*, April 2, 1989, p. 2. See also R. A. Stone, *Social Change in Israel: Attitudes and Events 1967–1979* (New York: Praeger, 1982); and Y. Yishai, *Land of Peace: Whither Israel?* (Stanford, Calif.: Hoover Institution, 1987).

2. The field work for the surveys was done by the Dahaf Research Institute. The surveys were prepared and conducted by the National Security and Public Opinion Project of the Jaffee Center for Strategic Studies at Tel Aviv University, directed by the author.

3. See Juan J. Linz and Alfred Stepan, eds., *The Breakdown of Democratic Regimes* (Baltimore: Johns Hopkins University Press, 1978).

4. Sartori argues with himself about whether parties of the center are characterized by immobilism or by mediation, thereby brokering the demands of the extremes. Whatever his conclusion, it is relevant here. Giovanni Sartori, *Parties and Party Systems* (Cambridge: Cambridge University Press, 1976), 135.

4

Extremism, Intensity, and Apocalyptic Warnings: Prophetic Policy Advocacy in Modern Israel

Ira Sharkansky

It is as though God Himself had said to the Jewish people, "Since, in your anger at Hadrian's intention to erect a shrine on My holy mountain, you showed no compassion for the lives of My children in pursuing the Bar Kokhba Rebellion, I have decreed that the Temple Mount not be in the your hands."[1]

This quotation does not come from ancient history or a contemporary religious visionary. It was written by a secular professor of international relations at a distinguished university. Earlier in his career he was a general in the armed forces, the commanding officer of military intelligence, and an advisor to the prime minister.

A prophetic style of policy advocacy is prominent in modern Israel.[2] Jeremiah would be an appropriate candidate for a patron saint, if the moderns were inclined to choose one.

Jeremiah was extreme in both style and substance. He positioned himself alongside the flow of pedestrians at the gates of Jerusalem and the Temple, and he decried the sins of the people and elites. He attacked the rulers' pursuit of advantages in international policies, and he urged that they remain loyal to Babylon.[3]

Jeremiah was explicit in detailing the punishments that would ensue from a continuation of wayward behaviors. Time and again he proclaimed that God "will make Jerusalem heaps, a lair of jackals...the cities of Judah a desolation, without an inhabitant."[4]

Despite the Jewish tradition that prophecy ceased from the time of the First Temple's destruction, modern Israel features prophetic policy advocates on issues large and small, at widely different points of the ideological spectrum. The individuals singled out in this chapter do not claim to be speaking for the Almighty. In this, they differ from the biblical prophets. Yet they act as if they have the Lord's power of attorney.

A prophetic style appears among trained technocrats as well as ordinary citizens. Some of the practitioners are religious, but others are overtly secular. What unites them is their reference to historic Jewish traditions; their willingness to confront beliefs and practices widely accepted by the mass and the elite; and the extreme nature of their descriptions, plans, or predictions. They deal in catastrophe or miracles. They offer radical solutions for Israel's problems. There is no middle ground or modesty in what they express.

MODERN PROPHETS

One of Israel's best-known writers, Amos Oz, travelled throughout the country in order to locate individuals who could articulate its range of opinions.[5] A number of his contacts expressed themselves in prophetic terms.

Oz quotes religious Jews who settled in the territories occupied as a result of the 1967 war. For them, holding that land is a holy mission. Their settlements represent the fulfillment of God's destiny for His people, and they will ensure the physical security of the nation in international politics.

One settler reminded Oz that the prophet Amos had been a farmer in the same site, and he had predicted the rebirth of Israel. According to the settler:

If you'd look at our community . . . you'd see with your own eyes the fulfillment of the prophecy. . . . You'd have to be completely blind, God forbid, not to see that this is the beginning of the Final Redemption.[6]

Another of Oz's contacts was a secular moshav resident. He was especially critical of the pampered Jews of the diaspora, who criticize Israel for not being gentle enough with the Arabs. To him, the work of Zionism is not done. He told Oz that it is necessary to bring even the *feinschmeckerim*[7] to Israel, perhaps by force. "Even if I have to blow up a synagogue here or there (to move them on)."

Oz composed one chapter from a discussion that he had with religious settlers in the West Bank. This was his opportunity to be prophetic. Oz attacked the close-minded religiosity of the settlers, and he asserted that his own secular humanism is also integral to the Jewish tradition.

The Jewish people have a great skill of creating destruction. We are perhaps the world champions of destruction. Of course, people can assert that all the destruction that they impose on themselves comes as a decree from heaven.... But our skill at destruction is not a decree from heaven.... Our characteristic demand for thoroughness, totality, to invent an ideal to accomplish fully, or to break our heads against the wall in failure.[8]

Prophetic Technocrats

Some of Israel's sophisticated technocrats express themselves in a prophetic style. Three prominent examples are Yehoshafat Harkabi, Meron Benvenisti, and Emanual Wald. Each of them earned doctorates from elite universities, and each has held ranking positions in military, governmental, or academic institutions. They lecture in prestigious forums and publish with serious presses or research centers. Each warns of a major disaster that will befall Israel if his own plea for reform is not heeded. Like the biblical Jeremiah, the work of each could profit from a careful editing. They combine detailed analysis along with polemics that reach beyond their facts and leave a skeptical reader to wonder about their conclusions.

Yehoshafat Harkabi

Professor Harkabi is prophetic in the style of his writing, even while the substance of his argument supports pragmatism in policy-making. A former head of military intelligence, he is emeritus professor of international relations at the Hebrew University of Jerusalem. He publishes extensively, and he appears regularly on Israeli radio and television.

Harkabi warns Israelis against those who revere the heroic religiosity and nationalism of the Bar Kokhba rebellion against the Romans in 132–135 C.E. To him, those who praise Bar Kokhba overlook the virtually total destruction of Jewish life in the region of Judea following the rebellion.[9]

For Harkabi, political realism is a value with religious significance. It is the ideal way to ensure the survival of God's people.[10] Bar Kokhba was guilty of irrational warfare that was bound to end in disaster. He did not consider the strategic setting. He failed to take account of the prevailing peace in the Roman Empire, the capacity of the Empire to focus massive resources in suppressing the rebellion, and the Romans' concern not to let a rebellion against the Empire go unpunished.

Harkabi is not primarily concerned with Bar Kokhba. That ancient figure provides a lesson for the unrealistic people of today. They are the nationalistic and religious zealots who would decide by themselves that the West Bank will be Israel's possession.

The contention that without ruling the West Bank Israel cannot survive weakens Israel's very right to exist ... such a stance may conjure up and inject new life into the old anti-Semitic image of Jews' claiming for themselves exclusive rights ... leaving the West Bank without sovereignty negates the current world order which is based on the sovereign division of territories.[11]

Harkabi predicts disaster if the zealots do not stop, or if they are not stopped by more reasonable Israelis.

The existence of the Jewish people is not a given. . . . Our deeds and our blunders will have considerable impact not only on the fate of those who dwell in Israel, but in a large measure on the entire Jewish people. Having chosen statehood, our destiny is, to a considerable degree, in our own hands, more than at any time since Bar Kokhba. This new situation demands not myths, but sobriety, much self-criticism, and severe critiques of the historical circumstances in which we find ourselves.[12]

Harkabi returned to these themes in a recent book that takes account of the Lebanese war, the Arab uprising, and other events in Israel and the Arab world.[13] He continues to see a grave situation with dire consequences. He writes about disasters of recent years, "the increasingly degenerate standards of Israeli civic and political life," and "fiascos" of political leaders that have bequeathed "a dangerous and misleading world view."[14] "What is at stake is the survival of Israel and the status of Judaism. Israel will soon face its moment of truth. The crisis that faces the nation will be all-consuming."[15]

The principal messages of Harkabi's new book are that Likud-dominated governments have been deluded by unrealistic goals and that Israel must deal with the PLO in order to establish a Palestinian state in the occupied territories.

Meron Benvenisti

As a deputy mayor of Jerusalem, Meron Benvenisti worked in behalf of creating ethnic boroughs that would contribute to the political stability of Israel's capital. He earned a doctorate at Harvard's Kennedy School and then dedicated himself to assessing the situation in the occupied West Bank. His reports, published by the American Enterprise Institute for Public Policy Research, make as much sense as anything amidst the tangle of data pertaining to demography, housing, transportation, and public expenditures.

Along with his research, Benvenisti employs the harshest of terms. He sounds like a Jewish prophet when he expresses moral compulsion, describes a decline in the standards of his people, and predicts national disaster if his warnings are not heeded.

Benvenisti refers to the Israelis as conquerors, and he compares them to the medieval autocrats who plundered the lands they occupied.[16] He terms the new settlers parasites, in contrast with the earlier pioneers who created productive agricultural units.

The national ethos . . . is deliberately reinforced and strengthened, not to instill renewed ideological motivation but to do just the opposite, to facilitate sheer consumerism and to exploit it. The consequences of distorted institutional and value systems may prove the heaviest price Israel pays for its West Bank settlement policies.[17]

Writing in 1984, Benvenisti saw the Palestinian cause as all but lost. His hope for the Palestinians and the Jews lay in enlightened Jewish Zionism. In his view, the Jewish ideology must awake from its own "fossilized" condition and recognize that the Palestinian evil—even though it may have been killed—will haunt Israel from the grave.

A new equilibrium between nationalistic objectives and humanistic values must be found. Zionism cannot escape the fate of other great liberating philosophies. Its failure to adjust to changing realities may turn it into a dark force.[18]

Benvenisti's latest book reads as if it had been written quickly during the first month or two of the Arab uprising that began in December 1987.[19] The self-centered nature of the work bears some resemblance to the books of the biblical prophets. Benvenisti does not claim to be speaking for God, but he does return time and again to his own previous writing. Some quotations of himself go on for several pages.

Benvenisti likens the 1987 uprising to the Yom Kippur War of 1973. The Israeli leadership of 1973 misread the signs of Egyptian and Syrian preparation and paid for their errors with a costly war. The leadership of 1987 misread the signs of domestic unrest. Benvenisti asserts that Arab unrest is increasing and that much of it is not connected with the PLO. To him, this means that Israelis are missing the point, and perhaps an opportunity to save their country, by their outmoded condemnation of PLO terror as the source of their security problem.

Benvenisti's despair appears in his lack of solution. Once he loathed the right-wing Likud bloc for its intense commitments to spreading Jewish settlements. New he concedes that all major Jewish political groupings, including his own Labor movement, are set against Arab aspirations by virtue of their commitment to Zionism and to the state dominated by Jews that it implies. He mentions briefly that he supports a territorial division between Israelis and Palestinians, but he then refrains from specifying solutions that neither Jews nor Arabs seem ready to accept.

Emanual Wald

While he was a colonel in the Israel Defense Forces (IDF), Emanual Wald, who holds a doctorate in public administration from Syracuse University, was asked by the chief of the General Staff to formulate proposals for the military in the coming decade, based upon his analysis of its performance in Israel's recent wars.

Wald earns a place in this discussion about modern prophets for his extreme attack on one of the most sacred cows of the Israeli establishment, for his perception of a deterioration in the quality of his nation's leaders, and for his prophecy of a national disaster if his prescriptions are not implemented.

Israelis view the IDF as their protection from annihilation. Most citizens enter its service at the age of eighteen, and men remain active in the reserves until they are in their fifties. Israelis know at first hand about the cumbersome military bureaucracy and about snafus in training and combat. However, they also recite the good works of the IDF in holding off a number of Arab armies in 1948, capturing Sinai in 1956, achieving stunning victories in the 1967 war, crossing the Suez Canal in 1973, and rescuing Israeli hostages at Entebbe in 1976.

Wald claims that the IDF is a conservative, self-satisfied, incompetent organization with a growing record of operational failures.[20] He writes that avoiding blame for a mistake has replaced an aggressive pursuit of objectives as the Israeli military norm.[21] The officer corps has become a mediocrity that fears self-criticism, and it cannot learn from its previous mistakes.[22] He describes members of the General Staff as concerned primarily with bureaucratic wars meant to ensure resources for their own branches of the service and to provide prestige for the victors. The product of these bureaucratic wars is an army equipped with too much of the wrong hardware, whose expense deprives important services of needed resources. Much of the equipment is likely to be ineffective when it is actually used in combat.[23]

Wald also describes a naive strategy of defending the status quo, which has been an obsession of ranking politicians and the military command throughout the forty years of Israel's existence. This simplistic policy frees both the politicians and the soldiers from thinking about more creative ways to solve the country's security problem.

Because of irrational postures, the outlook becomes enslaved to a Moloch of absolute defense, stuck in failure and rejecting all logic.... Therefore, they ... putter amidst breakable tools of power that corrode ... victory goes to the cursed tools that become obsolete: this leads to failure and the drowning of power in the sea.[24]

At various points Wald ridicules the IDF policy of minimizing casualties as an excuse that is used by commanders who do not achieve their objectives: "the prominent unwillingness of field officers to take chances, that derived from faulted professionalism and low motivation, excused by the slogan that saving lives is more important than saving ammunition."[25]

Wald's assessment of the IDF did not fall on receptive ears. He resigned from the military when it became apparent that the chief of staff would not bring his report before the General Staff for a formal review.

One of Wald's problems was the style of his presentation. If there was truth in his conclusions, they were presented in a way that minimized their impact. The targets of his criticism could too easily dismiss his book as poorly argued. Time and again he accused the officer corps and the General Staff of professional incompetence, without considering in a systematic way viewpoints other than his own.

Another of Wald's problems lies in the fact that the army he describes as incompetent is widely viewed as successful.

Meir Kahane and Yeshayahu Leibowitz

The late Rabbi Kahane and Professor Leibowitz are two figures on the fringes of Israeli politics who have demonstrated that the prophetic style is available to opposite poles of policy advocacy. The expressions of both have been heavily laden with references to Jewish history. Both are religious Jews, and both have preferred a wholly Jewish state. Kahane would have achieved his goal by expelling non-Jews; Leibowitz would give over to a Palestinian state a substantial part of the territory currently controlled by Israel.

The tirades of Rabbi Kahane showed some resemblance to the most simplistic of the biblical figures. Kahane cited the Books of Ezra and Nehemiah to support demands to ban marriages between Jews and non-Jews and to require the termination of those that exist. Kahane also would have required the departure of all non-Jews who refused to accept a subordinate citizenship without political rights.[26] The secular center and left of the Israeli spectrum branded Kahane a racist and outlawed his message. His party was banned by the Electoral Commission from the 1988 election campaign because of its racist messages.

Leibowitz, a professor of chemistry at the Hebrew University of Jerusalem, has made a name for himself outside of the laboratory. He appears frequently on Israeli television, usually in rumpled clothes with his eyeglasses askew.

Soon after the end of the Six-Day War in June 1967, Leibowitz began to warn his countrymen about the moral costs of military occupation. To him, it is impossible to realize Jewish values in a binational state where the Jews are military occupiers. He has directed his harshest tones at religious and nationalist Jews who advocate the settlement of Jews in the occupied territories, or the absorption of those territories into Israel. The scenario that he projects is continued Jewish-Arab conflict and a brutalization of the Jewish state by those who seek to achieve an upper hand by force.

Internally [Israel] will become a state of...concentration camps for people like me, and externally it will sink into apocalyptic wars with the whole Arab world from Kuwait to Morocco.[27]

Perhaps it is an exaggeration to use the powerful symbol of the Old Testament prophets in this discussion of individuals who are active in contemporary Israeli politics. Yet the metaphor captures the extremity and intensity of their expressions, their evoking of dire threats for those who resist their message, and their use of historic themes or symbols in criticizing existing policy. Of the figures mentioned here, Kahane and Leibowitz seem to fit the prophetic metaphor most closely. Wald is perhaps the most distinct from the metaphor, insofar as his argument is almost completely secular, and he is least attracted to ancient themes and symbols. Yet even he belongs on the list of those who recall the prophetic tradition. He criticizes Israel's most cherished institution (the IDF) in the most extreme terms. If the army truly is as weak as he claims, then Israelis must expect a fate similar to the residents of Jeremiah's Jerusalem.

SOURCES OF EXTREME EXPRESSION

Israelis who contemplate a career as policy advocates may hearken to the style of prophets that they have studied in school. Or the style of Israelis' political discourse may have something to do with similarities in the settings that spawned Jeremiah and other biblical prophets and those who emulate them 2,500 years later.

Jeremiah described powerful adversaries in Babylon to the east and Egypt to the west. Judah was weakened further by internal divisions between Jews who adhered to the God of Moses and those who followed other gods. The setting of contemporary Israel is hardly more enviable than that of the ancient country. Most neighboring states are hostile, and a Palestinian national movement mounts terrorist attacks against Israel and Jewish institutions overseas. There are domestic divisions between religious and secular Jews, and between Jews of different ethnic origins.

An extremism of political expression may reflect the biblical prophets' roots in a weakened polity that was dependent on outsiders and in the later statelessness of the Jews. Life in a regime controlled by someone else—without the need to decide among contending demands for limited resources—may have kept the Jews from learning to be satisfied with modest goals or what is attainable.[28]

The Holocaust and Israel's wars have raised the specter of national annihilation. They add realism to the threats of dire consequences by modern policy advocates.

The culture of the Jewish people may help to explain the appearance of modern Jeremiahs. The Israeli political scientist Ehud Sprinzak describes an extremism in Israeli public life that he traces to the pressures that existed in the prestate period of Jewish settlement in Palestine and in European and Middle Eastern communities where the Jewish settlers originated.[29] It is possible to add two millennia to the beginning of Sprinzak's history and to link the beginning of Jewish insecurity to the golden ages of biblical prophecy.

Another Israeli political scientist, Gadi Wolfsfeld, shows that Israelis are given to more extreme forms of political expression than people in several other Western democracies: Austria, Finland, Germany, Great Britain, Italy, the Netherlands, Switzerland, and the United States. In response to survey questions that asked about the best way of doing something about an unjust law, Israelis were more likely than residents of these other countries to say, "demonstrate," and less likely to indicate that they would undertake a quiet action like contacting a political leader or initiating a petition.[30]

Wolfsfeld cautions against an overly simple view of Israel's political culture. Rather than finding an extremity of expression as a fixed entity in Israel, he shows that it increased markedly during the 1970s and 1980s. There was also an increased incidence of discontent during that period and a decreased sense that major political institutions were meeting the citizens' needs.

A political-economic perspective provides other insights into the prophetic style of contemporary Israelis. It also reinforces Wolfsfeld's finding of a recent increase in extreme styles of political expression. Economic conditions worsened significantly after the Yom Kippur War of 1973.[31]

The connection between Israel's economic problems and the extreme political expressions lies in the absence of slack resources and the resulting pressure on policy advocates to more extreme expressions in order to get some of what is available.

A combination of extensive security commitments and aspirations to offer social services of West European quality has created a situation where public sector expenditures have been larger than the gross national product.[32] This means that Israel's policy-making is a zero-sum game. What one player wins must come out of what is available to others. There are also noneconomic shortages in Israel's policy arenas. The energy of ranking policymakers is overloaded by problems in the fields of security, economic management, and social services.

In such a setting, policy advocates compete for attention and resources by claiming that theirs is a desire of the most critical dimensions. Any less of a claim may ensure a hapless place toward the end of a long list of priorities. The pressing emergency overcomes the absolutely necessary. Modesty must give way to hyperbole in describing problems, offering solutions, and warning about the failure to accept the prescriptions that are offered.

As this chapter was being prepared for publication in the last weeks of 1990, the prominent items on the public agenda symbolized Israel's penchant for awesome problems. The Arab uprising, into its fourth year, showed no signs of relaxing the pressure on domestic security. Saddam Hussein was variously threatening to make Tel Aviv his first target, or to burn half of Israel. Two hundred thousand immigrants arrived during 1990, and 400,000 more were projected for 1991. These immigrants would increase the country's population by nearly 15 percent in two years and test its capacity to provide housing, jobs, and social services for the newcomers.

The extreme style of policy advocacy is self-perpetuating. Modest claims about new issues have little appeal when government forums and the news media are filled with advocates seeking to outperform one another in their claims of imminent disaster.

Israel's successes also push policy advocates to extremities. Israel's founders were successful beyond what could have been predicted by a policy analyst. The Jews were a miserable people, ridden with internal disputes, with no territory or military power. Yet they succeeded in acquiring an independent country in a place where they had been a minority of the population a generation earlier. Since 1948 Israel had stood out from the 100 or so other new countries for its economic growth, social programming, and military success, all the while maintaining a democratic regime.

History has encouraged Israeli politicians and their critics to think big. A record of outstanding success creates a faith in additional miracles that haunts contemporary policy analysts who would urge caution.

Politicians may be pushed to extreme plans by opportunities to invest other peoples' money in their dreams. Diaspora Jews helped finance one project of the 1980s to link the Mediterranean with the Dead Sea. This was halted only when it was seen to threaten both the fragile economy of Israel and its physical environment. Even the American government seemed to expect miracles in the Promised Land, as shown by its willingness to underwrite the Lavi military plane.

DO PROPHETS SUCCEED?

The record of the biblical prophets and their modern counterparts had been mixed, at best.

Some outspoken policy advocates have had a measure of success. Their golden age may have coincided with the cabinets led by the Likud bloc of Prime Minister Menachem Begin after the elections of 1977 and 1981. During that time, the settlement of Jews in the occupied territories moved forward dramatically under the leadership of individuals who spoke in terms of religious and national missions of the greatest importance. Minister of Defense Ariel Sharon was called by some the Jewish Napoleon. He is said to have undertaken the war in Lebanon at least partly for the purpose of remaking the politics and demography of Lebanon and turning Palestinian aspirations from Israel to Jordan.[33]

Harkabi, Benvenisti, and Wald have not been successful. The chief of the IDF General Staff refused to schedule a discussion of the report written by Emanual Wald. The settlement of Jews has gone forward in the West Bank despite the warnings of Harkabi and Benvenisti. The pace of new settlement slackened after 1984, but this was due to economic constraints rather than a policy decision on the merits of the issue. Benvenisti's latest book offers no solutions for Jewish-Arab tensions; rather, it despairs at the lack of communication between Jews and Arabs, which both reflects and reinforces their competing definitions of history and justice.

Meir Kahane was the target of legislation to outlaw racist political parties. Yeshayahu Leibowitz expects to end up in a concentration camp created by Jews.

Jeremiah's record was not much better. He illustrated the failure of those whom Martin Buber terms the true prophets by virtue of criticizing the political establishment.[34] Jeremiah earned an important place in Jewish history, but he did not persuade the people of Judah or their rulers to change their ways. They continued with their idolatry, sexual licentiousness, and the pursuit of advantage in international politics. It was for these reasons, according to the biblical text, that they lost God's support and their country.

IMPLICATIONS FOR ISRAELIS AND
ISRAEL WATCHERS

The extremity and intensity of Israeli policy advocates is not a trait that can be dismissed out of hand as the expressions of secular crackpots or spiritually motivated individuals who have tuned out the secular world. The style transcends the religious sector, even though it may have its roots in the biblical prophets. There are examples among secular technocrats who have succeeded in competitive career struggles as well as among religious demagogues and visionaries.

For Israelis, the prophetic tradition creates a great deal of noise. It also may produce a heady feeling of democratic morality. Yet the incessant criticism of the political establishment precludes a degree of satisfaction with existing policies that could remove them from the agenda and give the country a rest. Prophetic criticism of current policies may push officials to optimal aspirations, even while Israel's intractable problems of security and economic weakness suggest that the fate of Israeli politicians is to avoid grand illusions of meeting fully the demands of foreign or domestic protagonists.

Israel's style of politics may affect the nature of policy. An example appears in the intense quarrels among cabinet ministers, several of whom demand budget priority for new projects, usually in a condition when the budget is already in deficit and the annual rate of inflation is well into double figures. During the 1977–85 period, the competition over nonexistent resources finally pushed the annual rate of inflation over 1,300 percent.

However, there is no compelling evidence that Israel's style of policy advocacy leads inevitably to extreme decisions. Indeed, the prophetic component in Israeli politics may work to moderate policy, despite the shrill nature of its style. Figures like Leibowitz, Harkabi, and Benvenisti may blunt extreme policy recommendations by heightening moral ambiguities and by recalling historic examples of national disaster that followed bold moves.

Impasse among policymakers may also be a product of extreme claims on various sides of compelling issues. Israel's failure to resolve the nature of the West Bank and Gaza after twenty-three years of occupation owes something to the extreme and divergent postures taken by Jews, as well as to intransigent Arabs.

For Israelis and for those who watch them, the extremity and intensity of policy advocacy produces a vexing problem of distinguishing sincere analysis and demands from the hyperbole that may be meant only to achieve for its practitioners a place on the cabinet's agenda. There are no apparent patterns to allow predictions as to when the prophetic style will appear, or when it will be successful in achieving its purported demands.

To a policy technocrat who is schooled in precision and the control of emotions, it may appear that the prophetic tradition makes a negative contribution to contemporary Israel. It does not make policy-making easy for Israelis or for those who must deal with them. Yet the style is deeply ingrained, and it seems unlikely to disappear. Its roots go back to the biblical prophets and have been reinforced by miserable historical experiences. It is part of modern Israel's connections with its history that help to unite the people and allow them to withstand severe problems. It is a piece of the Israeli reality to be accepted with other goods and bads.

EPILOGUE: A CAVEAT ABOUT ISRAEL'S RELIGIOUS SECTOR

The lack of religious politicians' monopoly of a prophetic style of policy advocacy suggests a caveat relevant to other issues, beyond the nature of political style in Israel: Religious figures are assigned roles by Israel watchers that they do not deserve.

Religious politicians are not necessarily fanatic, and they do not necessarily pursue stereotyped roles with respect to the occupied territories. During the period of 1977–84, when religious parties were at their historical height of political power, they acted nonetheless in pragmatic and flexible ways like secular politicians. Even while they demanded policy changes in line with religious doctrine and spoke in otherworldly terms, they were satisfied with more money for religious schools, housing, and other social services. They might have deserved increased allocations on the simple criteria of their numbers and their pent-up demands from the years when they did not receive governmental allocations on the same per capita basis as secular Israelis.[35]

In the same perspective, it is appropriate to question the claim that religious extremism characterizes the phenomenon of "settler politics" in Israel, or adds substantially to the intransigence of the Shamir government. It is unlikely that a majority of Jews who have settled in the occupied territories are religious. The Likud government wanted to put as many Jews as possible in the territories and realized that there were not enough politically motivated or religious Jews to meet their needs. What characterized the greatly increased movement of Jews to the territories during the Likud governments of 1977–84 was the construction of suburbs within commuting distances of Jerusalem and the Tel Aviv metropolitan area, connected to those cities by new roads. Many settlers are secular middle class or upwardly mobile working class intent on a

sizeable home available for less money than in established urban neighborhoods. Their reasons for resisting a transfer of the territories to Arabs
are home ownership and financial security rather than any religious
doctrine. Some of these new settlers left their homes when they found
that the problems of living amidst hostile Arabs outweigh the advantages.

Most of Israel's religious Jews do not live in the occupied territories.
Many of the Israelis who fit the designation of ultra-Orthodox are ambivalent with respect to the retention of those territories. Leaders of
Agudat Israel supported Israeli withdrawal from the Sinai in keeping
with the Camp David agreement. One rabbi expressed his ambivalence
about the occupied territories by stating that continued occupation was
not worth the loss of one Jewish life; however, withdrawal would not be
justified if it led to the loss of one Jewish life. Small ultra-Orthodox
movements continue to oppose the rule of a Jewish government in any
of the Promised Land.

Shamir himself, who is secular, pursued a coalition with the Labor
party after the 1988 elections partly to free himself from dependence
on the religious parties. His previous behavior suggests that he would
resist surrendering the territories regardless of religious issues.

NOTES

1. Yehoshafat Harkabi, *The Bar Kokhba Syndrome: Risk and Realism in International Relations*, ed. David Altshuler, trans. Max D. Ticktin (Chappaqua, N.Y.:
Rossel Books, 1983), 83.

2. This chapter draws extensively on the author's *Ancient and Modern Israel:
Explorations of Political Parallels* (Albany: State University of New York Press,
1991).

3. Jer. 10:2; 17:5–7.

4. Jer. 9:10.

5. Amos Oz, *A Journey in Israel: Autumn 1982* (Tel Aviv: Am Oved, 1986),
in Hebrew. A political scientist is tempted to compare his book to those of Robert
E. Lane, e.g., *Political Ideology: Why the American Common Man Believes What He
Does* (New York: Free Press, 1962).

6. Amos Oz, *In the Land of Israel*, trans. Maurie Goldberg-Bartura (London:
Harcourt Brace Jovanovich, 1983), 71.

7. A derivation from the German meaning "epicures," usually used in a
condescending manner.

8. Oz, *A Journal in Israel* (Hebrew version), 111–12.

9. Harkabi, *The Bar Kokhba Syndrome*.

10. Ibid., 123.

11. Ibid., 172–76.

12. Ibid., 113–14.

13. Yehoshafat Harkabi, *Israel's Fateful Hour*, trans. Lenn Schramm (New
York: Harper & Row, 1988).

14. Ibid., xi.

15. Ibid., xix.

16. Meron Benvenisti, *The West Bank Data Project: A Survey of Israel's Policies* (Washington, D.C.: American Enterprise Institute, 1984), 34.

17. Ibid., 58–59.

18. Ibid., 69.

19. Meron Benvenisti, *The Sling and the Club: Territories, Jews and Arabs* (Jerusalem: Keter Publishing, 1988), in Hebrew.

20. Emanual Wald, *The Curse of Broken Tools: Decline of Israel's Military and Political Power (1967–1982)* (Jerusalem: Schocken Books, 1987), in Hebrew.

21. Ibid., 78.

22. Ibid., 123, 139, 126.

23. Ibid., 131.

24. Ibid., 239–40.

25. Ibid., 78.

26. For example, see Rabbi Meir Kahane, *They Must Go: How Long Can Israel Survive Its Malignant and Growing Arab Population?* (Brooklyn, N.Y.: The Jewish Idea, 1981).

27. Yeshayahu Leibowitz, *On Just About Everything: Talks with Michael Shashar* (Jerusalem: Keter Publishing, 1988), 24. In Hebrew.

28. Maurice Samuel, *The Gentleman and the Jew* (New York: Knopf, 1950).

29. Ehud Sprinzak, *Every Man Is Right in His Own Eyes: Illegalism in Israeli Society* (Tel Aviv: Kibbutz Artzi Hashomair Hazair, 1986), in Hebrew. See also his "Fundamentalism, Terrorism, and Democracy: The Case of Gush Emunim Underground," Washington, D.C.: The Wilson Center, Occasional Paper, September 16, 1986 (mimeo).

30. Gadi Wolfsfeld, *The Politics of Provocation: Participation and Protest in Israel* (Albany: State University of New York Press, 1988).

31. A change in economic conditions traceable to the war and postwar resupply is evident in measures of reduced growth of the economy and personal income; in increases in balance of payments deficits and foreign debt; in increased defense expenditures, government domination of the economy, and inflation. For details, see Ira Sharkansky, *The Political Economy of Israel* (New Brunswick, N.J.: Transaction Books, 1987).

32. For an explanation of this bizarre condition, see Sharkansky, *The Political Economy of Israel*, Chapter 3.

33. Sharon is said to have planned the war in such a way as to weaken the support for the PLO in Israel's occupied territories, to bring about the overthrow of Jordan's King Hussein by Palestinians, and to obtain the declaration of a Palestinian state in place of Hussein's kingdom. Shai Feldman and Heda Rechnitz-Kijner, "Deception, Consensus and War: Israel in Lebanon" (Tel Aviv University, Jaffee Center for Strategic Studies, 1984), 3.

34. Martin Buber, *Israel and the World: Essays in a Time of Crisis* (New York: Schocken Books, 1948), 116.

35. Ira Sharkansky, "Religion and the State in Begin's Israel," *Jerusalem Quarterly* (Spring, 1984). Similar is Ira Sharkansky, *What Makes Israel Tick? How Domestic Policy-Makers Cope with Constraints* (Chicago: Nelson Hall, 1985), Chapter 4.

5

The Religious Parties as a Support System for the Settler Movement

Stewart Reiser

This chapter analyzes two interrelated forces in Israeli society: the religious parties as one part of the sociopolitical support system of Gush Emunim and the settler movement.

The first section, on the religious parties, concentrates on the reasons for their electoral expansion of power in 1988, their future growth potential, and their policy orientations and priorities. The second section analyzes the issue of continuity and change within the settler movement in reaction to the intifada as well as to the official government and IDF reactions to the uprising. This discussion includes structural and demographic changes, the more public organization and use of settler militias, settler vigilantism, the possible resurgence of a fringe Jewish underground with both Jewish and Arab targets, and, finally, the political implications of these extrasystemic activities. Certain aspects of the PLO diplomatic campaign warrant integration into the analysis.

THE MEANING OF THE RESURGENCE

The percentage of the Israeli electorate that voted for the four religious parties in 1988 was approximately 50 percent higher than in the previous election, held in 1984. In itself, the increase to 18 seats should not be the focus of attention. The aggregate of religious mandates has vacillated between 10 and 18 seats since the first election in 1949. There were 18 religious seats following the 1959, 1961, and 1969 elections. As recently as 1977 there were 17 religious seats. The return to 18 seems great because it followed two elections, those of 1981 and 1984, wherein the religious parties went into the downside of their cycle, registering 10 and 12 seats, respectively.

The more significant factor is that the growth of the religious vote has not been within the religious Zionist camp, which is represented at the polls by two parties: the hawkish National Religious Party, or MAF-DAL, and the dovish MEIMAD, which failed to attract enough of the electorate to earn a Knesset seat. (MEIMAD received 15,783 votes, or 0.7% of the electorate.[1]) The increase occurred almost exclusively in the three ultra-Orthodox, or haredi, parties: SHAS, Agudat Israel, and Degel HaTorah.

There seems to have been two sets of reasons, each with several components, for the stabilization of the National Religious Party at 5 votes (they had won 6 in 1981 and 4 in 1984), which has been, along with its secular counterpart Tehiya, the political support system for Gush Emunim within the Green Line and, at the same time, the more than doubling of the ultra-Orthodox seats from 6 to 13 between 1984 and 1988. The latter growth was caused, in part, by the entry of thousands of usually apolitical Ashkenazi ultra-Orthodox into the electoral system, including women nonvoters. The entry was largely, although not wholly, caused by intrareligious strife between ultra-Orthodox sects. This strife was characterized by the intervention of a particularly charismatic American rabbi, the Hasidic leader of the Habad movement, Lubavitcher Rabbi, Menachem Mendel Schneerson, and the financial funding and organizational efforts of the Habad movement in behalf of Agudat Israel. Schneerson's major rival, within Israel, Rabbi Eliezer Schach, was instrumental in the creation of two of the other haredi parties, the Sephardi SHAS and the Ashkenazi Degel HaTorah. The conflicts that were played out reflect centuries of rivalry between the Hasidic and *Misnagdim* approaches to scholarship and holy law.

A brief historical background of the haredi movement may be helpful for an understanding of the particular place that they occupy in contemporary Israel. The term *haredi* means pious, anxious, zealous, or those who feel awe. The haredi movement, which began in the eighteenth century, was a defensive reaction to the major transformation European Jewish life faced. The transformation itself was guided by two forces. One was the emancipation, which allowed individual Jews to leave their autonomous, minority, community and move into the mainstream of several European states. The second was the Jewish enlightenment, or *haskalah*, which exposed Jews to mainstream Christian, and increasingly secular, culture. One consequence of these two forces was total assimilation. Another was acculturation, the attempt by Jewish individuals to embrace both cultures simultaneously. It was under these circumstances that Reform, Conservative, and Orthodox Judaism formed.

Each represented or characterized a different degree of or, conversely, resistance to acculturation.

The haredi, or ultra-Orthodox, opposed the many forms that Jewish acculturation took. For this reason, the ultra-Orthodox were totally anti-Zionist. Zionism, or Jewish nationalism, represented another manner of serving or bridging the two cultures since it accepted, or asserted, the premise that the Jews were a nation that deserved secular sovereignty. Most important, the ultra-Orthodox opposed the secular nationalists as people who were forcing the hand of the Messiah by reestablishing Eretz Yisrael.

From a distance, the haredim appear quite similar. There are, however, important distinctions and divisions amongst them that came into play rather sharply in the recent election. The Hasidim stress the *Tsadic*, or holy teacher and leader. The powers of the Tsadic for his community go beyond legal interpretation and guidance. His charisma can be so great that the community occasionally believes in his ability to perform miracles. The Misnagdim, on the other hand, are Judaism's version of the strict constitutionalists, or strict Talmudists. It was this movement that started the yeshiva, or school, where the Torah was taught. This conflict over how to preserve Judaism in the face of assimilation and acculturation lasted for two centuries in Europe. In addition, within each approach, or school, there were the expected subdivisions and rivalries based upon geographic locations and personality conflicts.

In the twentieth century, the Holocaust made these two movements ally, but not unify, against the forces of acculturating Jewry. A group of the more liberal, or acculturated, Orthodox organized the Mizrahi, or religious Zionist movement. This group took the political form of MAFDAL, the National Religious Party, which is not considered haredi, and which historically has been one of the major actors in the creation of Israel and its political system since 1949. The Agudat Israel movement formed in Europe to give shape to the needs of the various currents of the haredi population. Tens of thousands of those who belonged to the Agudist movement migrated to Palestine before, and after, World War II. The Holocaust shifted the attitude of most of the haredi, as represented by Agudat Israel, from being anti-Zionist to what could be more aptly termed non-Zionist. To the Agudists, Israel represented a haven for Jews but not the culmination, nor even the start of the new Messianic era. In short, it was a place for the body but not the soul of Jewry.

The geographical shift of Jews from Europe to the United States and to Palestine/Israel this century altered the nature and position and roles of the haredi and their yeshivot. In Europe the yeshiva student was a privileged elite protected by the broader Jewish community, particularly the haredi, from the stresses of the wider social economy. His role was to study and perpetuate Jewish law and custom. He would be financially provided for, albeit at a modest level, by his family and the wider community. However, the yeshiva did not prepare the student for the outside world; when the student married, he had to leave the school. The system was costly and relied upon charity.

The move to the United States and Israel brought this sector of Judaism into societies where the state provided social benefits and a higher standard of living than it had previously experienced in Europe. This enabled the Orthodox families to keep their sons in yeshivot of even higher levels of education. An entirely new structure, called the *kollel*, was created in Israel, which allows a married student to stay in school rather than drop out and enter the mainstream economy. The student need not support his wife and growing family. This constituted a revolution in the world of the haredi.

It is necessary to understand this evolving set of financial arrangements to know why Agudat Israel, a non-Zionist party, joined the Likud government in 1977. Agudah had never before helped form a government or served in a cabinet, although the party had always won several seats in the parliament. The increased financial strains placed upon the kollel system by the growing haredi population made Agudat Israel join in order to look out for the financial interests, actually one of the major pieces of the infrastructure, of its constituency. The recent struggle between SHAS, Degel HaTorah, Agudat Israel, and MAFDAL was and will remain a struggle over patronage and funding for their own educational institutions and subsidized housing. This financial struggle was enhanced by the historical conflicts within the haredi world, as well as severe personality clashes between their leaders.

While the Eastern, or Sephardi, Jewish community never went through this history of emancipation and acculturation in the Ottoman Empire and therefore never formed their own counterpart to the haredi reaction, the Sephardim came to Israel and went to religious institutions and schools run by Lithuanian Misnagdim and East European Hasidim. As a result of this, some Sephardim even speak Yiddish and dress in the black garb that characterizes European haredim. However, as in many other components of Israeli society, the Sephardim were kept in a subordinate position within the haredi world.

The 1988 campaign that included "blessings and curses" by respective rabbis, door-to-door campaigning, video cassettes, and the flight to Israel of perhaps thousands of New York–based haredim who have joint American-Israeli citizenship, at the request of Rabbi Schneerson, mobilized many thousands of Ashkenazi haredim, particularly women, who had never participated in the Israeli political system. These numbers swelled the mandates registered by Agudat Israel and its Ashkenazi rival Degel HaTorah, a party that was created almost at the last minute by Rabbi Schach to counter Schneerson and the Hasidic "onslaught." The future participation of these particular constituencies depends to a large degree upon Schneerson's decision about whether to intervene again in Israeli electoral politics.

This assessment is compounded by the fact that Agudah clearly over-played its hand in the postelection negotiations. It was Agudist politicians who insisted upon Likud "party discipline" from Prime Minister Yitzhak Shamir over the issue of the "Who is a Jew" amendment; Agudah, of the four religious parties, pressured the entire system most for this issue. This pressure was one of several factors in the recreation of the National Unity Government, which neutralized the right and left wings of the system and blunted all of the demands of the religious parties. Given this outcome, it is reasonable to conclude that such an enormous effort coupled with such minimal returns (as well as the enmity that the haredi engendered throughout the entire Israeli political system and among American Jewry who believed that national issues such as the intifada, the American peace initiative, and so on should top the agenda) will discourage the Ashkenazi haredi leadership from repeating such an ambitious foray into electoral politics. This is not to say that Agudat Israel and Degel HaTorah will not continue to maintain from 5 to 7 seats between them; rather, since the recent expansion was set off by such an anomalous set of circumstances and the political and economic payoffs were so low, it is reasonable to believe that these two ultra-Orthodox parties may have peaked and that competition in the future will return to smaller pragmatic struggles over patronage and budgets, particularly after the passing from the scene of their two aged spiritual mentors. The same phenomenon of peaking is probably also true for the National Religious Party, MAFDAL, but for other reasons. However, it cannot be said for SHAS, the Sephardi Guardians of the Torah. Before we turn to SHAS, a short discussion of MAFDAL's present and future is in order.

As stated, the National Religious Party entered the 1988 Knesset with 5 seats. It had lost some of its small dovish constituency to MEIMAD, which, as noted, did not attract enough votes to attain a seat. At the same time, Morasha, a small, breakaway, right-wing religious nationalist party, remerged with MAFDAL. MAFDAL also attracted a good deal of Arab and Druze support, almost 8,000 votes,[2] because the party em-phasized religious educational issues during the campaign—issues that still concern a large sector of the Israeli Arab and Druze populations. However, it must be noted that, with all of this movement into and out of the party in 1988, this once vibrant force in Israeli politics, the original "third force," appears to have reached a plateau. Without elaborating on MAFDAL's history, in the 1970s the younger generation of leaders of religious Zionism pushed the party toward the political right in an effort to become a new centrist party, similar to the Christian Democrats in Europe, and to capture the religious, or traditionalist, voters of the Likud. The strategy backfired. By taking Likud's and Tehiya's positions on the occupied territories, many MAFDAL voters whose nationalism was more politically important than their religious sentiments shifted toward Likud. At the same time, in the late 1970s, MAFDAL began to ignore the sensitivities of its Sephardi constituency, which was demonstrated when the party central committee placed only one Sephardi candidate among the top 10 (i.e., safe) seats in the national election lists. MAFDAL started losing some of this constituency to ethnic religious parties, first TAMI, then SHAS. Thus, MAFDAL made two major errors. It tried to become a religious version of Likud or Tehiya and lost to each, particularly to Likud. Second, the party began to act toward the Sephardim as had Labor and lost to TAMI and SHAS.[3]

What this seems to imply is that MAFDAL's future resurgence as a political party may be somewhat limited since there are by now many homes for religious Zionists.[4] These include Likud, SHAS, perhaps Tehiya, and even the Labor Alignment, for religious doves, if MEIMAD continues *not* to become a force on its own. If MEIMAD does catch on, it will be as an alternative to MAFDAL because of its peace position, and it will attract religious doves from Labor. If this analysis is correct, it would seem that the National Religious Party will no longer act as a bridge between the secular and orthodox of Israel nor function as a third political and moral force; indeed, it can look forward only to a future of increased marginality. Quite the opposite, however, can be said for SHAS.

SHAS, which has grown since 1984, from 4 to 6 Knesset seats, has become the third largest party in Israel. This growth is reflective of other, wider sociopolitical characteristics occurring within Israel. The second reason for the increased aggregate of the religious vote is the continued "migration" of traditional, albeit non-ultra-Orthodox, Sephardi voters to the SHAS party. The Sephardim's shift to Likud in 1977, although it started much earlier, transformed Israel into a two-party or two-bloc system. The continued shift of many lower income Sephardim from Likud to SHAS and, to a lesser extent, to Agudat Israel, rather than any of the more rightist secular parties, reflects a continued ethnic resurgence, a rejection of the Israeli melting pot, discontent in the socioeconomic programs of the Likud, and earlier, deeper disenchantment with the Labor Alignment.

In my estimate, of all of the above-mentioned phenomena that are related to the recent increase in the religious vote, the ongoing shift of the Sephardi electorate reflects the most important political trend—the trend that is most likely to continue and most likely to have the greatest impact on the issues of war and peace, territorial compromise, and relations with the Palestinians.

All four religious parties demanded major increases in funding for their constituencies. All failed. SHAS, whose platform is largely tuned to the feelings of discrimination among the lower income Sephardim in development towns and the poorer sections of Israel's larger cities, has again won the Interior Ministry which, in turn, has control of the funds for the development towns where many working-class Sephardim live and remain underemployed. (In fact, SHAS received 16% of the votes in development towns which had voted heavily for the Likud in the elections prior to 1988.[5]) A continued perception of ethnic discrimination, accompanied by an even tighter austerity budget, managed by the Ashkenazi-led Labor and Likud National Unity Government, will probably reinforce the continuation of the political migration of the Sephardic working class, which began from Labor to Likud in the 1960s and 1970s and into ethnoreligious parties, such as TAMI, in 1981, and then SHAS, in 1984 and 1988. SHAS has the greatest growth potential of all the religious parties because it plays to the socioeconomic needs of an already politicized segment of Israeli society, a segment whose identity as well as economic well-being are at issue.

SHAS's importance will increase as long as the overall stalemate or deadlock in Israeli politics continues. This overall deadlock between the Nationalist and Liberal camps began in 1981. However, whereas Likud had 48 seats in 1981 against the 47 mandates of Labor that year, the overall level of the tie, or deadlock, has dropped over the last two elections. Likud and its allied parties totalled 46 in 1984, with Likud itself dropping to 41; Labor and its allies totalled 46 in 1984, with Labor itself dropping to 44. Labor fell to 39 seats this election, and its left-center allies (the Citizens' Rights Movement, MAPAM, and Shinui) lost 4 seats. These four did not shift to the Arab bloc (one possible explanation) since the Arab bloc itself rose from 7 in 1984 to 8 in 1988; one of these, the Arab Democratic party, was the breakoff from Labor. Likud, in 1984, lost some of its constituency to rightist allies, such as Tehiya; however, in that same election, Likud began to lose some of its Sephardic constituency to SHAS. Thus, of the two major blocs, the Nationalist camp has more or less stabilized between 1984 and the present, although between them Likud and Tehiya have lost 4 seats and Moledet and Tzomet have gained 3, bringing the Nationalist camp to the same aggregate as in 1984. Labor and its allies in the Liberal bloc have declined.

One likely explanation of the electoral shift is that the two liberal parties that lost votes, Shinui and MAPAM, lost them to Labor while, at the same time, a greater amount of the more conservative Labor voters shifted to Likud (perhaps due in part to the intifada). Likud, however, lost a seat in this election, and those voters shifted either to SHAS, Agudat Israel, or a secular rightist party. The wild card in these calculations is the segment of the electorate that was to cast its vote for the Kach party of Meir Kahane.

Kach had one seat in the 1984 Knesset. Polling that took place prior to Kach's prohibition from participation in the election varies as to the party's share of the electorate. One poll (*Hadashot*) claimed that Kach maintained only 1 seat; most others ranged from a low estimate of 3 to a high estimate of 5 or 6. A secret poll conducted by Likud in August 1988 indicated that Kahane would receive 6 or 7 seats in the Knesset. In another poll, Modi'in Ezrahi found that the 5 seats that Kach would have won before it was disqualified would now be divided among Likud, which would gain 3; Moledet, 1; and SHAS, 1.[6]

In fact, Likud lost 1 seat. Some of Kach's constituency went to Moledet. Perhaps if we assume that Kach would have won 3 or 4 seats, Moledet was a clear beneficiary of Kach's disenfranchisement. Moledet, a new secular party, was one of only two parties that called for the transfer of the Palestinians from the territories. It won 2 seats. Tzomet was the other party that called for transfer; it grew from a single seat to 2. Tehiya, calling for annexation and the creation of Greater Eretz Yisrael, but not transfer, lost 2 seats.

It seems that the two parties of the national right that had major working-class Sephardi constituencies, Likud and Kach, lost in two directions, to very hard-line secular parties, such as Moledet and Tzomet, or to ethnically oriented religious parties, such as SHAS or Agudat Israel. It seems reasonable to contend that the non-ultra-Orthodox, albeit traditional, working-class Sephardi voter probably feels comfortable shifting between secular parties that convey nationalistic images, themes, and positions but that stress traditional Jewish values, on the one hand, and religious parties that emphasize ethnic identities as well as religious law, on the other.[7]

The complaints of this stratum of Israeli society range widely, but one clear criticism is that they have experienced the Israeli melting pot as a continuing set of demands by the Ashkenazi founding fathers that they accept the values, and identities, of the veteran elite. In return, in their estimate, they were relegated by both secular Zionist movements and the Nationalist and Liberal blocs, particularly the latter, into being the permanent proletariat of Israel. In short, they were encouraged to surrender their traditional values of the patriarchal family, the Torah, and their traditional rituals for insufficient socioeconomic mobility. In my estimate this will remain a long-lasting feature of the "class demography" in Israel, and internal Likud party politics will tend to reinforce the continued migration of the Sephardi working class to SHAS. Likud is doing everything that it can, perhaps inadvertently, to alienate its Sephardic constituency.

The last election witnessed the reinforcement of the Yitzhak Shamir–Moshe Arens camp within Likud. Without going into policy content, it appears as if Shamir has made a decisive mark on the hierarchy of Likud at the expense of the Ariel Sharon and David Levy camps. The upcoming generation behind Arens and Shamir are men like Ronnie Milo, Dan Meridor, Ehud Olmert, Benjamin Netanyahu, and Benny Begin. Many of these men unquestionably are men of high calibre; however, most of the young Likud stars come from the Ashkenazi educated elite, and those who have lost out are the Sephardi protegés of the Levy and Sharon camps who drew particularly well in the development towns of Israel. Given the slight rise in mysticism among the poor Sephardim and the fact that SHAS is becoming the haven and support system for these people, who are facing increasing socioeconomic challenges, it is reasonable to speculate that although SHAS may not become to Likud what Likud became to Labor in the 1970s, SHAS has unlimited growth potential and may become the third political force in Israel.

THE POLICY IMPLICATIONS OF THE RESURGENCE

Historically the agenda of the haredi parties has fit within two categories: to encourage religious legislation for the Jewish state and to increase state funding for their separate housing, kollel, and educational infrastructures. Their approach to Zionism has always been reserved, although the haredi for the greater part are no longer anti-Zionist. However, for the vast majority of haredi of Ashkenazi background—most ultra-Orthodox are of European background—the Zionist movement and the state of Israel do not signify the beginning of the Messianic era for Jewry or for the world. Israel as a modern state has little theological significance.

The position and security of the haredi community within Israel is their top priority, and their campaign platforms before elections as well as their stated political agenda during coalition negotiations following elections reflect these priorities. As the haredim vie for increasingly scarce financial resources, the struggle intensifies. This last election partly reflected the competition for state subsidies for housing and educational institutions among the three ultra-Orthodox parties.

While the three haredi parties do not view the territories as a top priority, SHAS, Degel HaTorah, and Agudat Israel do have policy orientations toward them if not set policy positions. These orientations are flexible and loose since they do not emanate from any structured set of theological principles; rather, the principles include a love of the Eretz Yisrael matched by a perhaps greater commitment to the cause of peace and the saving of lives. Balanced against these perhaps conflicting principles are the desires of the leaders of the haredi parties, particularly SHAS, to retain the loyalty of their newly acquired constituency, many of whom are more nationalistic, or "hawkish" than the religious party leadership.

Most Israeli, and some American, analysts fall into one of two camps regarding the "natural" alliance partner for the religious parties. Many see Israel divided between the Liberal and the Nationalist camps, with the haredi parties, in addition to MAFDAL, automatically and naturally part of the Nationalist bloc. This group of analysts include people of both the left and right, by Israeli definition. At the same time, more than a few analysts, mainly of the "peace camp," claim that the real place of the haredi parties is within the Liberal camp, where MAFDAL itself stayed from 1948 to 1967 in an easy alliance with Labor, and in uneasy coalition for another decade before the shift to Likud in 1977. These analysts do not base their position on this "ancient history," but instead they point to the dovish positions of much of the rabbinical leadership of Agudat Israel, SHAS, and Degel HaTorah, as well as the dovish reputation of one of the major spiritual mentors of the latter two, Rabbi Schach.

As noted earlier, these positions are based, at least in part, on the fact that the Zionist movement and the state of Israel historically have had no religious or Messianic significance to the ultra-Orthodox of Judaism. This is not to say that there is no great love of Eretz Yisrael. Rather, the state of Israel as a manifestation of the modern Zionist enterprise, or occupying all of the Land, is not the highest priority of the haredi community, and it is balanced against other priorities in an insecure world of limited resources. Therefore, those analysts claim that the "natural home" of the three haredi parties will be with Labor at the crucial moment. They explain the propensity of these parties to look first to the Likud for a coalition based on the Nationalist camp's greater sympathy for the religious and financial requirements of the ultra-Orthodox. This mode of analysis states that, because the territories and Jewish settlements therein are not the priority to the haredi, they will pay the price on larger national issues and go with either camp that accedes to their religious legislative desires and the financial needs of their community, which do top the hierarchy of their priorities.

There is much to be said for this mode of analysis, and it is necessary to point out that only MAFDAL, of the four religious parties who won seats in the 1988 election, made demands for increased settlements, housing, road infrastructures, and so on within Judea, Samaria, and the Gaza Strip. The demands of SHAS, Agudat Israel, and Degel HaTorah were strictly for various portfolios in the government, increased state funding for religious education and the kollel and housing systems for the ultra-Orthodox community, as well as religious legislation, including the "Who is a Jew" law and Rabbinical Court laws. These parties made few demands regarding the territories, their legal status, the settlements within them, or any issues concerning Gush Emunim, with the exception of statements concerning the government's handling of the intifada.

During the negotiations for the formation of the new government, the three haredi parties shifted from one side to the other with Agudat Israel actually signing a "final agreement" with Labor.[8] Rabbi Avraham Ravitz, the party head of Degel HaTorah, also shifted from the pro-Likud position to one that favored Shimon Peres. He finally favored the continuation of a National Unity Government but one that, again, stipulated a rotating leadership. Throughout, it was clear that Ravitz's emphasis was on traditional haredi values, those that strengthened the insular community from the forces of secularism that surround them.

Although Rabbi Ravitz has displayed some hawkish tendencies during interviews and claims that Degel HaTorah's spiritual mentor, Rabbi Schach, also has a love for Eretz Yisrael,[9] it seems reasonable to conclude that Degel HaTorah should not be ruled out as a supporter of a moderate, carefully thought out peace initiative that includes territorial concessions. Rabbi Schach has always shown great fear of alienating the Jewish people of Israel from those in the United States as well as from the American government. In fact, one reason that Ravitz shifted toward Labor in the final stages of the coalition negotiations was the damage to these relations within the international Jewish community that was being caused by Agudat Israel's demand for the "Who is a Jew" amendment. Degel's constituency, almost exclusively Ashkenazi haredi, will not present themselves as an obstacle to territorial compromise since they do not see the state of Israel, with or without Judea and Samaria, as ushering in the Messianic era. The foreign policy positions of the other three parties are more complicated, particularly in the case of SHAS, and to a certain extent Agudat Israel, because there is a certain ideological distance between the party leaders and their more hawkish constituencies.

SHAS's rabbinical leadership, Rabbis Yitzhak Peretz and Ovadia Yosef, conducted a campaign that was more hawkish than expected on the basis of their actual sentiments regarding national issues. Peretz campaigned on "putting down the intifada," and he took a more nationalist stance than in any time in the past. The gains made by SHAS were in part due to the redistribution of power between the secular right wing, Likud and Tehiya, and some gains from the Kach constituency. Thus, when Rabbi Yosef and Arye Deri, the rising young star of SHAS, wanted to join Labor in coalition, when it appeared that Likud would not accede to SHAS's religious and financial demands, these leaders held back because they feared alienating their newly won electorate. These leaders, who also look to Rabbi Schach for spiritual guidance, as does the leadership of Degel HaTorah, will be torn between their inclinations toward compromise, based on religious and personal principles on the one hand, and their fear of losing some of their expanding constituency on the other. Thus, despite calls to put down the intifada during the campaign, the actual foreign and defense policy platform of SHAS read, "The borders of Israel were stipulated in our holy Bible and the longing for a return to Zion and a greater Israel has never ceased. However, it is the duty of Israel's leaders to persist in putting an end to the bloodshed in the region through negotiations for peace."[10] In fact, party spokesman, Zvi Yaacovson, posed the issue in a manner to which security experts could well relate: "If it can prevent the death of one Jew to return the territories, they will be returned. But not if it will cause the death of two others."[11]

Interior Minister Arye Deri accompanied the former Sephardi chief rabbi and major SHAS supporter, Ovadia Yosef, to Egypt at the end of July 1989, where the latter stated to Egyptian President Hosni Mubarak, that halacha justifies territorial compromise. Yosef delivered a rabbinical pronouncement that asserted that, although there is no question as to the sanctity of the Land of Israel, "it is permissible to sever limbs when that is deemed necessary for preservation of human life."[12] This analogy is the code utilized by religious doves to proclaim the value of pikuach nefesh. The declaration by the Sephardi religious luminaries caused such a stir in Israel that the current chief rabbinate issued a halachic decision that the Torah forbids making territorial concessions in the Land of Israel.[13] In sum, SHAS, at the time of reckoning, will be caught between several principles pulling it toward peace, including Yaacovson's cost-effective analysis, and their perceived need to hold onto an electorate that could propel the party into the position of third most powerful in the state.

The foreign policy views of this constituency are important. The lesser educated, working-class Sephardi population, in general, is more hawkish, or anti-Arab, than either their Ashkenazi or more highly educated Sephardi counterparts.[14] However, this hawkishness is derived from many complex historical reasons, such as having lived as a Jewish minority within and under a Muslim Arab majority and more recent resentments against the elite Ashkenazi peace movement that appears, in their estimate, to care more for improving Jewish-Arab relations, by Israeli concessions to the latter, than with improving Ashkenazi-Sephardi relations within the Jewish community.

The majority of those Sephardim who are relatively hawkish are rarely so because of a mystical Messianic tie to Greater Eretz Yisrael, as are the supporters of mainly Ashkenazi Gush Emunim. There were right-wing religious Zionists among the Sephardim who voted for SHAS. There probably were more than a few. However, those who truly wanted to support what Gush Emunim stands for voted for the extremely hawkish platform put forward by Avner Shaki of MAFDAL during the 1988 election (60% of MAFDAL voters are Sephardim[15]). One must add that those Sephardim who voted for SHAS rather than MAFDAL this election did not avoid MAFDAL because of ethnic alienation. Shaki, who headed the National Religious Party list, is himself of Sephardi background.

In short, several of SHAS's leaders, such as Deri, will vacillate between their ideals, which are not exactly dovish but do show sympathy toward a territorial compromise for a peace treaty, and their perceived needs to hold onto their constituency, which is rightist but not Messianic by nature. Others, such as Rabbi Peretz, are of a more rightist inclination but do not appear to be in the ascent within the party hierarchy as does Deri who has Rabbi Yosef's full support and who, in turn, has the greatest grip on the loyalties of SHAS's constituency. The party cannot and should not be ruled out as a possible supporter of a peace initiative that includes some form of territorial compromise. Unlike the original haredi party, Agudat Israel, SHAS is readying and positioning itself to be a major Israeli player on the broad national field, and its positions will reflect these ambitions, rather than those of a party with narrow, single-issue concerns. This ambition, which can be realized only with a continued constituency expansion, will play to the grass-root desires of this constituency, and this may temper any lean toward a very moderate approach to peace negotiations.

A similar, but not identical, assessment can be made for Agudat Israel. Agudah did not run on a Nationalist platform. However, given the nature of the campaign, which consisted of the use of "blessings and curses" by Rabbi Schneerson, Habad, and Baba Baruch, a perhaps significant percentage of the 3-seat gain by Agudah was also from the working-class Sephardi community. Just as SHAS will, so will Agudat Israel face the dilemma of choosing between their more dovish Talmudic principles and the fear of losing some of their newly won constituency. Agudah's problem may be of a different nature than that facing the leadership of SHAS. Whereas the political rabbinical leaders of SHAS, as well as their spiritual guide, Rabbi Schach, are fairly dovish and very concerned about the isolation of the Jewish people, the recent spiritual mentor of Agudat Israel, Rabbi Schneerson, is extremely hawkish and a long-time advocate of a Greater Israel. Schneerson opposes the surrender of any territory, attributed the capture of Jerusalem and the rest of Judea and Samaria in 1967 to Habad's endeavors to see to it that all members of the IDF pray each day, and communicated his desire during the 1973 war that the IDF capture Damascus. Some prominent Agudists, such as Avraham Verdiger, followed Schneerson's lead. At the same time, however, others such as MK Rabbi Menachem Porush, called for the primacy of the principle of pikuach nefesh. Given Agudah's newly mixed constituency and Rabbi Schneerson's ideological position, Agudah, like SHAS, will be on the fence when an Israeli government is faced with a vote on national issues of war and peace and historical boundaries.

Finally, there is MAFDAL, the original bastion of religious Zionism. MAFDAL's leadership is somewhat divided on the national issue. However, its constituency is not. Those religious Zionists who wanted to recreate a moderate religious center had their opportunity when the MEIMAD ran several former MAFDAL political figures, including one as prominent as Yehuda Ben-Meir. MEIMAD attracted only 0.7 percent of the Israeli vote, failing, this time around, to enter the Knesset. Given this choice between religious Zionist parties, it is safe to say that those voting for MAFDAL were not ambivalent about the party's positions on the territories, expanding the settlement drive, and the peace process. Avner Shaki, party leader at the time, ran MAFDAL's most nationalistic race and may even have attracted some of Kach's loose voters even though MAFDAL did not advocate the expulsion of the Arab population.

It is at the leadership level that there exist some political, and perhaps some ideological, splits, rather than within the electorate at large. Following the national election, MAFDAL held a party election on December 26, 1988, to determine which of its leading ministers, former party leader Zvulun Hammer or then leader Avner Shaki, would take the religious affairs portfolio in the National Unity Government. Hammer won by an extremely large margin. In fact, he polled more than the aggregate of his three opponents, which included Shaki. Shaki had won an earlier party vote, by a very narrow margin, at the start of 1988, which placed him at the top of the MAFDAL list, and he subsequently pulled the party platform farther to the right. Whether the more recent party election that gave Hammer the cabinet portfolio is interpreted as one for party leadership or not, it may represent a possible shift toward a more moderate foreign policy. Another party rightist, Yosef Shapira, also did very poorly in the December vote. While it may be too early to elaborate on this point, Hammer is very close personally and, perhaps ideologically, to Yehuda Ben-Meir and Yehuda Amital, who started the dovish MEIMAD party. It is quite possible that at least Hammer and perhaps one other of the five MAFDAL ministers in the Knesset would cautiously, although sincerely, weigh a peace proposal that includes settler rights in territories abdicated to Palestinian sovereignty. MAFDAL has had a broad national agenda for decades. However, it has failing banking and religious agricultural settlement systems, as does the Labor Alignment, and it has neglected its infrastructure within the Green Line as the party has concentrated on supporting Gush Emunim over the past decade.

MAFDAL may or may not have hit a historical dead end within Israel. Its ideological quest to become the third force for the state has certainly failed, and it appears that, in the future, its major competition will be SHAS and not the secular right-wing parties such as Likud and Tehiya. If MAFDAL decides to compete, on the grass-roots level, with SHAS for the traditional Sephardi population, rather than continue its quest for Greater Israel, as it has for the past decade, then it will have to concentrate on the educational and financial needs of what will constitute this grass-roots constituency. This shift in emphasis, if it is to be attempted, can be undertaken in coalition with Labor as well as Likud. This is not to suggest that Hammer's victory over the hawkish Shaki is the start of a pronounced move toward the center of Israeli politics. Rather, it indicates that there are strong mixed feelings about continuing on a relentless hawkish path within the party and that Hammer and perhaps others in the parliament might show flexibility on the issue of Palestinian political rights and the settlements in the territories.

This former point may be worth pondering. Yasir Arafat's somewhat veiled statement that the Israeli state will not be without Palestinian Arabs (it contains many already) and that the future Palestinian state need not be without Jews can only be a purposeful opening to Israel's concerns about the retention of part of the settler system within the territories. Thus, it is possible that part of a settlement could include the "right of Jews to live within" what they will consider the Greater Land of Israel, but will not be the state of Israel, areas that could make up part of either a Palestinian state or a Palestinian-Jordanian confederation.

THE SETTLER MOVEMENT, THE INTIFADA, AND THE NATIONAL ELECTION

The renewal of the National Unity Government in 1988 achieved several negative objectives; it obstructed the confluence of several forces within Israel's political society that had assertive agendas to pursue. In short, it "clipped the wings" of the Israeli left and right, on the one hand, and neutralized the demands of the religious parties, on the other. A narrow government of center-right-religious blocs, the only mathematical option to a National Unity Government, would have left Labor in opposition, and the demands of the radical right within the government would have polarized the Knesset, probably strengthening the dovish wing of Labor and making Labor's leftist allies more vocal. Replacing Yitzhak Rabin as defense minister with one from Likud would have driven Peace Now into the streets, perhaps on a massive scale. The triumph of the pragmatic wing within Likud, composed of Arens and the next generation from Herut including Meridor, Olmert, and Milo, all contribute to strengthening Prime Minister Shamir's policy of immobilism in the face of all the threats of the intifada. The following section considers the settler movement's reactions to the intifada and the government's reactive policies. It attempts to assess the settler movement's attitudes and reactions in several manners. First, the demographic changes occurring within the territories during the intifada are discussed. Second, the results of a survey taken to determine settler attitudes toward withdrawal and antigovernment resistance are considered. Third, militia organization and vigilante activity are examined.

DEMOGRAPHIC CHANGES IN THE SETTLER COMMUNITY IN THE FACE OF THE UPRISING

Israeli opponents of Gush Emunim were quick to conclude that the intifada has stemmed the momentum of Jewish settlement in the occupied territories. Their logic was, and to a large extent still is, that there are two types of settlers: a hard nucleus of fanatics, whose presence in the territories constitutes a religious or historical personal experience for them and a much larger number of more secular Israelis who moved to the territories to reap the material and fiscal benefits of living in pleasant surroundings and government-subsidized housing. For the latter group, the surroundings are no longer pleasant and, although their old subsidized mortgages and loans are still intact, the real estate values have dropped owing to the Arab uprising, and further settlement for like-minded Israelis is being discouraged by austerity cuts in the various ministry budgets that have been the mainstay of Gush Emunim. These Israelis may have spouted an ideology similar to that of the true believers, but the rhetoric was a cover or an addition to the material benefits for which they really relocated. They were not and are not prepared to put their families through the demands and real self-sacrifice that will be warranted in the face of a deteriorating situation.

This appraisal was reinforced by actual settler activity during the first several months of the intifada. There was a good deal of talk about leaving among members of the latter category, and an undisclosed number of families did leave.[16] There was also a halt in Jewish settlers moving into the territories. However, by early spring this turned around, and movement out halted and movement in picked up again. Table 5.1 indicates the difference in the rate growth of 1988 as compared to the earlier non-intifada years.

As can be seen, the 1988 percentage increase is the same as the preceding year, approximately 10.5 percent, and the absolute increase of 7,000 is actually 500 more than the previous year despite the fact that there was some emigration and no immigration for the first three or four months of 1988. These figures do not support any assertion voiced by Gush Emunim that there has been a major groundswell of support for the beleaguered settler community. At the same time, they also clearly do not support the point of view of Gush's opponents within Israel that the movement is hemorrhaging.

The location of the settlers is important to our analysis as can be seen in the findings of the survey summarized in Table 5.2. The table indicates

Table 5.1
Jewish Population on the West Bank (end of year)

Year	Total	Absolute Increase	Percentage Increase
1976	3,176	-	-
1977	5,023	1,847	58.1
1978	7,361	2,338	46.5
1979	10,000	2,639	35.3
1980	12,424	2,424	24.2
1981	16,119	3,695	29.7
1982	21,000	4,881	30.3
1983	27,500	6,500	30.9
1984	44,146	16,646	60.5
1985	52,960	8,814	20.0
1986	60,500	7,540	14.2
1987	67,000	6,500	10.7
1988	74,000	7,000	10.5

Source: Meron Benvenisti and Shlomo Khayat, *The West Bank and Gaza Atlas* (Jerusalem: West Bank Data Base Project, 1988), p. 32, Table 1. The update for 1988 comes from *The Jerusalem Post*.

Table 5.2
Distribution by Metropolitan and Rural Areas

	1982	1984	1985	1986
Metropolitan areas	57.7	80.1	83.2	84.8
Rural areas	42.3	19.9	16.9	15.2
Total	100.0	100.0	100.0	100.0

Source: Meron Benvenisti and Shlomo Khayat, *The West Bank and Gaza Atlas* (Jerusalem: West Bank Data Base Project, 1988), p. 33, Table 4.

the distribution trend of the settler population this decade, but it does not include the very latest figures.

The growth in the urban, or suburban, settlements has far outdistanced the growth in the rural settlements that are more ideolocally inclined and situated within or surrounding areas heavily populated by Arabs. This not insignificant increase of settlers since the intifada belies either or both themes that the Israeli peace camp held concerning the potential for Gush Emunim's growth. One assertion was that the state of Israel had already significantly exhausted its "reservoir of fanatics" who were willing to move into the territories. The second was that the intifada had destroyed the material appeal to the nonideological, or nonfanatical, secularists.

The attitudes of both groups were researched in a survey conducted in August 1988 by Rina Dagani among 400 family heads in eleven western Samaria settlements, following nearly ten months of the intifada.[17] Although all surveys are imperfect, these results are very similar to the author's own, much more impressionistic, conclusions derived from several years of interviews with members and leaders of Gush Emunim.

SETTLER ATTITUDES IN THE FACE OF POLITICAL CHANGE

The Dagani survey separated the sampled settlements into four categories: urban secular, Ar'iel, Alfe Menashe, and Ginnot Shomron; rural secular, Ma'ale Shomron, Sha'are Tiqva, Sal'it, and Barqan; urban religious, Elqana and Qarne Shomron; and secular settlements inside the Green Line but on the border of Samaria, such as Oranit and Kokhav Ya'ir. The survey did not interview rural religious settlers. (The reader would be safe to assume that the overall trends would have been in a more militant or hawkish direction than they were in Dagani's study.) The research goals were to understand the motives for settlement in Samaria, to attempt to define the "typical" settler, and to see if, and how, the religious settler differs from his secular counterpart.

The results were as follows. In response to the question, "How would you react if the government decided to evacuate the settlements in return for a peace agreement?," 45 percent replied that they would agree to be evacuated in one way or another. Of these, 5 percent said that they would leave after lawful protest; and 5 percent, after they received appropriate compensation.

Approximately 26 percent of the interviewed replied that they would object categorically to any form of evacuation, even to the extent of civil war. The principal objectors to leaving Samaria came from the religious settlements. About 50 percent of the religious respondents threatened to resort to active resistance and civil war. (Approximately 75% of the settlers in Samaria are secular.) However, there was a very high level of support for an even harsher iron fist policy in the secular settlements of Alfe Menashe, as a result of the Molotov cocktail death of a family in that settlement.

Finally, in response to the question, "Are you acquainted with a family in your settlement which is considering leaving the place?," 20 percent admitted knowing such families; 30 percent knew at least four families who wished to leave the settlement. The majority of those wishing to leave reside in urban secular settlements.

The author's own discussions with settlers, particularly in Judea, prior to the intifada and as recently as December 1988, have indicated a strong core of mainly, but not exclusively, religious settlers willing to fight the

Arab population and even to resist the IDF if a settlement included evacuation. Their overriding rationale would be to "up the psychological ante" to such a degree, by showing that Jews would be willing even to resist a Jewish army to stay on the land, that the Israeli government would lose its political resolve. Thus while the government would attempt to deal with settler opposition and resistance as criminal acts of violence against the state, the militants within Gush Emunim would attempt to elevate the issue to the top of the national agenda and draw in as many supporters as possible from within the Green Line or, conversely, bring down the government through demonstrations, perhaps violence, in Israel's cities. As the intifada approached its second year, other small voices were emerging from among the settler community. These, perhaps, reflected both fatigue and a sense of limits and indicated that some of the community might see the work of Gush Emunim over the past two decades as *this generation's* contribution to the overall development of Greater Eretz Yisrael, leaving future work for future generations. This would imply that territorial compromise might be considered so long as full evacuation of the existing settlements is not.[18]

SETTLER MILITIAS AND VIGILANTISM

While many of the settler community are taking a wait-and-see attitude toward the National Unity Government's position regarding elections for the Palestinian inhabitants of the occupied territories, the more militant wing of Gush Emunim regard the plan as a prelude to national betrayal. However, many of the settlers are very disgruntled at the limited commitment for additional settlements within the budget. A lesser, albeit significant, number of settlers feel that the IDF is not doing enough to secure the roads and settlements against the intifada. These fairly widespread sentiments have led to several phenomena, some of which are potentially serious. First, there has been a dramatic rise in vigilante activity, accompanied perhaps by the emergence of a second "Jewish underground," this time with Israeli Jewish, as well as Palestinian Arab, targets. There is insufficient proof at this point to determine whether there is an unorganized structure behind the new wave of Jewish terror. Second, there has been the organization of militias, even outside and beyond the control of the Judea and Samaria Council of Settlements. Third, there have been clashes between the IDF and settlers.

Organized settler militia activity began in Judea. By the spring of 1988 the Committee for Security on the Highways, unofficially known as the "Kiryat Arba patrol," was "arresting" Arabs and conducting searches at bus stops well beyond the jurisdiction of their settlements. Halhoul, north of Hebron, was the site of an altercation between settlers, on the one hand, and IDF soldiers and television journalists, on the other, in April

1988. (Kach has a particularly strong support in the Hebron-Kiryat Arba region). By mid-summer settler activity spread to Samaria where they had previously maintained relative restraint.[19]

The heavily armed settlers are only occasionally disarmed by the IDF, usually following an incident, and the settlers in Hebron have established, in response to IDF confiscations, the Association for the Protection of Hebrew Arms.[20] Basically, this is merely a surfacing of a phenomenon that has been in operation underground for years, the provision of weapons outside of official security channels.

However, conflicting reports of a major settlers' militia did not emerge until mid-February 1989. Two members of the opposition party, the Citizens' Rights Movement, Yosi Sarid and Dedi Zucker, wrote to Attorney General Yosef Harish warning him that there was a "fully equipped" settlers' militia, based in Ariel, that was regularly engaged in "punitive, intimidatory and relatiatory" missions. Sarid and Zucker said that the militia was made up of companies, each of which draws its manpower from a particular locality. The companies are commanded and coordinated from a sophisticated communications headquarters that controls the entire West Bank. There are supposedly five operational bases: Ariel, Ginot Shomron, Ma'alel Shomron, Kedumim, and Yitzhar settlements. The headquarters staff is made up of settler leaders, some of whom double as senior members of the settler organizations.

The companies are equipped with modern weapons and communications equipment that operates on different network levels. Most of this equipment was, and is, supplied to the settlers, for self-defense, by the IDF. Sarid and Zucker insist that the headquarters staff have drafted a range of contingency plans for most political and security scenarios and that these include "confrontations with the IDF if circumstances so warrant."[21] General Ehud Barak, IDF deputy chief of staff, in a testimony to the Knesset claimed that he was "unaware of settlers having established any militia" and stated that while individual settlers cause damage to Arab property and break the law there are no grounds for considering this a group phenomenon.[22] Yisrael Harel, chairman of the Council of Settlements in Judea, Samaria, and Gaza, also denied the validity of any of Sarid's assertions.

However, Sarid was the Knesset member who had the strongest evidence concerning the existence of the Jewish underground in the early 1980s and was one of the first to publicize this information at that time. There were public denials by the political and security hierarchies at that time also. Other members of both the IDF and the Council of Settlements are much more supportive of Sarid's claims. After having to use tear gas, in early February, to drive armed settlers out of an Arab village, the commander of the troops in Judea and Samaria, Brigadier General Gabi Ofir, chaired a debate at the IDF's Central Command to discuss the institutionalization and activities of the settler militia. Both IDF sources and Ron Nahman, head of the Ariel local settlers council, admit that the militia does exist, that it operates beyond the control of the parent body Judea and Samaria Council of Settlements, and that it can mobilize hundreds of armed settlers at very short notice.[23]

This form of organization and activity is the major and most potentially explosive settler reaction to their perception that the situation in the territories is insoluble as it is currently being handled and that the state organs are themselves not providing sufficient responses. On the fringes, at this point, but with potential for growth, are two other marginal phenomena, each probably connected to the disenfranchised Kach party. One is the reemergence of a Jewish underground which calls itself Sicarayim; the second is the establishment of the "State of Judea" which, its founders claim, will come into being if and when the IDF withdraws from the territories.

Sicarayim, or those who individually attribute their acts to an organization by this name, initially chose Jews as their targets. These earlier targets—of arson—included peace activists, poll takers, and newscasters.[24] Their actions appear to be emerging out of the militants' anger that there seems to be a substantial body of Israeli public opinion that holds that Israel should talk to the PLO in order to resolve the intifada. Sicarayim later took credit for the April 10 fatal shooting of an Arab, outside the Jaffa Gate entrance of Jerusalem. This may have been in response to earlier disturbances when Arab demonstrators threw stones at the Western Wall.

As of now, there still remains the question of whether these half dozen violent incidents are the unconnected work of isolated extremists or the vanguard action of an armed underground network with an agenda that will intensify inside Israel as well as in the territories if and when the parties approach a solution. To date, Israeli police appear to be treating it as if it were another underground that is attempting to popularize its mission through the manipulation of the media.

On October 18, 1988, the Israeli Supreme Court ruled the Kach party ineligible to run in the national elections. Three months later, the movement declared its intention to form a State of Judea in the territories of Judea, Samaria, and Gaza. In his original 1985 article calling for the establishment of this entity, Kahane asserted that it would take place in the event of an Israeli withdrawal, or when it appeared that steps toward Palestinian autonomy were serious. In the event of these occurrences, Kahane claimed that there would be a forced takeover by armed Jews who would form the new state.[25] If events reached this point, the creation of the state would not constitute a breach with the ideology of Gush Emunim, which holds that there should be no dividing line, of any nature, between the Jews within the current state of Israel and those in the territories since all of the land constitutes Greater Israel. Kach's maneuver would constitute a desperate last stand after the government abandoned Gush Emunim. How seriously should outside policymakers, or Israelis, view this marginal phenomenon?

The real issue is not a paper Judean state. The real issue is what type of resistance Kach and the more militant fringe of Gush Emunim will be able to muster in the face of the start of an implementation of Palestinian autonomy. Given the earlier part of this section, it appears that there already exist armed and organized militias operating outside the auspices of the Council of Settlements. In addition within the official settler movement, there are many religious and secular settlers who claim to be willing to resist what they define as a threat to their home and holy land. Kach will do its best to mobilize rightist forces within the Knesset and in the cities within the Green Line in an attempt to bring down the government and reverse the process. The strategy will not be to beat the IDF; rather, it will be to raise the cost of a government victory to such a degree that the government will not be willing or able to pay the price.

It appears likely that a Labor government committed to a faster pace of withdrawal may engender this form of extralegal opposition more than either a Likud or National Unity Government committed to a gradual process beginning with elections and leading toward Palestinian autonomy. However, once the fanatical right-wing perceives that Shamir is not practicing total immobilism and delay, but is merely slowing the process to a pace that will test the good will and intentions of the Palestinians, as well prepare the Israeli center for a form of Palestinian self-determination, one should expect the start of atrocities by Kach and settler militias to disrupt the process. It will be at these stress points, long before Israel is at a point of withdrawal, that a series of crises will arise. The militants will not wait for a last-minute demonstration, such as at Yamit.

Under these circumstances, Israel's religious parties will have their commitment to Greater Israel put to the test. Under this scenario, the IDF will necessarily intensify its policing duties against the settler militias in the face of Jewish-initiated incidents as Jewish, as well as Palestinian, casualties mount. At the same time, the governments of both Israel and the United States should be expected to stand firmly by the respective obligations that they made to one another, as well as to Jordan and the Palestinian community. If at the earliest stages there is room for compromise regarding the continued existence of the more substantial settlements within the territories, an issue that Arafat appeared to have tentatively introduced into the marketplace of ideas, then Israel and the United States have a good chance to isolate the fanatics from the center-right of Israeli politics. None of the secular parties to the right of Likud, such as Tehiya, Moledet, and Tzomet, will support any move toward autonomy that could lead to Palestinian self-determination; nor would the two major parties be able to count on most of the Knesset members of the National Religious Party, although Zvulun Hammer and one other might join. However, the Knesset support for Greater Eretz Yisrael from among the members of SHAS, Agudat Israel, and Degel HaTorah is neither broad nor deep, and it is completely conditional upon the price that this support entails in other areas that have much greater priority.[26]

NOTES

1. See Don Peretz and Sammy Smooha, "Israel's Twelfth Knesset Election: An All-Loser Game," *Middle East Journal* 43, no. 3 (Summer 1989): 390, Table 1.

2. *The Jerusalem Post*, November 7, 1988, 2.

3. These developments are discussed in further detail in Stewart Reiser, *The Politics of Leverage: The National Religious Party of Israel and Its Influence on Foreign Policy* (Cambridge, Mass.: Center for Middle Eastern Studies, Harvard University, 1984).

4. Menachem Friedman, professor of sociology at Bar-Ilan University, Tel Aviv, has expressed this opinion in several forums and in the Israeli press. Friedman's field of expertise is Israel's ultra-Orthodox community.

5. Robert O. Freedman, "Religion, Politics, and the Israeli Elections of 1988," *Middle East Journal* 43, no. 3 (Summer 1989): 414.

6. For the polls that refer to Kach's standings see *Hadashot*, August 22, 1988, 1; *Ma'ariv*, October 21, 1988, A1–2; *Yedi'ot Aharonot*, October 7, 1988, 1; *Davar*, July 17, 1988, 1; and *'Al Hamishmar*, October 27, 1988, 2.

7. According to Sammy Smooha, a poll conducted for him in April 1988 by Dahaf indicated that "70.6 percent of Orientals indicated that they would vote for 'right' parties and 29.4 percent for the 'left.' Among Ashkenazi voters the breakdown was 35.4 percent 'right' and 64.6 percent 'left'." Peretz and Smooha, "Israel's Twelfth Knesset Election," 401, note 39.

8. As pointed out by Robert Freedman, "Agudat Yisrael opposed Israel's annexation of the Golan Heights in 1981, claiming that it was an unnecessary provocation." Freedman, "Religion, Politics, and the Israeli Elections of 1988," 411.

9. See for example the interview in *The Jerusalem Post*, International Edition, October 15, 1988, 8.

10. *Yedi'ot Aharonot*, October 26, 1988, 4; SHAS election advertisement subtitled "Main Points of Platform."

11. *The New York Times*, November 8, 1988, 6.

12. *Middle East International*, no. 356, August 4, 1989, 12.

13. *The Jerusalem Post*, July 28, 1989, 1.

14. Smooha's data, cited in note 7 does not hold either the education level or occupation of the respondents as constants, although the original Dahaf survey may do so. Peretz and Smooha, "Israel's Twelfth Knesset Election."

15. Freedman, "Religion, Politics, and the Israeli Elections of 1988," 411.

16. Arye Ofni, deputy head of the Samaria Regional council, and Uri Ari'el, secretary-general of the Council of Settlements in Judea, Samaria, and the Gaza district, acknowledged that several people left settlements at the start of the uprising and that there was an accompanying halt in settlers coming in for the first four months. *The Jerusalem Post*, September 20, 1988, 2.

17. The results of the Dagani research can be found in *Ha'aretz*, November 10, 1988, 13. Dagani is a city planner and project director with Geocartography-Land Space Research Ltd. Co.

18. The author has been made aware of these "voices" through indirect sources and has not been able to confirm either the degree to which they reflect wider settlement sentiments or the depth of their conviction.

19. *'Al Hamishmar*, July 13, 1988, 2.

20. *'Al Hamishmar*, August 3, 1988, 1.

21. *The Jerusalem Post*, February 13, 1989, 1. Also see *'Al Hamishmar*, February 10, 1989, 1, 10; and *Al-Fajr*, February 20, 1989, 3.

22. IDF Radio, February 14, 1989.

23. *'Al Hamishmar*, February 10, 1989, 1, 10.

24. See *The Los Angeles Times*, March 28, 1989, 6; and *The Jerusalem Post*, April 22, 1989, 2.

25. *Ma'ariv*, November 29, 1988, 9. Also see *The Nation*, January 19, 1989, 3; and *The Jerusalem Post*, January 17, 1989, 2, for Kahane's principles for the new state.

26. On April 24, 1989, the founding ceremony of the Eretz Yisrael Front was held at the settlement of Bet Arye. In a live interview on Jerusalem Domestic Service (Radio), Tehiya MK Professor Yuval Ne'eman stated that the Eretz Yisrael Front, which is the Knesset's support system for the Council of Jewish Settlements in Judea, Samaria, and Gaza, consists of thirty members. Of these, according to Ne'eman, there are eighteen or nineteen Likud members, *two MAFDAL members, one each from SHAS and Agudat Israel*, and the remainder from Tehiya, Moledet, and Tzomet. (Italics added by author.)

6

The Israeli-Jewish Presence in the Territories: Historical and Cultural Roots

Chaim I. Waxman

In much of the mass media as well as in scholarly analyses, Israel's continued military and civilian presence in the West Bank and Gaza Strip is viewed as a major, if not *the* major stumbling block to a resolution of the Arab-Israeli conflict which is widely understood as essentially being an Israeli-Palestinian conflict. In many writings, the Israeli settlers in the Administered Territories are viewed as wholly irrational, religious zealots imbued with an extreme spirit of Messianism, who are willing to go to any lengths—civil war and, if necessary, even the risk of world war—to increase Jewish settlement in the territories and thereby hasten the arrival of the Messiah. Until these extremists are overcome and Israel leaves the territories, it is further asserted, there cannot be any resolution of the conflict.[1]

This chapter contends that, although the above-cited characterization may be psychologically beneficial to some spectators of the Arab-Israeli conflict, it is replete with distortions and factual errors and can do nothing to further actual peace efforts. Since a complete analysis should be impossible within the context of this brief presentation, this chapter focuses on who the settlers are, what their reasons are for settling, what the extent of their support is within Israel, and whether their presence precludes a just and peaceful resolution of at least the Israeli-Palestinian component of the Middle East conflict.

The Israeli Jews who live in the region of the areas that are beyond the pre-1967 unofficial borders of Israel, the Green Line, are not simply a small group of hothead extremists. According to the most recent credible estimates, more than 200,000 Israelis now live in the areas captured during the Six-Day War. As Table 6.1 indicates, in 1988 an estimated 110,000 Jews were living in those parts of Judea that were actually annexed, developed, and incorporated into the city of Jerusalem; an additional 81,700 were living in Judea, Samaria, the Gaza district, and the Golan Heights. These numbers, which increase annually, demonstrate conclusively that the Israelis living beyond the Green Line are not simply a small, basically insignificant group of zealots and militants.

In addition, the overwhelming majority of them are not either political or religious fanatics. Some of them are there for reasons completely unrelated to ideology. They are there for a very understandable, pragmatic reason—housing is considerably cheaper there. Additionally, since the government of Israel supports Jewish settlement in the territories both ideologically and economically, residing in the territories is not viewed by many of the residents as a challenging political act. Moreover, most of those residing in the territories and, indeed, most Israelis, view their decision to live in whatever part of the territories they choose as an inherent right and as perfectly legitimate and duly sanctioned within both traditional Zionism and international law. On the contrary, they argue, the attempt to prevent any further Jewish settlement of the areas and to remove those already there is antithetical to the dictates of history and law. Failure to acknowledge their rights to live in the territories, they believe, frequently stems from not having an even elementary familiarity with the long history of the area or with Jewish history and culture.

From a Jewish perspective, which has broad support both within Israel and within Jewish communities around the world, the right of Jews to live in Judea and Samaria is based on their more than 3,000-year-old deep connection and direct involvement with the area. It is a right which has been self-evident not only to the vast majority of Jews but also to the Western world at large. Indeed, it was on the basis of that historical right that the Balfour Declaration was issued in 1917, and that right was reiterated by the League of Nations in 1922 as well as by the United Nations in 1948. Eretz Yisrael, the Land of Israel, of which Judea and Samaria are the heart, has been a central component of Judaism and Jewish culture since early biblical times. Hebron, in Judea, and Shechem (Nablus), in Samaria, are among the most ancient biblical cities and are part of the very core of the "Promised Land," as is Beersheba, city of the tomb of the matriarch, Rachel, a site which has long had an even more special and a deeper meaning for Jewish mothers. Judea and Samaria are the crux—though certainly not the totality—of the land that was the birthplace of the Jewish people, which they (and others sometimes, as well) have historically viewed as promised to the Jewish people.

Although the destruction of the Temple and the loss of Jerusalem to

Table 6.1
Jewish Population over the Green Line: Jerusalem, Judea, Samaria, Gaza District, and Golan Heights

	1986	1988
Jerusalem		
New neighborhoods		
East Talpiot	12,200	
French Hill	9,100	
Gilo	25,200	
Neve Yaakov	14,300	
Old City	2,200	
Pisgat Zeev	2,400	
Ramat Eshkol, Givat Hamivtar, Maalot Dafna	15,000	
Ramot	23,800	
	104,200	110,000
Judea		
Towns		
Efrat	1,600	1,750
Givat Zeev	3,900	4,250
Kiryat Arba	4,500	5,000
Maaleh Edumim	12,400	13,000
Regional Councils		
Gush Etzion	3,400	3,500
Hebron Hills	1,000	1,300
	26,800	28,800
Samaria		
Towns		
Alfei Menashe	1,800	2,000
Ariel	5,900	8,500
Elkana	1,900	2,000
Emanuel	4,000	4,500
Maaleh Efraim	1,100	1,300
Regional Councils		
Samari	9,300	12,000
Benjamin	5,800	8,500
Jordan Valley	2,000	3,200
	31,800	42,000
Gaza Regional Council	1,800	1,900
Golan Heights	8,700	9,000
Total	173,300	191,700

Source: *Survey of Arab Affairs* (Jerusalem: Jerusalem Center for Public Affairs), no. 13, August 15, 1988, p. 9.

Rome in 70 c.e. resulted in the end of Jewish sovereignty in the Holy Land and the onset of the dispersion of Jews and Jewish communities in distant countries throughout the world, the Holy Land, Eretz Yisrael, was never far from the consciousness of Jews during the almost 2,000-year absence of Jewish sovereignty in the land. Throughout almost that entire period, Eretz Yisrael played a central role in traditional Jewish culture. Small Jewish communities there persevered, aided by contributions from diaspora Jewish communities. Some diaspora Jews managed to visit Eretz Yisrael; others actually managed to move there on a more permanent basis. And, for Jews around the world, the Holy Land and the dream of return were imbedded in daily religious rituals and prayers as well as in law and lore.

Three days each year in the Jewish ritual calendar were set aside as fast days commemorating a significant part of the destruction of the Temple and the loss of the Holy Land. Likewise, the loss of Jerusalem is symbolized in the rituals of the Jewish marriage ceremony. The daily prayers are recited facing east, toward Jerusalem. The service of the Passover feast, the Seder, concludes with the prayer, "Next year in Jerusalem!" For the vast majority of Jews, who were in the diaspora, these served as constant reminders of the Jewish title to and yearning for the land. The daily prayers and rituals have continuously sustained the persistent yearning both for being in Eretz Yisrael and for the ultimate Messianic redemption (Waxman 1989, 27–38). And, as indicated, some Jews remained in the land long after the Romans and subsequent conquerors: The Byzantines, Califates, Crusaders, Mamluks, Turks, and finally the British all left. The only time that there were no Jews there was during the nineteen-year period from 1948 to 1967, when Jordan occupied Judea and Samaria, the West Bank.

Since 1967, at least until the intifada, the Palestinian Arab uprising in the territories that began in December 1987, the overwhelming majority of Israelis residing in the territories have been opposed to efforts aimed at driving Palestinian Arab residents from there. Except for the few who supported Meir Kahane and his Kach movement, the Israelis in the territories hoped for an accommodation that would allow both the Jews and the Arabs to live there. Since the intifada, there has been a decrease in the numbers of those who view such an accommodation as feasible. This became evident in the election to the Knesset in 1988 of the Moledet party, which advocates the "peaceful" transfer of the Palestinian Arabs from the territories, and of the Tzomet party, which maintains a very hard-line approach to the Palestinian Arabs. But even in that election, Moledet candidates were the choice of but a small minority of residents in the territories (*Nekudah* 1988). In contrast to the notion of transfer, there was, a number of years ago, even a proposal by Tehiya, a nationalist political party which enjoys wide support within the territories, to grant

Israeli citizenship to any Palestinian Arab in the territories. Although many Israelis (and others) on the political left tend to view this proposal as insincere and cynical, it should be noted that a very similar proposal was part of the platform of Ezer Weizman's Yahad party during the 1984 election campaign in Israel, and Weizman is perceived as being dovish on the issues of Palestinian Arabs and the territories.

On the other hand, there are Israelis on both sides of the Green Line who cannot understand the moral validity of a peace proposal that precludes the possibility of a continued Jewish presence in the territories. As one Israeli, who emigrated from the United States and now lives in Efrat, recently put it, "Can Jews aspire to live anywhere in the world, but not in or near Hebron, Bethlehem, Nablus, and Jenin? Is Jewish-Arab coexistence possible only on one side of the 1967 Green Line, but not on the other?" (Bedein 1989). The problem for those such as Bedein is that policymakers in Washington, D.C., and elsewhere frequently view all settlers as followers of Meir Kahane and his Kach party, which advocates the immediate annexation of the territories and the removal, by force if necessary, of all Palestinian Arabs from the territories. The available empirical evidence, however, indicates not only strong opposition among the residents of the territories to Meir Kahane and his policies, but also that the vast majority are neither fundamentalists nor Messianists—at least, they are not any more than most Orthodox Jews. They do believe that that right to dwell in the territories as well as in all of Israel is religiously legitimated, if not ordained, and they do believe that ultimately the Messiah will redeem the entire land as well as the entire Jewish people. Those are basic precepts within traditional Judaism. Indeed, there was a distinct Messianic component to the ideas and writings of the forerunners of Zionism in the first half of the nineteenth century, and many of the Jewish masses in Eastern Europe were subsequently attracted to the Zionist movement because they saw it as the vehicle for the fulfillment of many of those Messianic aspirations.

Unquestionably, it was within the air of a broader prevailing Messianic anticipation that the founding fathers of religious Zionism, Rabbi Zvi Hirsch Kalischer (1795–1874), the Ashkenazi, and Rabbi Yehuda Chai Alkalai, the Sephardi, emerged as authoritative critics of the popular notion that the Messiah would arrive suddenly through a momentous act of Divine intervention. Four years before the widely anticipated date of the redemption, Kalischer wrote a letter to Anselm Rothschild, the head of the Frankfurt am der Oder branch of the Rothschild family banks, in which he turned to Rothschild for assistance. Perhaps the most novel aspect of Kalischer's approach was in his conviction that the Messiah would arrive through natural processes and by human efforts:

No one should think that the redemption of Israel and our Messiah, whom we await each day, will arrive through God's sudden descension upon Earth saying to His people, "Go out," or that He will suddenly send His Messiah from Heaven to blow on a big *shofar* over the dispersed of Israel....

The beginning of the redemption will be through natural causes and by the will of the governments to gather some of the dispersed of Israel to the Holy Land....

Then, when many of the dispersed of Israel will be in the Holy Land and Jerusalem, the Merciful One will comfort us to bring about for us complete redemption and everlasting happiness. At that time, there will be wars over the Land of Israel, and then will arrive [the Redeemer]. (Raphael 1974, 211–12)

After his lengthy discussion of the Messiah and redemption, Kalischer suggested to Rothschild that he buy a different piece of land for Muhammad Ali, the Egyptian ruler who then controlled Eretz Yisrael, so that Ali would give the land to the Jews, where, through the help of many wealthy Jews, they would be able to establish a government of Israel and build up the country for the many dispersed Jews who would flock to it.

Although Rothschild's response, if any, is unknown, it is known that Kalischer subsequently wrote to Sir Moses Montefiore, apparently in 1839, and also to Albert Cohen, the manager of philanthropic funds of the Rothschild family in Paris, in 1860. In that same year, 1860, Kalischer joined an organization founded by Dr. Chaim Lurie, the Society for the Colonization of Palestine in Frankfurt am der Oder.

The uniqueness of Kalischer's Messianism, as indicated above, lies in his espousal of the natural process of the redemption, and the fact that he combined his vision with pragmatism, that is, he suggested specific ways to settle the land and undertook efforts to realize those suggestions. He not only wrote to wealthy Jews in an effort to enlist their financial assistance in building up the land, he also detailed the directions which that building should take. It is significant that two of his suggestions, the establishment of an agricultural cooperative as the economic foundation of settlement and the establishment of an agricultural school in Eretz Yisrael, were both seconded by Moses Hess and became realities in later years. The latter was realized when the Alliance Israelite Universelle founded the well-known agricultural school, Mikveh Israel, in 1870, and the former, with the adoption by the Palestine Office of World Zionist Organization of an emphasis on agricultural development in the early 1900s (Waxman 1989, 40–42).

Kalischer's slightly younger contemporary, Rabbi Yehuda Alkalai (1798–1878), was born in Sarajevo, Serbia, and was reared within the Sephardi tradition of the Balkans, and authored numerous books in which he elaborated on his convictions with regard to the imminent onset of the Messianic era. To participate in the process of redemption, he called upon his fellow Jews to manifest their repentence by the establishment of a tithe for the rebuilding of Jerusalem and for the beginning of a Jewish return to Eretz Yisrael, the first step of which was to be the migration of 22,000 Jews to the Land. This, of course, would require governmental support, and Alkalai was confident that such would be forthcoming. He also urged every Jew to send one of his children to settle in Eretz Yisrael.

In 1871, Alkalai himself went to live in Jerusalem where he continued his efforts to organize Jewry for the support of the rebuilding of Eretz Yisrael. In an article written that same year, he tells of his success in organizing Ashkenazi and Sephardi leaders of Jerusalem for the establishment of a branch of *Kol Yisrael Chaverim* (all of Israel are brothers), an organization founded in Paris in 1860, of which Alkalai was an enthusiastic supporter. The Jerusalem branch had as its explicit objective assisting the poor in the settling and building of the Land. Likewise, he was an avid supporter of the Society for the Colonization of Palestine in Frankfurt am der Oder and of the agricultural school, Mikveh Israel (Waxman 1989, 42–45).

The third of the three "true forerunners of Zionism" (Katz 1986) was Moses Hess (1812–1875). Born in Bonn, a descendant of rabbis—his paternal great-grandfather was a rabbi in Mannheim and his maternal grandfather was a rabbi near Frankfurt—Hess was a secular Jew who, in his youth, became estranged from Jews and Judaism, married a non-Jewish woman who had been a prostitute, was an editor of the *Rheinische Zeitung* and a prominent figure in the German radical movement, and was "the first German Communist." He developed a relationship with Karl Marx, who was a regular contributor to the *Rheinische Zeitung*, through their mutual interest in the philosophy of G.W.F. Hegel and socialist theory and praxis; he was known by his friends as "the communist rabbi" (Avineri 1985).

According to his own account, it was Hess's reactions to the notorious blood libel in Damascus, in 1840, that led him to write *Rome and Jerusalem*, which was first published in 1862. Be that as it may, the book was revolutionary in that it asserted that Jews are a national entity, and he advocated the establishment of a Jewish national home in Eretz Yisrael. When Theodor Herzl read the book, in 1901, he proclaimed, "Everything that we have tried is already in his book" (Patai 1960, 3: 1090). Hess averred that Jewish nationality consists of "a unity which cannot be separated from the heritage of my forefathers, from the Holy Land and the Eternal City, from the birthplace of the faith in the Divine unity of life and the pact of brotherhood which will be taken between all peoples" (Hess 1983, 29).

Despite the vast differences in the backgrounds of Hess, Kalischer, and Alkalai, they shared a common belief in the dawning of the Messianic era in the nineteenth century. For Hess, that century marked the "spring-time" of human history and was characterized by the liberation and regeneration of oppressed nations and classes, and it was the destiny of the Jewish people, in their own liberation and regeneration, to play a pivotal role in the universal process of liberation. Although Hess was unique, and most of the secular Zionist leaders neither adhered to nor proclaimed such Messianic notions, it is, nevertheless, the case that a large percentage of the masses of Jews were attracted to Zionism because of their Messianic beliefs, and these were fed upon by the fact that "modern [Jewish] nationalism leaned heavily on the old messianism, and derived from it much of its ideological and even more of its emotional appeal" (Katz 1986, 91). One manifestation of this was the widespread perception among the Eastern European Jewish masses of both Theodor Herzl and David Ben-Gurion as the Messiah (Patai 1960, 1: 310; Bein 1970, 201–2; Ben-Gurion 1970, 34; Pearlman 1970, 224–34).

Since its inception, there have always been within the religious Zionist movement two very different perspectives on the Zionist endeavor: one views the resettlement as part of the Messianic process; the other denies any Messianic element in Zionism (Luz 1988, 227–55; Nehorai 1988). In either case, virtually all religious Zionists believe that living in Eretz Yisrael under Jewish autonomy has religious significance. Initially, at least among the leadership, it may well be that the Messianic perspective of Zionism was the minority. However, since the Balfour Declaration, and especially since the establishment of the State of Israel, the Messianic perspective has increasingly been the dominant one. This does not mean that religious Zionists are political Messianists, however. The vast majority subscribe to the belief that the Messianic process is a gradual one, and their sense that the Zionist endeavor is part of that process is more of a belief than a firm conviction. With Israel's swift victory in the Six-Day War, the reunification of Jerusalem, and the capture of all of Judea and Samaria, it was not only religious Zionists, but many secular Israelis as well who perceived in the unfolding of events an element of Messianism. But that did not make them political Messianists either.[2]

Moreover, there is no evidence that there is any inherent conflict between the beliefs of religious Zionism and modern, democratic political values. Indeed, the historic inseparability of Judea and Samaria from Eretz Yisrael and, therefore, the right of Jews to settle in the territories have been basic principles of the Likud. The establishing of Jewish settlements there has, therefore, been supported by the government of Israel. Prior to the Ninth Knesset elections in 1977, in which Menachem Begin's party was victorious, such governmental support was much more selective; since then, it has been quite broad.

Nor is there any evidence that the religious settlers have unanimously been unconditionally opposed either to any territorial compromise or Palestinian Arabs remaining in the territories. Among them, there is a range of positions on these issues as there is within the National Religious

Party, and there have been changes over the years since 1967 in the relative strengths of the various positions. Within the NRP, for example, the 1973 convention adopted the position that "the NRP cannot assume any share in governmental responsibility if a peace plan is submitted by the government involving the relinquishment of parts of Eretz Israel, the heritage of our fathers." A number of subsequent NRP conventions did not adopt that position. Then, an even more recent convention went further to declare that

the religious historical right of the Jewish people to sovereignty over Eretz Israel is a fundamental principle in the educational thought and activity of the movement, with strict care and responsibility for the well-being and completeness of the people.... No part of the land will be ceded to a foreign government ... and not one Jewish settlement will be uprooted from its place.

While insisting that "no national independent Arab entity will be established in Eretz Israel," the convention called for efforts to reach "honorable coexistence and resolution of the demographic problem by means of continuing the process of the return to Zion and the growth of the people in its land." It also called for the "strengthening and enhancing of the settlements and establishing new ones, in the Gallilee, in the Golan, Judea and Samaria, the Jordan Rift, the Negev and the Gaza Strip" (Azrieli 1990, 11).

In my own studies of American-born Israelis in the territories (Waxman 1984/85; 1989, 150–68), I found that even after having formulated ideological attachments to the area, these American Israelis retain their rather liberal social, political, and religious attitudes and values in that respect. For example, most of those whom I interviewed were very positive in their attitudes and feelings about American society and culture, and they were also highly committed to and supportive of one of the basic values of American political culture—democracy. When asked for their attitudes and feelings about democracy as a basic value, 50 percent indicated that they were strongly supportive of the value and indicated no qualifications; another 29 percent stated that they support it, but with qualifications. Less than 15 percent rejected democracy for Israel, on the grounds that "Democracy is not a Torah concept," "I want a religious state in Israel," "I hope for a Jewish monarchy in Israel," or, as one male stated, "Democracy is fine for the United States. In Israel, I would now like to see a military junta."

Also, although most of my interviews were conducted prior to the arrest of the so-called Jewish underground, the group of settlers that was charged and convicted of having committed a number of violent actions against Palestinian Arabs in the territories, 20 percent were conducted just after the arrests. Those interviews contained additional questions to probe the respondents' reactions to the alleged activities of the underground. Virtually all of those questioned strongly condemned the underground on legal and pragmatic grounds, and many on moral grounds as well. This was the case not only among those unaffiliated with Gush Emunim, but even among some of its strongest adherents. For example, a thirty-three-year-old mother of five who went on aliya in 1972, moved to a settlement in 1975, and is actively involved with the settlement movement responded:

If it turns out that there is truth in all of the allegations, I am opposed when it comes to harming innocent people. Not only were those actions mistaken, they were bad, very, very bad. The principle is, number one, you're not allowed to harm innocent people, and number two, you're not allowed to take the law into your own hands when you have a sovereign government.... The danger to undercut the government by taking the law into your own hands is very serious. ... I think, in terms of the basic ideology and principles of Gush Emunim, no reexamination is called for. With respect to actions, on the other hand, I think that there are attitudes we might have unconsciously or deliberately passed on, consciously or unconsciously, that have given messages, not just to our children but to ourselves, our neighbors, our society, that there are times when taking the law into your own hands is a good thing. And they confuse it because this country doesn't have a long tradition of democracy and what we used to call, "the legitimate limits of protest." They don't understand that. They think that if you are right, then to the end. So you can even sit in a bunker and blow yourself up if they say they're taking away Yamit, and you can throw soldiers off roofs, as some lunatic fringe said.... It's not that they're really lunatics. It's just that they don't understand what are the legitimate limits of protest. In a democratic system there's some point at which you say that I've come to the end. Now I've done all that I can and there's nothing more that I can do.... You can't hurt your own army; you can't hurt other people; you can't undercut your own government.... There are some things that you just can't do, and that's when you have to fold up with your tail between your legs and go home, back to the drawing board, and say, "How come I couldn't influence?" (Waxman 1979)

It is not only the majority of Americans among the settlers who could not have been in the past and certainly cannot now be characterized as political Messianists; neither can the general population of today's Jewish residents in the territories and, indeed, even some of those who have played leadership roles in Gush Emunim, the ideological movement of settlement. They may be more hard-line than the average Israeli was, but the overwhelming majority of them are not political Messianists. Moreover, it is not at all clear that today they are all that much more hard-line than the average Israeli Jew. According to a detailed report of a study by Elihu Katz, who heads Israel's Guttman Institute of Applied Social Research, there was a hardening of Israeli attitudes on the subject of Arab-Jewish relations, and especially on the issue of a Palestinian state, even before Iraq's invasion of Kuwait, in August 1990, and the support for Iraq expressed by PLO leaders and many Palestinian Arabs in the territories. Katz found, in July 1990, "that Israeli Jews divided roughly into 30 percent 'doves' and 70 percent 'hawks.' Moreover, the 70 percent "hawks" were "really made up of 30 percent "security hawks" and 40 percent "ideological hawks" (Goell 1990).

Nor are all of the leaders of Gush Emunim political extremists. Although some clearly are, there are others who have manifested political beliefs and behavior more moderate than those of the average Israeli. Thus, for example, even with the hardening of positions among many Israelis as a result of the intifada, a prominent figure in Gush Emunim, Rabbi Menachem Fruman, who serves as the rabbi of Tekoah, a settlement in Judea, created a stir in Israel in September 1989, when he met and held conversations with Feisel Husseini, a leading proponent of the PLO in the territories. Despite the efforts of some of the most extreme activists in Gush Emunim to have Fruman condemned and excluded from the movement, he subsequently had a televised discussion, with other settlers, of his meetings with Husseini. During the discussion and in several interviews with newspaper reporters at the time of his conversations with Husseini, Fruman insisted that his political positions in no way precluded the possibility of establishing a polite, cordial relationship between Husseini and himself. While neither was persuaded by the other to alter his initial position, their ability to engage in a personal dialogue is indicative of characteristics incommensurate with the stereotype of the radical extremist. Fruman's dialogue, subsequent televised discussion with other settlers, and his continuing as spiritual leader of Tekoah all suggest that not only he but also many other settlers have much broader and more complex perspectives than those commonly associated with either political Messianists or religious fundamentalists.[3]

During 1988 and early 1989, dire predictions were made by many of those opposed to Jewish settlement in the territories that the settlers, being politically extremist and unstable in any case, would set up vigilante squads in response to the intifada. These predictions, however, have not materialized. On the contrary, despite living under the constant threat from the stones and rocks that are regularly thrown at Israeli vehicles in the territories—the minimum damage from such rocks and stones is broken windows and auto body damage—there have been very few reported cases of vigilantism. Moetzet YESHA, the Council of Settlements, publicized very explicit clarifications with respect to legally permitted and prohibited action to be taken when one is the victim of stoning (Moetzet YESHA 1989), and the evidence suggests that such instructions have been followed. The overwhelming majority of Israelis living in the territories have adapted to their predicament but not by violence or by fleeing. They have developed a variety of ways of better protecting themselves and their vehicles, such as by installing special reinforced glass or plexiglass, and they have learned to live with those conditions.

More recent and perhaps even more conclusive evidence of the heterogeneity of opinions among Israelis in the territories—not only those of American background—can be found in the distribution of votes in the November 1988 Israeli national elections. Analysis of the available returns indicates that Likud received the largest number of votes of those who voted in the territories, followed by the National Religious Party and Tehiya. The new party, Moledet, which advocates the transfer of Arabs from the territories, also received a significant number of votes. However, so too did the non-Zionist religious parties, Agudat Israel and SHAS, as did even Ma'arach (Labor) and MEIMAD, the religious Zionist peace party which did not receive a sufficient number of votes to win even one seat (*Nekudah* 1988). Not only did Moledet receive a minority of votes in the territories, there is reason to assume that the majority of those in the territories are opposed to the very idea of transfer (Berkovitz 1989).

Moreover, the firm belief in the validity of the Jewish claim to Judea and Samaria and the Jewish right to settle there is shared by many Israelis who do not live in the territories. That is clearly the position of both the Likud and Tehiya parties, although it may be presumed that some of those who voted for either of those parties favor retaining Israeli control of the territories for strategic, but not necessarily ideological, reasons. On the other hand, a not insignificant number of Labor party members staunchly maintain that Jews definitely have historical rights to Judea and Samaria. Indeed, in the 1984 Knesset elections, Labor as well as Likud "said *no* to the PLO, *no* to removing settlements from Judea and Samaria, and *no* to a Palestinian state" (Torgovnik 1990, 39). By mid-1990, evidence indicated that the attitudes of Israeli Jews, in general, were hardening against the notion of Israel's ceding the territories (Goell 1990).

Given both the magnitude and the depth of the Israeli Jewish ties to the territories, it would be highly unrealistic to envision an Israeli withdrawal from there similar to the Israeli withdrawal from Sinai. Wrenching as the latter was for many Israelis, the Israeli presence in the Sinai was much smaller and had no historical foundation. As has been discussed above, the situation with respect to Judea and Samaria is very different. Many more Israeli Jews live there, the Jewish presence in the area has a 3,000 or more year history, and the area is of very deep and ancient religious significance. With conditions such as these at play, it would seem that a much more realistic approach toward a peaceful resolution would be in the direction of some form of ultimately shared rule for the territories. Various proposals along these lines have been made in the past (e.g., Elazar 1982). The current explosive situation should lend urgency toward movement in that direction.

NOTES

1. It is not only non-Israeli observers who portray the settlers in these terms. Some of the most prominent Israeli intellectuals, who are at the forefront of the Israeli peace movement, frequently use rhetoric which portrays the settlers in demonic verbal caricatures. On the settlers and the settlement movement, Gush Emunim, see Aran 1986; Lustick 1988; Newman 1985; O'Dea 1976; Raanan 1980; D. Rubinstein 1982; A. Rubinstein 1984; Rudik 1989; Sprinzak 1986; Tal 1984.

2. Except for a small minority who would be willing to challenge, defy, and possibly even engage in armed conflict with Israel's government and army, and who might, therefore, qualify as political Messianists, the overwhelming majority of Jewish residents of Judea and Samaria are loyal, law-abiding citizens. Though they might attempt to pressure the government into particular policy decisions and actions, they utilize legitimate channels for this purpose.

3. Nor is Fruman alone among the rabbis in settlements who play leadership roles in Gush Emunim and whose positions are much less extremist than one would imagine from the stereotypes. Another prominent example is Rabbi Yoel Ben-Nun, the rabbi of Ofra, who has frequently issued strong public criticisms and even condemnations of extremists in Gush Emunim, such as Rabbi Moshe Levinger of Hebron. See, for example, Ben-Nun's article, "If We Persist on the Road of All or Nothing We Will Get, as in Sinai, Nothing."

REFERENCES

Aran, Gideon. "From Religious Zionism to Zionist Religion: The Roots of Gush Emunim." In *Studies in Contemporary Jewry*, edited by Peter Y. Medding, 116–43. Vol. 2. Bloomington: Indiana University Press, 1986.

Arian, Asher. *Politics in Israel: The Second Generation.* 2d ed. Chatham, N.J.: Chatham House, 1989.

Avineri, Shlomo. *Moses Hess: Prophet of Communism and Zionism.* New York: New York University Press, 1985.

Azrieli, Yehuda. *The Knitted-Skullcap Generation.* Jerusalem: Avivim, 1990. In Hebrew.

Bedein, David. "Israeli Policy Goes Beyond Die-Hard Ideologues." "Letters," *The New York Times*, November 5, 1989.

Bein, Alex. *Theodore Herzl.* New York: Atheneum, 1970.

Ben-Gurion, David. *Memoirs.* New York and Cleveland, Ohio: World, 1970.

Ben-Nun, Yoel. "If We Persist on the Road of All or Nothing We Will Get, as in Sinai, Nothing." *Nekudah* 132 (July 31, 1989): 22–23, 38–39. In Hebrew.

Berkovitz, Dov. "We Shall Not Stoop to the Depths to Which Amos Oz and His Friends Reached." *Nekudah* 131 (June 30, 1989): 19. In Hebrew.

Elazar, Daniel J. *Judea, Samaria and Gaza: Views on the Present and Future.* Washington, D.C.: American Enterprise Institute, 1982.

Goell, Yoseph. "Polls Show a Hardening of Attitudes Towards Arabs and PLO State," *The Jerusalem Post*, International Edition, August 25, 1990, 10.

Hess, Moses. *Rome and Jerusalem, and Other Jewish Writings.* 1862. Reprint. Jerusalem: Zionist Library, 1983. In Hebrew.

Katz, Jacob. *Jewish Emancipation and Self-Emancipation.* Philadelphia: Jewish Publication Society, 1986.

Liebman, Charles S., and Eliezer Don-Yehiya. *Civil Religion in Israel: Traditional Judaism and Political Culture in the Jewish State.* Berkeley, University of California Press, 1983.

Lustick, Ian S. *For the Land and the Lord: Jewish Fundamentalism in Israel.* New York: Council on Foreign Relations, 1988.

Luz, Ehud. *Parallels Meet: Religion and Nationalism in the Early Zionist Movement, 1882–1904.* Philadelphia: Jewish Publication Society, 1988.

Mahler, Gregory S. *Israel: Government and Politics in a Maturing State.* New York: Harcourt Brace Jovanovich, 1989.

Moetzet YESHA. "To the Resident Who Drives and Walks Along the Roads." *Nekudah* 130 (June 2, 1989): 17. In Hebrew.

Nehorai, Michael Zvi. "Rabbi Reines and Rabbi Kook: Two Approaches to Zionism." In *Yovel Orot: The Thought of Rabbi Abraham Isaac HaCohen Kook,* edited by Binyamin Ish Shalom and Shalom Rosenberg, 209–18. Jerusalem: World Zionist Organization, Torah Education Dept. In Hebrew.

Nekudah. "Final Count of the Results of the Elections in Judea, Samaria and the Gaza Strip." 125 (December 28, 1988), 40–41. In Hebrew.

Newman, David, ed. *The Impact of Gush Emunim: Politics and Settlement in the West Bank.* London: Croom Helm and New York: St. Martin's Press, 1985.

O'Brien, Connor Cruise. *The Siege: The Saga of Israel and Zionism.* New York: Simon and Schuster, 1986.

O'Dea, Janet. "Gush Emunim: Roots and Ambiguities: The Perspective of the Sociology of Religion." *Forum* 2, 25 (1976): 39–50.

Patai, Raphael, ed. *The Complete Diaries of Theodor Herzl.* New York: Herzl Press and Thomas Yoseloff, 1960.

Pearlman, Moshe. *Ben Gurion Looks Back.* New York: Schocken, 1970.

Raanan, Zvi. *Gush Emunim.* Tel Aviv: Sifriyat Poalim, 1980. In Hebrew.

Raphael, Yitzchak, ed. *The Writings of Rabbi Yehuda Alkalai.* Jerusalem: Mossad Harav Kook, 1974. In Hebrew.

Reich, Walter. *A Stranger in My House: Jews and Arabs in the West Bank.* New York: Holt, Rinehart and Winston, 1984.

Rubinstein, Amnon. *The Zionist Dream Revisited.* New York: Schocken, 1984.

Rubinstein, Danny. *On the Lord's Side: Gush Emunim.* Tel Aviv: Hakibbutz Hameuchad, 1982. In Hebrew.

Rudik, Yohai Baruch. *Eretz Geulah: Ideological Roots of Religious Zionism, Gush Emunim, the Jewish Underground, and the System of Their Relations with the Secular World in the State of Israel.* Jerusalem: Institute for the Study of the Teachings of Rabbi A. I. Kook, 1989. In Hebrew.

Sprinzak, Ehud. *Gush Emunim: The Politics of Zionist Fundamentalism in Israel.* New York: American Jewish Committee, Institute of Human Relations, 1986.

Tal, Uriel. "Totalitarian Democratic Hermeneutics and Policies in Modern Jewish Religious Nationalism." In *Totalitarian Democracy and After: International*

Colloquium in Memory of Jacob L. Talmon. Jerusalem: Israel Academy of Sciences and Humanities, Magnes Press, 1984, 137–57.

Torgovnik, Ephraim. "The Incumbent's Electoral Politics under Adverse Conditions." In *Israel's Odd Couple: The 1984 Knesset Elections and the National Unity Government,* edited by Daniel J. Elazar and Shmuel Sandler. Detroit, Mich.: Wayne State University Press, 1990, 27–41.

Waxman, Chaim I. "American Israelis in Judea and Samaria." *Middle East Review* 17, no. 2 (Winter 1984/85): 48–54.

———. *American Aliya: Portrait of an Innovative Migration Movement.* Detroit, Mich.: Wayne State University Press, 1989.

7

The Embeddedness of the Arab-Jewish Conflict in the State of Israel: Demographic and Sociological Perspectives

Calvin Goldscheider

One framework for viewing the demography of Israel and the occupied territories relates to what may be called the *embeddedness* of the Jewish-Arab conflict. The argument is that the internal ethnic-religious conflict in the State of Israel is most problematic precisely because it is normalized; it is embedded in the demographic and social structure. The conflict is an integral part of the ways in which the institutions of the State of Israel have been, and are, organized and how the younger generations of Jews and Arabs are socialized and taught about each other. The core of the conflict is profound because it is linked to patterns of everyday life, not to the rare event; it is part of the ways in which Jews and Arabs in Israel compete for economic and political resources, and how they live and think. Because the conflict does not simply reflect the ideologies of political elites but is embedded in the society and its institutions, it is not transitional. To understand this embeddedness we need to examine the demographic evolution of Israeli society in all its complexities. We focus here on the demography of Jewish and Arab populations within Israeli society and on the ethnic-religious divisions with each community; we also examine the historical evolution of these populations and their likely trajectories in the near future.

Demographic processes have shaped and continue to shape the Jewish-Arab conflict in ways that are long standing but have become more acute in the recent period. These processes influence social, economic, and political policies and are linked to the most fundamental issues of Zionism and Arab nationalism; they are related to issues of territory and autonomy and in turn to national integration and economic development. Demographic processes were at the heart of the Jewish settlement of Palestine and are at issue in the Jewish resettlement of Jerusalem and the West Bank (Judea and Samaria). They have been central to the Jewish-Arab conflict for over a century and continue to influence the Palestinian issue today; they were central to the political issues of the 1988 elections in Israel in more profound ways than in the past and are likely to be critical in the political arena—Israeli, Palestinian, and international—in the future.

Moreover, demographic issues have become so embedded in the ideology and politics of Jewish-Arab communities and so linked to social structure and institutions that only revolutionary population changes can alter the basic patterns. At least in the short run, such demographic revolutions are rare and difficult to predict (or to manipulate through policies and programs). It is likely therefore that the demographic underpinnings of the Jewish-Arab conflict will remain salient at least for the next generation. If the conflicts associated with Arab-Jewish relationships are transitory and idiosyncratic, time and normalization will reduce, if not eliminate, the tensions. If the issues are only political and personal, then political change and the silencing or elimination of individuals will go far toward the resolution of the conflict. On the other hand, when the tensions and conflict are embedded in the social, demographic, cultural, political, and economic spheres of society, social institutions reinforce intergroup conflict.

The overlap of socioeconomic, residential, and ethnic differences between Jewish and Arab communities within Israel have also become translated into ways of thinking. The links between ethnicity, power, and social class are transmitted generationally. Hence, policies directed to changing the demographic and social structure are likely to reduce the intensity and depth of the conflict. In contrast, the argument that there will be a firm basis for a peaceful resolution of the conflict when Arabs and Jews "desire" peace or when representative leadership is located implies that, if there is no peace, someone does not want it, that desires are the major obstacles to a peaceful resolution, and that the absence of leadership remains the major impediment to peace. The conflicts between Arab and Jew within Israel, however, are not simply a question of desires or even a question of interests. Even if a political settlement between Arabs and Jews is reached, the embeddedness of the conflict will continue as a major obstacle to sustained peace and peaceful relationships between ethnic and religious groups.

In order to clarify the demographic embeddedness of the Arab-Jewish conflict, we shall review the changing demographic contours of majority-minority relationships. This includes an investigation into the changing size, growth, and ethnic composition of the Jewish and Arab populations,

the demographic formation of these communities—particularly the evolution of immigration patterns—the differential fertility of Jewish and
Arab populations, and the changing relative population proportions of
each, now and in the future. At the same time we shall explore issues
of socioeconomic inequalities within and between the Jewish and Arab
populations and relate these inequalities to demographic processes as
well as to the individual views of Arabs about Jews and Jews about Arabs.
The embeddedness of the conflict emerges clearly when both the com-
munity-demographic and individual-perceptual levels are compared and
integrated. The demography of the State of Israel and the territories
occupied by Israel should be viewed in broad social science contexts, for
demography is not simply the recital of statistics, and population problems are not limited to the sensational. Demographic analysis encom-
passes more than issues of the so-called demographic time bomb of Arab-
Jewish population growth patterns and their relative sizes in the State
of Israel.

THE CURRENT DEMOGRAPHIC PICTURE

We begin our examination of the embeddedness of the conflict by
outlining the current demographic profile of the Jewish and Arab populations in Israel.[1] At the end of the 1980s, the State of Israel had a
population size of 4.5 million, of which 82 percent were Jews, 14 percent
were Moslems, 2.2 percent were Christian, and 1.7 percent were Druze
(Table 7.1). Over time, the Jewish population has become increasingly
"Oriental," from Asian and African origins: In 1948, about 15 percent
of the Jewish population of Israel was Oriental; by the end of the 1980s,
the proportion had increased to about 54 percent. To be sure, the changing ethnic composition involves the complexities associated with the specific countries of origin within both the Oriental and Western Jewish
population, the changes generated by the length of exposure to the
country, generation status, and marriage between ethnic groups. Nevertheless, the identification of two socioethnic groups within the Jewish
population in Israel reflects one major axis of continuing differentiation
and inequality. The Oriental-Western division remains of primary importance in terms of differential power and economic resources, residential concentration, educational attainment, women's roles, and social
status. The shift toward a larger proportion of Orientals within the
Jewish population is therefore of significance because it is one basis of
social inequality; ethnicity in Israel is not simply a distinction reflecting
cultural differences.

At the same time that the Jewish population of the State of Israel has
become increasing Asian-African, the Arab population has become increasingly Moslem. At the end of the 1980s, about 800,000 non-Jews

Table 7.1
Population of the State of Israel, by Religion, 1948–1987, and Population Projections to the Year 2000 of Israel with and without the Populations of Judea and Samaria and the Gaza Area (in thousands)

	1948	1955	1965	1975	1985	1987	2000	2002*
Total	882	1,789	2,598	3,493	4,266	4,407	5,370	7,447
Jews	717	1,591	2,299	2,959	3,517	3,613	4,212	4,212
Non-Jews	165	198	299	534	749	794	1,169	3,235
Moslem	114	136	212	411	578	615	924	X
Christian	X	43	57	80	99	103	122	X
Druze	X	19	30	42	72	76	113	X
Percent Jewish	81	89	88	85	82	82	78	57

Sources: Central Bureau of Statistics, *Statistical Abstract of Israel*, various issues; population projections were adapted from the data in the *Statistical Abstract of Israel*, Vol. 39, 1988, Tables 2.20 and 17.4

Data for the year 2000 are for the State of Israel and for the year 2002 for Judea and Samaria and the Gaza area. The column marked 2002 includes projections for the population of Israel as well as Judea and Samaria and the Gaza area.

were living in the State of Israel, of whom 78 percent were Moslem (almost entirely of the Sunni branch of Islam), 13 percent were Christian, and 9.5 percent were Druze. In contrast, 69 percent of the non-Jewish population in 1948 were Moslem. By the end of the 1980s, there were an estimated 1.4 million Arabs (almost all Moslem) and about 60,000 to 70,000 Jews living in the territories administered by Israel (the West Bank, including Judea and Samaria and the Gaza Strip). Together, the population of the State of Israel and the territories administered by Israel had a 63-percent Jewish majority out of a population size of 5.8 million in 1987.

This snapshot demographic profile needs some historical context in dealing with the relationships between Jews and Arabs within Israel. We turn to an overview of immigration patterns.

Immigration

Immigration has been a major strategy of nation building in the State of Israel. The processes, patterns, and policies of immigration to the State of Israel have been unique. The conditions preceding and following the Holocaust and World War II in Europe, the emerging nationalism among Jews, the conditions of Jews in Arab-Moslem countries, and the existence of an expanding Jewish community in prestate Palestine are particular circumstances that influenced the immigration of Jews. In addition, Jewish immigration has retained an ideological centrality in Israel and has been and continues to be of overwhelming importance in the formation and development of Israeli society.

Immigration to Israel was rooted for centuries in Jewish religious ideology and, from the middle of the nineteenth century, in secular Jewish nationalism, Zionism. The beginnings of modern international immigration to Palestine, and subsequently to Israel, may be traced to the end of the nineteenth century, when organized groups of Jewish immigrants entered Palestine to build a national Jewish homeland.[2]

There were ambiguous British political commitments to Jewish and Arab nationalism throughout the prestate period. The emergence and strengthening of the Zionist movement, with an emphasis on immigration, settlement, and development, occurred along with the growing momentum of Arab nationalism. During the entire mandate period, British policy was directed solely to Jewish immigration. There were no clear policy guidelines on Arab immigration to Palestine; there were flows of migrants from neighboring Arab countries, mostly labor migration, often seasonal and temporary, in response to economic opportunities in Palestine. Most of the demographic growth of the Arab population came through natural increase; immigration was the primary source of Jewish population growth.

Against the background of the immigration restrictions placed by the British, the growing pressures to find a refuge for the Jewish survivors of the Holocaust in Europe, and the increasing political influence of the Zionist organization, new policies and patterns of immigration characterized the first period after the establishment of the State of Israel. Two documents are important sources for understanding the formal context of Israel's immigration policy. The Declaration of Independence stated that "The State of Israel is open to Jewish immigration and the Ingathering of Exiles" (passed on May 14, 1948) and was combined with the first order enacted by the provisional government to abolish the British restrictions on immigration and to define retroactively "illegal" Jewish immigrants as legal residents of the country. Together, these represented the foundation of Israel's immigration policy during the first two years subsequent to statehood. The Law of Return, enacted on July 5, 1950, granted to every Jew in the world the right to immigrate and settle in Israel, with minor exceptions related to health and security. These formal regulations do not convey the main thrust of Israel's policy, which was to actively encourage and subsidize the major phases associated with the immigration process.[3]

The patterns of immigration and the countries of origin of the immigrants to Israel, which have fluctuated since statehood in 1948, can be divided into several main periods (Table 7.2 and 7.3). The first period, from 1948 to 1951, can be referred to as the period of mass immigration. This was the most critical period in terms of the initial sociodemographic, economic, and political development of Israel, and it continues to have consequences for every aspect of social life. The period was characterized by a very high volume and rate of Jewish immigration from diverse countries. In the three years after the establishment of the State of Israel, immigration doubled the size of the Jewish population. Initially, the immigrants were of European origin—Jewish refugees coming to a predominantly European-origin society; in 1948, 85 percent of the 100,000 immigrants were of European origin. But this country-of-origin pattern changed as Jewish immigrants from Arab countries joined this stream: In 1949 and 1950, about half of the immigrants were from Europe; by 1951, over 70 percent of the immigrants were from Asian and North African countries, mainly Iraq, Iran, and Libya. The primary determinants of this mass migration were political and economic, with some mix of religious Messianism among the Jews from the traditional communities of Asia and North Africa.[4]

The second major stream of immigration to Israel began in the mid-1950s, when over half the immigrants were from North African countries, particularly from Morocco, Tunisia, and Egypt. This period witnessed the imposition of selective quotas and immigrant regulation in an attempt to control the negative economic impact of rapid, large-scale

Table 7.2
Number of Immigrants and Rate of Immigration, by Year of Immigration, 1919–1985, Palestine and Israel

	Palestine			Israel	
	Immigrants			Immigrants	
Year	Number (000s)	Rate	Year	Number (000s)	Rate
1919	1.8	32	1948	101.8	229
1920	8.2	135	1949	239.6	266
1921	8.3	115	1950	170.2	154
1922	8.7	106	1951	175.1	132
1923	8.2	91	1952	24.4	17
1924	13.9	146	1953	11.3	8
1925	34.4	283	1954	18.4	12
1926	13.9	93	1955	37.5	24
1927	3.0	20	1956	56.2	35
1928	2.2	14	1957	71.2	41
1929	5.2	34	1958	27.1	15
1930	4.9	30	1959	23.9	13
1931	4.1	24	1960	24.5	13
1932	12.6	69	1961	47.6	25
1933	37.3	185	1962	61.3	30
1934	45.3	177	1963	64.4	30
1935	66.5	201	1964	54.7	25
1936	29.6	80	1965	30.7	14
1937	10.6	27	1966	15.7	7
1938	14.7	32	1967	14.3	6
1939	31.2	72	1968	20.5	8
1940	10.6	23	1969	37.8	15
1941	4.6	10	1970	36.8	14
1942	4.2	9	1971	41.9	16
1943	10.1	21	1972	55.9	21
1944	15.6	29	1973	54.9	20
1945	15.3	29	1974	32.0	11
1946	18.8	33	1975	20.0	7
1947	22.1	36	1976	19.8	7
1948	17.2	72	1977	21.4	7
			1978	26.4	8
			1979	37.2	12
			1980	20.4	6
			1981	12.6	4
			1982	13.7	4
			1983	16.9	5
			1984	20.0	6
			1985	10.6	3
			1986	9.5	3

Sources: Dov Friedlander and Calvin Goldscheider, *The Population of Israel* (New York: Columbia University Press, 1979), Table 2.6; *Statistical Abstract of Israel*, various years.

Note: The rate of immigration is per 1,000 mean Jewish population; until May 14, 1948, immigration is to Palestine; after May 15, 1948, immigration is to Israel.

Table 7.3
Immigrants by Continent of Origin and Period of Immigration, 1919–1985, Palestine and Israel

	All Countries (000s)	Percent	Asia	Africa	East Europe	Central European Balkan	Other West
1919-23	35.2	100.0	5	*	84	7	4
1924-31	81.6	100.0	12	*	78	6	4
1932-38	197.2	100.0	9	*	60	27	4
1939-45	81.8	100.0	18	*	34	44	4
1946-48	56.5	100.0	4	*	68	26	3
1948	101.8	100.0	5	9	54	29	3
1949	239.6	100.0	31	17	28	22	3
1950	170.2	100.0	34	15	45	4	2
1951	175.1	100.0	59	12	26	2	1
1952-54	54.1	100.0	25	51	12	5	8
1955-57	164.9	100.0	6	32	23	6	3
1958-60	75.5	100.0	18	18	56	2	6
1961-64	228.0	100.0	9	51	32	1	6
1965-67	60.8	100.0	18	20	47	2	13
1968-73	247.8	100.0	13	14	44	2	27
1974-79	156.8	100.0	8	5	63	1	23
1980-84	83.6	100.0	8	19	41	1	30
1985-88	46.2	100.0	12	13	42	1	33

Sources: Dov Friedlander and Calvin Goldscheider, *The Population of Israel* (New York: Columbia University Press, 1979), Table 2.6; *Statistical Abstract of Israel*, various years.

*Combined Asia and Africa, over 90 percent from Asian countries. East Europe includes USSR, Latvia, Lithuania, Poland, Romania; Central Europe includes Germany, Austria, Czechoslovakia, Hungary; Balkan includes Greece, Bulgaria, Yugoslavia; Other West includes other European countries, United States of America, South Africa, and Oceania.

immigration. The occupational skills and educational background of these immigrants differed significantly from those of earlier European-origin streams; migrants arrived with fewer occupational skills and lower levels of education and were not easily integrated into the labor market. Nevertheless, 165,000 immigrants arrived between 1955 and 1957.

The third immigration wave, which began after the 1967 war, mostly came from Eastern Europe (the Soviet Union and Romania) and from Western countries, mainly the United States. These were, and continue to be, the major Jewish population centers outside of Israel and therefore the potential sources of new Jewish immigration. Between 1972 and 1979, 267,582 immigrants arrived in Israel, 51 percent from the Soviet Union and 8 percent from the United States; of the 94,279 immigrants to Israel, from 1980 to 1985, 13 percent were from the Soviet Union, 9 percent from Romania, 14 percent from the United States, and 15 percent from Ethiopia. In 1986, 9,505 more immigrants arrived: 18 percent were from the United States and 14 percent were from Romania—the only two countries contributing at least 10 percent of the immigrants to the State of Israel—the rest of the immigrants arrived from over forty-five different countries.[5] Restrictions on the emigration of Jews from the Soviet Union and the option of alternative destinations (particularly to the United States) reduced the flow of Russian immigrants to Israel until 1989.

A new pattern of immigration from the Soviet Union began to occur in 1990, as significant numbers of Jews started to leave the Soviet Union to immigrate to Israel. Changes in immigration policy in the United States have reduced the number of Russian Jews who are able to immigrate to the United States. During the period from 1989 to 1990, an estimated 100,000 new Russian Jewish immigrants arrived in Israel. This volume is clearly a sharp increase from the previous period: Not since the 1950s has there been such an annual volume of immigration to the State of Israel.

The potential for increased numbers of immigrants from the Soviet Union is great; an estimated one million Jews, or more, still live there. What proportion of the Jewish population of the Soviet Union will immigrate to Israel and what proportion of those immigrating will remain in Israel are open questions. Much will depend on the Soviet policies of emigration, the American policy of restrictions on Soviet immigration to the United States, the economic capacity of Israel to integrate the new immigrants, and the social and political conditions in Israel.

At the end of 1990, there were clear signs that the Soviet immigrants in Israel were experiencing housing and education problems, along with short-run employment and related economic difficulties. There are still problems of housing for previous waves of immigrants and their children who continue to live in substandard conditions. As in the past, there is a high probability of negative reaction against the government subsidies that this immigration stream will receive, particularly among the Asian and African ethnic groups. It is too soon to know how tensions between the recent immigrants from the Soviet Union and the previous waves of immigrants from Asian and North African countries will be resolved. It is also unclear what influence the adjustment of the first 100,000 Soviet immigrants will have on future immigration to Israel from the Soviet Union and out-migration from Israel.

The long-term impact of immigration to Israel on the Jewishness of these immigrants is clearly positive and fulfills the Zionist mission of being a country for the ingathering of Jewish populations. It is likely that the longer run economic impact of the Soviet immigrants on Israeli society will be positive as well, given the high levels of education and occupational skills of many of the immigrants and their high socioeconomic aspirations for the next generation. The real unknowns about this new wave of immigration are how many Jews living in the Soviet Union will immigrate to the State of Israel. Given the choice of destination, many have in the past turned to the United States as a haven. For those emigrating from the Soviet Union in the 1980s, well over half, and in the late 1980s, close to 90 percent, rejected immigration to Israel to immigrate to the United States. But with the closing down of the American option, there are fewer places to go outside of the State of Israel. Some European countries may ease their immigration restrictions, but it is not clear how many of the Soviet out-migrants will opt to go somewhere other than Israel.

It has become clear that information flows in both directions to and from Israel and the Soviet Union. Therefore the degree of integration, the ability to find jobs and housing, the schools, and the Israeli-Arab conflict will have an impact on the potential amount of further immigration and on the possible return migration or forward migration of the Soviet Jews who have already arrived in Israel. Although these new immigration patterns will have an impact on Israeli society, some of the critical ethnic tensions within the Jewish population and between the Jewish and the Arab populations are unlikely to be altered by this immigration.

The volume, timing, and the ethnic origins of these immigrant streams to Israel had important implications for the demographic, social, economic, political, and cultural development of Israeli society. Each of these immigration streams was characterized by different patterns of selectivity; immigrants with different occupational skills, education, resources, and cultural backgrounds entered at different stages of the economic and social development of the country. The timing, the socioethnic composition, and the rate of immigration shaped the formation of the country as well as every thread of development—social, economic, political, and cultural. While the timing of immigration affected the initial adjustment of immigrants to the new society in terms of housing, economic opportunity, and settlement, contemporary differences between Asians and Africans and Europeans are not simply a function of the timing of arrival to Israel. Ethnic differences in economic, social, cultural, political, and demographic patterns extend to the second and third generations born in Israel. These differences relate primarily to the different socioeconomic background of these populations and their ethnic ties within Israel.

Occupational skills, educational background, family and ethnic ties of the European immigrants facilitated their relatively successful and earlier entry into Israeli society and their access to power, resources, and opportunity. Europeans could take advantage of their connections to the European-dominated society and economy. Asians and Africans came from societies that were less modern and were less able to compete with the Europeans in Israel. The timing of immigration and the cultural differences between groups reinforced these structural factors as well as community links which divided Israeli Jews. Immigration created two new ethnic communities among Jews in Israel—"European-Americans" and "Asian-Africans."

As in prestate Palestine, Arab immigration to Israel is restricted, and immigration to Israel is largely confined to the Jewish population. The major migration patterns occurred when the borders of the state were established in 1948 in only part of Palestine, and significant parts of the Arab Palestinian population became refugees in neighboring Arab countries. There was a substantial internal migration among Arab communities, and important distinctions among Israeli Arabs relate not only to religious differences but also to their internal "refugee" status.[6]

Immigration to Israel has resulted in the convergence of ethnic differences in some areas of social life as well as ethnic continuities in others. Emergent Jewish ethnic communities in Israel are significantly different from communities in places of origin. For example, occupational patterns have become more diversified for all immigrant groups; educational levels have increased; and mortality and fertility rates have declined sharply for those from Asian and African countries and have increased slightly among those from Western origins. Ethnicity among Jews in Israel does not reflect only the cultural legacy or the "primordial identity" of the past. Rather, ethnic communities are marked by differential socioeconomic advantage and access to resources, reinforced by discrimination and culture, often united nationally by externals, and differentially related to the Arab minorities in the State of Israel and in the territories administered by Israel.[7]

Perhaps the most important and most direct demographic consequence of these immigration patterns has been the sharp increase in the Jewish population of Israel. Had there been no immigration, the size of the Jewish population of Israel in the 1970s would have been less than one million instead of 2.7 million, and the proportion of Jews in the State of Israel would have been 65 percent instead of the actual 85 percent.[8] In contrast, the Arab minority within the State of Israel has grown by natural increase because immigration has remained in large part restricted to the Jewish population.

In addition to the effects on population size, immigration to Israel led to major and rapid declines in the mortality of the immigrants and has improved their levels of health care. There was an almost immediate decline in the mortality levels of Asian and African immigrants upon entry into Israeli society, where they were exposed to new and better health conditions. Life expectancy of the non–Western-origin Jewish population was 35 to 40 years in 1948; in the 1980s, life expectancy of Jews in Israel was 73 years, with no variation by ethnic origin. Over time, major reductions in the fertility levels of migrants from Asian and African countries occurred. The total fertility rate of this population dropped by 50 percent to 3.2.[9]

Most conspicuously, immigration has altered the ethnic origin composition of the Jewish population, moving it from an overwhelming Western-origin population to a balanced composition of Western and Oriental origins. Given the overlap of ethnic origin with social and economic resources, political orientations, and culture, the ethnic compositional shifts have had, and will continue to have, major implications for the social, economic, and demographic development of the society. Thus, in 1948, 85 percent of the Jewish population was of Western origins; by the 1980s, the Western-origin population had declined to 48 percent.

There have been major changes among all immigrant groups that have resulted in the emergence of new Israeli patterns, neither fully Western nor fully Oriental. Although ethnic cultural differences remain salient, and distance from the immigrant generation continues to be an important factor in understanding social change in Israel, the critical issues remain the structural features that differentiate ethnic groups in Israel. These include the overlap of ethnic origin with educational attainment, residential concentration, political behavior, and socioeconomic status. Higher levels of education and occupation continue to characterize European-origin populations of the third generation. Ethnic residential concentration continues by region (living in a development town versus a major urban center) that is linked, in turn, to job and educational opportunities. Ethnic concentration also characterizes residential patterns within neighborhoods of larger metropolitan centers. Continuing high rates of intraethnic marriages and ethnic self-identity may be observed, despite some increases in interethnic marriages over time.[10]

Intergenerational mobility has not closed the educational or occupational gap between immigrant groups. While every ethnic group has been characterized by social mobility, the gap has not diminished between ethnic groups. Thus, inequalities have persisted even with rapid development and economic growth (about 10 percent per year for the first thirty years following statehood) and the opening up of new opportunities within a relatively open stratification system. These inequalities, in turn, are linked to political changes in the government of Israel, particularly the strengthening of the right-wing political parties and the decline of labor and socialist control of the country.[11] The ethnic divisions within the Jewish population of Israel have implications for relationships with the Arab minorities within Israel and to the Arab populations in the territories administered by Israel on the West Bank and in the Gaza Strip.

While ethnic pluralism has emerged in Israeli society, there are also indications of increasing national unity and integration among the diverse immigrant streams. Educational and military institutions have been almost universal experiences for the Jewish population and have served as important mechanisms of national integration. The Hebrew language has become a major integrative force nationally, linking Jews of different national origins and with diverse linguistic backgrounds to each other and to the emergent national culture as well as past history. External hostilities and continuous wars with Arab countries have also resulted in the unification of the Jewish population of Israel.

Implications

Emerging from the review of immigration patterns are several critical and direct implications for the Jewish-Arab conflict within Israel. First, there has been a rather stable ratio between Jewish and Arab population size within the State of Israel. This is surprising since there has been an enormous increase in the Jewish population through mass immigration in the first three years of statehood and a continuing influx of Jewish migrants to Israel in the last three and a half decades. Between May 1948 and 1951, 687,000 Jews migrated to Israel, doubling the Jewish population; over 1.2 million Jews migrated to Israel in the three and a half decades after the end of this early mass immigration.

While the Jewish community increased in size through immigration, the Arab population increased through natural increase (the excess of births over deaths). In early 1948, when Palestine was within the British mandate, total population size was two million, one-third of which was Jewish. In mid–1948, when the State of Israel was established, it occupied only part of Palestine, and large numbers of Arabs emigrated (were forced out or fled, depending on one's point of view). Out of the 800,000 persons counted in the first census of Israel in 1948, 650,000 were Jews, 85 percent were European in birth or origin. The mass immigration of Jews in the three years following the establishment of the state increased the Oriental share of the total Jewish population from 15 percent to 33 percent. At the same time, the Arab population within the State of Israel increased in size through high birthrates and declining death rates; little Arab population growth came from net immigration. The high rate of Moslem fertility began a slow decline during the decade of the 1970s (Table 7.4). By the 1980s, Moslem fertility levels within the State of Israel had declined significantly. The total fertility rate of Israeli Moslems was 9.2 children in the 1960s, declining by 50 percent to 4.6 in 1987; the decline was from 4.7 to 2.6 children for Christian Arabs in Israel. These reductions in fertility reflect increases over time in levels of educational attainment, occupational achievements, and family-related changes, particularly the changing roles and statuses of women within the Arab community. The Arab populations of the administered territories continue to have very high fertility, and there are no clear signs yet of a decline in their fertility. In the late 1980s, the estimated crude birthrates were 41 per 1,000 for the Arab population in Judea and Samaria and 47 per 1,000 for those living in the Gaza area. Hence, the demographic ratio of Arab to Jewish population in the State of Israel has remained remarkably constant as Jewish immigration has balanced the high fertility of the Moslem-Arab population in Israel and major transitions in mortality and fertility among all population segments have occurred. Thus, data in Table 7.1 show that the percent Jewish was slightly over 80 percent in the State of Israel in 1948 and in the 1980s.

What about the future? Is there a basis for projecting a continuous balanced ratio of Jewish and Arab population in the State of Israel? What are the growth patterns associated with Israel's demographic mosaic? Several projections of Israel's population have been made and are instructive to examine not as predictors of what will be but as indicators of current patterns. All population projections are based on detailed assumptions about the future of those population processes that most directly affect the size and growth rate of the population. In preparing population projections for the Jewish and Arab communities of Israel, a series of maximum to minimum assumptions were made regarding the processes underlying population growth in order to have a broad range of possible combinations of fertility, mortality, and immigration. These were prepared separately for the populations living within the State of Israel and for the larger area under the administration of Israel.

Table 7.4
Total Fertility Rates, by Religion and Place of Birth, 1955–1987, State of Israel (number of births per woman)

	1955	1960	1965	1970	1975	1980	1985	1987
Total Population	4.03	3.95	3.99	3.97	3.68	3.14	3.12	3.05
				Jewish Population				
Born								
Europe	2.63	2.38	2.60	2.84	2.82	2.76	2.79	2.69
Africa–Asia	5.68	5.10	4.58	4.07	3.77	3.04	3.21	3.13
Israel	2.83	2.76	2.88	3.12	3.08	2.76	2.89	2.81
Total	3.64	3.49	3.47	3.41	3.21	2.76	2.85	2.78
				Arab Population				
Moslem	7.96	9.31	9.87	8.95	7.75	5.98	4.86	4.63
Christian	4.85	4.61	4.74	3.62	3.35	2.66	2.12	2.58
Druze	6.58	7.88	7.61	7.46	6.85	6.09	4.47	4.17

Source: Central Bureau of Statistics, *Statistical Abstract of Israel*, various issues.

Several demographic issues emerge from these projections that are related to our focus on Jewish-Arab relationships.[12]

1. What is expected to happen to the ethnic balancing among Israeli Jews? We have already noted the shift toward orientalization of the Jewish population of Israel, or the increase in the proportion of Jews from Asian and African origins. This pattern will continue in the future but at a very slow pace. While the rate of immigration to Israel from the Soviet Union beginning in early 1990 may involve several hundred thousand migrants over the next decades, there is likely to be long-run stability and balance in the size of the Western and Oriental Jewish populations in Israel. In large part this balance derives from the convergences in the reproduction patterns by ethnic origins, balanced by the relatively low rate of immigration to Israel from Europe and America, combined with the small number of Jews remaining in Asian and African countries. The most conservative estimate suggests that by the year 2015, the proportion of Israeli Jewish population who will be of Oriental origin will hover at around 60 percent. The range of likely possibilities is small and represents almost no basic change in current patterns.

2. What about the Jewish majority in Israel? Jews became the majority of the state's population after 1948, moving to 81 percent of the total population from 33 percent in the prestate period. By the 1980s, the proportion Jewish had edged upward to around 82 percent of the total population in the state. Most of this small change was due to the long-term impact of Jewish immigration. Since Israeli Moslem fertility had fallen considerably by the 1980s, the relative proportion of Jews and Arabs within Israel should remain between 76 percent and 79 percent through the year 2015, irrespective of any realistic assumption about fertility and immigration changes of either population. Thus, the majority-minority demographic issue within Israeli society is not likely to change significantly in the foreseeable future. With the increase in Soviet Jewish immigration, the proportion Jewish within the State of Israel will remain toward the upper end of this estimate.

3. What about the Jewish-Arab balance within Greater Israel? The demographic picture of Jewish-Arab ratios will be dramatically different if Israel annexes territory and the populations within the territories administered by Israel. Even unrealistic assumptions of increases in the rates of fertility and immigration of the Jewish population shrinks the proportion Jewish to less than 60 percent by the year 2015. In large part, the proportion Jewish in this Greater Israel depends on the continuing high levels of fertility of the Moslem population in the administered territories and the relative pace of immigration to Israel from the Soviet Union. It also depends on the policy of the Israeli government toward "encouraging" the Arab population to emigrate. The most likely combined assumptions will move the proportion Jewish to around 50 to

55 percent by the year 2015, when the total populations of Israel and the administered territories are considered jointly. A reduction of the Jewish demographic majority will occur even with some decline in Moslem fertility in the administered territories and with the net immigration of from 200,000 to 400,000 Jews from the Soviet Union.

Using carefully prepared estimates of the population of Israel and adding in the projected population of the territories of Judea and Samaria and the Gaza area, the Central Bureau of Statistics of Israel provides data for three estimates of the relative proportion of Jews and non-Jews. Including a range of Jewish immigration rates and emigration rates of Arabs from Judea and Samaria, these data show that, in a little over a decade (by the year 2002), the proportion Jewish will range between 55 percent and 58 percent.

The large increase in the immigration of Russian Jews to Israel will not significantly alter the population balance between Arabs and Jews in Greater Israel. While some politicians have argued that the new Russian immigration in the 1990s will "solve" the Jewish demographic problem of retaining the territories and the Arab populations within them, an analysis of the wider range of issues indicates that the demographic contribution of Soviet-Jewish immigration will not solve the demographic problem of the balance of Jewish and Arab populations in Greater Israel. Clearly, a large-scale influx of Jewish population will depend on how many come, how many stay, their future fertility, and what happens as a result to the migration balance among Arabs living in the West Bank and Gaza Strip. According to our best estimates, there are less than 1.5 million Jews in the Soviet Union. Assuming that from 200,000 to 300,000 Russian Jewish immigrants arrive in the last decade of the twentieth century, the proportion Jewish in Greater Israel will increase by only one or two percentage points (from 57% to 59%) by the year 2000. If half of the total Russian Jewish population immigrates to Israel in the next decade (650,000 to 750,000), the proportion Jewish in Greater Israel will hover at around 60 percent, only to decline to around 50 to 55 percent in the following decade. So the retention of territories and the Arab population as part of Israel will remain the basis of a demographic crisis for Israel's Jewish population under every reasonable and even unreasonable assumption about the influx of Soviet Jews.

Jews in the Soviet Union should immigrate to Israel for all the Zionist reasons that are imaginable. But it is fantasy to assume that this immigration will address the demographic problems of Jewish-Arab population ratios in Greater Israel. Surely the ideology that treats immigration to Israel as an imperative should not be converted to a policy of territorial-population expansion based on the political ideology of a Greater Israel. Immigration will not solve the demographic embeddedness of the Arab-Jewish conflict.

Whatever the range of political and administrative alternatives there are in dealing with the Arab populations of the West Bank and Gaza Strip, demographic issues are not far in the background. The extremes on all sides of the political issues, as well as the moderates, have used demographic issues to justify policy pronouncements. Clearly the political stalemate reflects compositional changes among Jewish Israelis (the Oriental-European divisions) as well as the demographic balances of Jewish and Arab populations within the state and in the West Bank and Gaza Strip.

The importance of these patterns within Israel goes beyond issues of politics and culture. Four decades ago, the Arab-Jewish conflict in Israel was between an overwhelmingly European, urban, educated, Jewish population and a divided, leaderless, isolated, agricultural Moslem community. In the 1980s, the Israeli-Jewish population is more likely to be from Moslem countries, recently educated and modernized, and economically mobile intergenerationally. The social position of the growing majority of Oriental Jews is below that of the Israeli-born of European origins and above that of Israeli Arabs. It is this social structural position of Oriental Jews, even for the second and third generations removed from foreign-born status, that becomes important in the determination of Jewish-Arab relations. Oriental "culture" or "mentality" is not the primary factor influencing the ways in which Oriental Jews relate to Israeli Arabs; nor are the "negative" experiences of foreign-born Oriental Jews with Arabs in countries of origin the key element in the current relationships between their children and grandchildren and the Arab minority in Israel. Rather it is the position Oriental Jews occupy in the social hierarchy within Israeli society that shapes in large part their relationship to the strata below them (i.e., the Israeli Arabs) and the strata above them (Israeli-born Jews of European origin).

Data on occupational and educational levels by generation among Israeli Jews illustrate the continuing hierarchy: While from 12 to 14 percent of first- and second-generation Asian- and African-origin Jews are in white-collar jobs, from 34 to 44 percent of first- and second-generation European-American origin Jews are in white-collar jobs. The proportion of first- and second-generation Asian- and African-origin Jews with thirteen or more years of education is between 10 and 12 percent compared to from 34 to 39 percent of the first- and second-generation European-American origin Jews. The lower levels and rates of intergenerational mobility among Israeli Moslems have been well documented as has their occupational segregation.[13]

The emerging Israeli-Jewish population is therefore interacting (at least formally) with an increasingly well-educated Moslem population working in urban-related industries, linked to Arab-Moslem populations in neighboring countries and throughout the world. The Israeli-Moslem population has limited political control over its own community, is relatively isolated residentially, and is restricted by the economic opportunities available. Israeli Arabs are increasingly in competition over social, political, and economic resources with the Oriental segment of the Jewish population. In such competition, the Israeli Arabs are rarely in a position to compete successfully. The structural positions of these groups within Israel, along with the changing ethnic demography, shape as well the attitudinal and normative patterns of how Jews view their relationship to Israeli Arabs and how Israeli Arabs view their future in Israeli society.

Population patterns have profound implications for Israeli society and for the people within it. Jewish-Arab relations have been based on, and continue to be based on, principles of mutual distrust. The Israeli government operates on the principle that Arabs are suspect and potentially disloyal. Formal and informal education raises generation after generation of Arabs and Jews not to trust each other. These patterns may be justifiable for a variety of reasons, particularly given the long history of war and terrorism in the area; however, even when understandable, the patterns have profound implications. Thus, for example, the continuous state of war and hostilities between Israel and her Arab neighbors has led to the geographic segregation of Arabs within Israel as well as to other forms of educational and occupational discrimination. Indeed, the treatment of the Israeli-Arab population as potentially disloyal to the State of Israel has been justified on this basis, as has the treatment of Arabs within the territories administered by Israel. The termination of the Arab-Israeli conflict would not automatically alter the embeddedness of such discrimination, since these patterns over time, and particularly over generations, have become institutionalized.

How does this distrust get translated into Jewish and Arab attitudes? Surveys in Israel show how deeply ingrained are these attitudes of distrust.[14] About two-thirds of the Jews believe that they cannot trust Israeli Arabs, and an equivalent proportion of Israeli Arabs believe that they cannot trust Israeli Jews. Each group perceives the State of Israel and the nature of the Arab-Jewish conflict in very different terms. Most Israeli Jews, for example, see the State of Israel as a Jewish homeland and want to maintain a Jewish demographic majority, with Hebrew as the sole national language, and they are supportive of continuous Jewish immigration to Israel. Most Israeli Arabs reject these views. Most Israeli Arabs reject the notion of Israel as a Jewish-Zionist state; most do not see an Arab state as an alternative model but envision a state based on a dual language and a dual culture, a state that recognizes equality and the legitimacy of sociocultural identities for Jews and Arabs.

In most cases, Jews in Israel believe that the state should prefer Jews to Arabs in all arenas of public policy. Only a small proportion of Jews subscribe to the notion of equal opportunity for all groups in areas of higher education, jobs, and financial support from the government. Fully one-third of Israeli-Jewish adults are not prepared to work with Israeli Arabs, and two-thirds are not prepared to have an Arab supervisor at their workplace. And while Israeli Jews express support for the rights of minority groups everywhere in the world in the areas of jobs, education, land ownership, and fair trials (particularly for Jews who are in the minority), they justify discriminating against the Arab minority in Israel in these same areas.

The implications of these and related attitudes are clear for Jewish-Arab relationships within Israel, for the tensions between Western and Eastern Jews within Israel, and for the potential conflict between Israeli Jews and Jews outside of Israel. As the Jewish population in Israeli society becomes more Oriental ethnically, the tensions between Jews and Moslems are likely to increase.

The demographic and attitudinal patterns imply serious challenges to policy. Population projections are not forecasts. They describe the current pattern, not what necessarily will be nor what is inevitable. But they are critical for considering new policy directions since the continuation of current policies will result in the population patterns that have been projected. These are few solutions to the Arab-Jewish conflict in Israel if the territories are incorporated within a Greater Israel and the Arab populations within them are retained. Given the current attitudinal profile of Jews and Arabs in Israel, the retention of the status quo will also accelerate the Arab-Jewish conflict within Israel. Neither Jews nor Arabs are going to leave their homes voluntarily, and few are building toward autonomy or minority independence.

Israel needs to deal constructively with its own ethnic pluralism and with its institutional relationship to the Arab minority within its borders in order to create a new basis for a pluralistic social order. If not, the growing orientalization of the Jewish population and the growing proportion of Arabs within Israel and the territories it manages will continue to polarize the society and exacerbate the conflict.

To the political demographic basis of the Jewish-Arab conflict must be added the religious basis on both sides. These religious divisions result in further embeddedness that is rationalized on the basis of holy texts and divine will, not simply on political and ideological grounds. The overlay of religious and political embeddedness onto the demographic issues seriously threaten future attempts at developing tolerance and sociocultural pluralism. And while the issues are national in scope, they are more extreme within the particular regions of the country where the demographic and ethnic composition is distorted in the direction of Jews or Arabs, Orientals or Westerners.

While the conflict is local, there are clearly international dimensions of the issue, from the support of the United States to the Jewish State of Israel, to the support of Arab states to the Arab population within Israel and to the Palestinian population within the West Bank and Gaza Strip. There is, of course, economic dependency of Israel on Western states, particularly the United States and on world Jewry; there is Arab dependency on international organizations, Palestinian organizations, and Arab states. So the local conflict has significant international dimensions and regional linkages.

The Arab-Jewish conflict has become embedded in Israeli society. While the roots of the conflict are to be located in history, the embeddedness of the conflict has more clearly emerged in the recent period. There are new factors in the Arab-Jewish conflict related to the types of embeddedness that make the situation in the last decade of the twentieth century different and more problematic than at earlier points in Israel's history. Ethnic compositional changes within the Jewish population, the growing proportion Moslem, the linkages among Moslems in and outside of Israel, and the generational transmission of mutual distrust are significant parts of the new embeddedness. The structural (social, economic, demographic, religious, and political) transformation of all the sectors of the Jewish and Arab populations has accelerated the conflict and heightened the tensions. The Jewish-Arab conflict within Israel will not likely be reduced by the continuation of current policies; more likely than not the conflict will become more extreme.

NOTES

An earlier and briefer version of this chapter appeared in *Middle East Review* 21, no. 3 (Spring 1989): 15–24. It has benefitted from suggestions by Alan Zuckerman and Frances Goldscheider at Brown University.

1. Some of the statistical presentation is documented in Dov Friedlander and Calvin Goldscheider, *Israel's Population: The Challenge of Pluralism*, Population Bulletin, Population Reference Bureau, Volume 39:2, 1984. More recent data are drawn from official data published by the Israel Central Bureau of Statistics. Unless otherwise indicated, I have relied on the *Statistical Abstract of Israel, 1989* as the latest reference for statistical data.

2. Calvin Goldscheider and Alan Zuckerman, *The Transformation of the Jews* (Chicago: University of Chicago Press, 1984).

3. Dov Friedlander and Calvin Goldscheider, *The Population of Israel* (New York: Columbia University Press, 1979).

4. Ibid.

5. Israel Central Bureau of Statistics, *Statistical Abstract of Israel*, Table V/4.

6. M. Al-Haj, *Social Change and Family Processes: Arab Communities in Shefar-A'm* (Boulder, Colo.: Westview Press, 1987).

7. Sammy Smooha, *Israel: Pluralism and Conflict* (Berkeley: University of Cal-

ifornia Press, 1978); Sammy Smooha, *Arabs and Jews in Israel* (Boulder, Colo.: Westview Press, 1989); Goldscheider and Zuckerman, *The Transformation of the Jews.*

8. Friedlander and Goldscheider, *The Population of Israel*, Table 7.6.

9. Friedlander and Goldscheider, *Israel's Population*, Table 4.

10. Calvin Goldscheider, "The Demography of Asian-African Jews in Israel," in J. B. Maier and Chaim I. Waxman, eds., *Ethnicity, Identity, and History* (New Brunswick, N.J.: Transaction Books, 1983), 273–89.

11. Asher Arian, *Politics in Israel: The Second Generation*, 1st ed. (Chatham, N.J.: Chatham House, 1985).

12. The themes for these projections and their details were developed in Friedlander and Goldscheider, *Israel's Population*. They parallel the conclusions of a similar set of projections published by the Central Bureau of Statistics in Israel. Both sets of projections are based on different sets of assumptions, but the conclusions are similar.

13. On the ethnic dimension in the Jewish stratification of Israeli society, see the excellent set of studies by Y. Nahon published by the Jerusalem Institute of Israel Studies (in Hebrew).

14. Sammy Smooha, "The Tolerance of the Jewish Majority in Israel Toward the Arab Minority: Comparative Perspectives," in A. Hareven, ed., *Is It Really Difficult to Be an Israeli?* (Jerusalem: Van Leer Jerusalem Foundation, 1983), 91–107. In Hebrew. See also Smooha's *Arabs and Jews in Israel.*

8

Demographic and Economic Forces Underlining Likud's Perspective of the West Bank

Fred Gottheil

When Zionists very reluctantly accepted the United Nations' Partition Plan for Palestine in 1947, giving them sovereignty over a small piece of western Palestine, they viewed their acceptance as a necessary cost of political compromise. That is to say, for the sake of national independence and regional peace, they were prepared to accept a geography far less than what they regarded as rightly theirs.

Their view of that fateful compromise is important. Our own understanding of the consequences of partition—and certainly the Arab Palestinian understanding—is that partition gave Jews a slice of Arab land. But most Zionists see that piece of history differently. To them, partition forced Jews to give up a part of *their* historic land.

FORTY YEARS LATER: LIKUD PHILOSOPHY

Likud settlement philosophy in the West Bank—Judea and Samaria, to most Israelis—is, in principle, consistent with traditional Zionist ideology. Willing to negotiate agreements that may end up limiting their sovereignty, they nonetheless insist on starting from the premise that, as a people, they have inalienable rights to settle anywhere in western Palestine.

For this reason, Israel insists that the West Bank is not enemy territory. As the nonaggressor in a war that undermined the armistice agreements of 1949, Israel argues that, once more, negotiation is required to establish in western Palestine secure and recognized boundaries. That is why

Israel refers to the West Bank as the Administered Territories, even though Westerners invariably call it the Occupied West Bank. Westerners chose not to call the West Bank occupied when it was taken by Jordan in 1948.

That is why Israel maintains that article 43 of the Hague regulations and article 64 of the Fourth Geneva Convention, which relate to conditions of "belligerent occupation," are not binding on Israel even though it chooses to abide by them. After all, the legal status of the area is still undecided. Jordan's sovereignty over the West Bank and Egypt's over Gaza was never recognized by Israel or by any other nation save the United Kingdom and Pakistan.

That is also why Likud insists on referring to the area as Judea and Samaria. These are, in fact, their only proper names, and they have been so since time immemorial. If Israel, Galilee, and Jerusalem are accepted names for identifiable geography, why not Judea and Samaria? Likud argues that our refusal to use these names distorts history and prejudices its case.

In this respect, Likud's views on the area differ in tone, if not in philosophy, from the views held by Labor. Labor shuns any reference to religious or inalienable rights to the West Bank; it prefers instead to make their claim to settlement on the grounds of national security.

To Likud, the security factor is obviously important, but it cannot be the source of its claim to settlement. Likud pushes the difference between its own philosophy and Labor's to bedrock: The legitimacy that Israel demands from its Arab neighbors can be justified only by the Jews' historic and religious identification with the geography. Undermining this identification undermines its own legitimacy. Menachem Begin has argued succinctly that if Israel has no rights to Hebron, it certainly does not have rights to Tel Aviv. The logic is understandable, if not compelling.

FROM PHILOSOPHY TO POLICY

However unduly this philosophical distinction with Labor is emphasized by Likud, it gets somewhat diluted, if not entirely lost, when it is translated into policy. After all, Shimon Peres, Labors' party leader, set out Labor's view on regional peace, security, and settlement in a document offered in April 1988. The document declares that there will be no return to the pre-1967 borders, that there will be no independent Palestinian state—not even on land evacuated by Israel—that the Jordan River will be Israel's eastern security border, that the Jewish settlements on the West Bank will stay, and that Jerusalem will remain united under Israeli sovereignty.

Although the document does not refer to religious or historical rights, to Palestinians, and perhaps to others, that omission is unimportant. What matters to them, ultimately, is what Jews do, not why they do it. On stated policy, then, Labor's own position does not allow Likud much room for fundamental differentiations.

But there are differentiations. Labor is more willing to use settlements as a bargaining chip, and it prefers to position them along West Bank borders and in unsettled areas, preferably away from Arab populations. Likud, on the other hand, opts for rapid expansion of settlements, with large populations forming cities and towns, and interspersing them among the Arab populations. The settlements, connected under the Likud government by an impressive network of east-west as well as north-south highways, have been integrated into Israel proper.

Labor's policy is low profile; Likud's, by design, is high profile. Likud is intent on sending out unambiguous signals. Yet, for both, the commitment is undeniable. According to Likud and Labor, if Arab Palestinians have a political future in the area, it will be only with a concurrent Israeli one, arrived at by mutual consent.

THE DEMOGRAPHIC BOGEYMAN

In the course of the protracted, exhausting debate within Israel on Israel's West Bank policy, the issue of demography is invariably used as if it were the deciding trump. Labor's dovish wing, championed at one time by Abba Eban, makes its case forcibly. If Israel insists on West Bank geography, it must absorb West Bank demography. That's trouble! It means giving up either Jewish political independence or Israel's democratic character. And because differential birth and death rates generate a population growth rate greater for the Palestinians than for the Jews, it becomes only a matter of time until Jews become a minority in their own land.

However convincing this demographic time-bomb argument may seem to be, it tends to fizzle out when confronted with empirical evidence. Even Meron Benvenisti, the Israeli former deputy mayor of Jerusalem and an outspoken critic of Israel's West Bank policy, takes issue with this demographic myth: "The so-called demographic threat, that is, the gradually increasing proportion of Arabs versus Jews, a notion that is widespread in Israel's dovish political thinking, is not upheld by the data."[1] He's absolutely right.

LOOKING AT THE DATA

Population growth is determined not only by birth and death rates, but also by migration patterns. These rates and patterns are continually

Table 8.1
Numbers of West Bank and Gaza Workers Employed in Israel, 1970–1988

	Number of Workers
1970	22,800
1972	57,900
1975	73,000
1979/80	81,800
1984/1985	92,800
1986/1987	103,300
1988	109,400

Source: *Bank of Israel, Annual Report, 1988*, Jerusalem, 1989, p. 85.

changing, reflecting changes in the political, cultural, and economic conditions in the region as well as changes in these conditions elsewhere.

For example, one of the principal factors checking Arab population growth in the West Bank is its relatively high rate of out-migration. This fact goes almost completely unnoticed. Most of the analysis on migration in the region focuses on Jewish immigration. Arab emigration from the West Bank depends not only upon the political, cultural, and economic conditions in the West Bank, but also upon those conditions in Israel and in the Arab world, particularly in the Arab oil-exporting economies.

Among West Bank and Gaza workers, as among workers almost everywhere, market forces dictate where they choose to work. Since 1970, Arab workers from the West Bank and Gaza have moved in increasing numbers from low-paying jobs in the West Bank and Gaza to higher paying jobs in Israel. Their numbers are shown in Table 8.1.

These numbers represent a 9.1 annual rate of increase in West Bank and Gaza workers employed in Israel. By 1987, these workers accounted for fully 39.2 percent of the total Arab labor force in the West Bank and Gaza. Of these workers, 45.6 percent were employed in Israeli construction, 14.5 percent in Israeli agriculture, and 18.1 percent in Israeli industry.[2] Two-thirds of them were classified as unskilled.[3]

This striking evidence of West Bank and Gaza workers' willingness to move from their own work environments to labor markets in Israel should undermine any confidence placed on population projections that are based strictly on natural rates of population growth—birthrates minus death rates—within the region. After all, demonstrated willingness to move in large numbers from labor markets in one region to labor markets in another is not far removed from willingness to move permanently from one region to another.

And Arab Palestinians have moved permanently out of the West Bank

Table 8.2
Net Migration Balance in the West Bank, 1968–1986

Year	Number	per 1,000
1968	-15,700	-25.6
1970	-5,000	-8.3
1972	-5,100	-8.2
1974	-2,700	-4.1
1976	-14,500	-21.4
1978	-9,400	-13.5
1980	-17,100	-23.7
1982	-7,900	-10.5
1984	-5,800	-7.3
1986	-5,100	-6.1
Total 1968-86	-149,900	

Sources: Meron Benvenisti, *The West Bank Data Project* (Washington, D.C.: American Enterprise Institute, 1984), p. 4. Data for 1982 to 1986 is drawn from *Statistical Abstract of Israel, 1988* (Jerusalem: Central Bureau of Statistics, 1988), p. 705.

and Gaza in large numbers as well. One of the most important variables contributing to their migration has been the political instability in the region. For example, as many as 170,000 people migrated out of the West Bank in the immediate aftermath of the 1967 war, accounting for 20 percent of the West Bank population.[4] That quick out-migration response was similar to the migration that followed the 1948 war. By 1982, there were as many as 600,000 Palestinians living in Saudi Arabia, representing, in part, these migrants and their subsequent offspring.[5]

Another factor contributing to out-migration is economics. Changing performances of the economies of Israel, the West Bank, the adjacent Arab states, and the Arab oil-exporting economies entice or curb migration. For example, when oil prices rise, the demand for foreign workers in OPEC economies increases, touching off migrations from non–oil producing Arab economies, including the West Bank.[6] Paradoxically, the Arab worker's propensity to migrate is also linked to Jewish settlement in the West Bank: the more Jewish construction in the area, the higher the demand for Arab construction workers which, in turn, dampens the economic pressures toward migration. Unlike the political factor, the economic factor is essentially continuous (see Table 8.2).

Look at the figures for 1980. The 17,100 migrants represented 2.37 percent of the total 1980 Arab West Bank population. This percent actually exceeded the 2.29 percent natural increase in the Arab West Bank 1980 population.[7] Although out-migration continues to 1986, the

Table 8.3
Gross Reproduction Rates, by Population Group, 1965–1969 to 1986

	Total Non-Jews	Moslems	Jews
1965-69	3.83	4.47	1.63
1975	3.31	3.76	1.56
1980	2.62	2.90	1.34
1986	2.07	2.25	1.37

Source: *Statistical Abstract of Israel, 1988* (Jerusalem: Central Bureau of Statistics, 1988), p. 120.

OPEC oil price collapse in 1982 may have contributed to the steady decline in migration numbers.

The high propensity of the West Bank population to migrate comes as no surprise. The West Bank experience is anything but unique. After all, millions of people have migrated from the less developed economies of Central and Eastern Europe, from North Africa, from other parts of the Middle East, and from East and South Asia. Many more millions migrate from rural areas to urban locations within their own economies. Their motivations are understandable: to achieve higher standards of living.

Declining Birthrates

The tendency for Palestinian birthrates to decline, too, tends to undermine the demographic charge that holding the West Bank will destroy Israel's democratic character (see Table 8.3).

The gross reproduction rates among non-Jews in Israel fell from 3.83 to 2.07, or by 54 percent. Even among the Moslem subset, the decline over the 1965–69 to 1986 period exceeded 50 percent. The gap in gross reproduction rates among Moslems and Jews falls rather dramatically, from [3.83/1.63 =] 2.74 in 1965–69 to [2.07/1.37 =] 1.64 in 1986. The slight increase in the Jewish rate, from 1.34 in 1980 to 1.37 in 1986, is explained, in part, by the immigration of religious Jews. There is no reason to assume that the downward movement in Moslem reproduction rates will not continue, narrowing further the rate gap between Moslem and Jew.

A recent study by Uziel Schmelz, one of Israel's leading demographers, dramatizes the change in Arab fertility rates. In Jerusalem, for example, he shows that Arab women now bear fewer than half the number of children they did twenty years ago. Moslem women in East Jerusalem averaged 9.7 children in 1967. The numbers dropped to 4.5 by 1983.

Table 8.4
Percent of Combined Israel and West Bank Population, Jews and Arabs, 1967–1987

	Jews	Arabs
1967	63	37
1977	65	35
1987	62	38

Source: Arnon Sofer, "Population Projections for the Land of Israel," *Middle East Review* 20, no. 4 (Summer 1988): p. 45.

On the West Bank, the decline in fertility has been less spectacular, but has still fallen to 7 children.

Population Shares Remain Relatively Unchanged

Combining persistent out-migrations and changing fertility rates in the region produces—what may be for some—a rather unexpected result, which is shown in Table 8.4.

These numbers have not gone unnoticed by Likud; in fact, Likud uses them to make its point. Benjamin Netanyahu, for example, is adamant about the political significance of these numbers. The charge generally made against Likud that time is working against Israel if it does nothing about the political disposition of the West Bank carries, for him, much less weight, if any weight at all.

The conclusions Likud draws from the data have not gone unchallenged. For example, Arnon Sofer, himself, argues that the relatively unchanging percentages presented in Table 8.4 are somewhat misleading. Although the percentages of Arab and Jewish populations in 1987 are similar to the percentages in 1967, the age compositions of the populations have changed. The 1987 Arab population is decidedly younger, with a greater percent falling within the childbearing age. Future populations, he argues, will reflect this difference.

But a younger population is also a more mobile one. Younger people, for example, are disproportionately represented among the migrant workers to the oil-rich economies. Their higher propensity to migrate out of the region is also linked to the intensity of political conflict felt within the region.[8] This fact is not lost on those who discount the importance of changing age compositions of the populations.

Coupling the younger population's demonstrated willingness to migrate with the expectation of still lower rates of fertility among West Bank Arabs undermines any forecast of substantive shifts in the percentages shown in Table 8.4. It becomes a matter of some conjecture whether past rates of population change are reliable indicators of the future. The demographic dragon, then, seems to have lost at least some, if not all, of its teeth.

DEBUNKING THE ZERO-SUM GAME IDEOLOGY

Economists do not agree on many things, but the one thing they do tend to agree on is that advantages gained in free trade between two regions typically accrue to both regions. This idea still fails to persuade people who are unprepared to appreciate its consequences. Interregional trade of goods, services, labor, and capital creates higher employment, higher wage rates, and higher standards of living in *both* regions. Interregional investments bring into the investment-receiving region not only higher employment and wage rates, but also new technologies that can contribute to the modernization of the region's economy.

Yet, in spite of overwhelming evidence and economic logic, there are still people who continue to view interregional trade, particularly among more developed and less developed economies, as a zero-sum game: What the developed region gains, the less developed region loses.[9] Israeli critics of Israel's West Bank policy and certainly West Bank critics of that policy share this zero-sum game view of Israel's economic relations with the West Bank.

LOOKING AT WEST BANK ECONOMIC DATA

But the most relevant data on the West Bank economy testify to the remarkable economic gains made in the West Bank since 1967. For example, consider a partial economic checklist offered in the *The West Bank Data Project*, a report of a team of scholars generally unsympathetic to Israel's control of the West Bank. The comparative data below draws mainly from the project's 1984 report which covers the period from 1967 to 1981. It has been updated by data offered in the *Statistical Abstract of Israel, 1988*.

1. Total West Bank and Gaza gross national product (GNP), as a percent of Israeli GNP, increased from 2.6 percent in 1967 to 5.5 percent in 1986.[10]

2. Real West Bank private consumption expenditure increased 8.8 percent per year between 1968 and 1980 and by 4.3 percent per year between 1981 and 1986.[11]

3. The percent of West Bank households possessing electric refrigerators increased from 13.8 percent in 1972 to 66.3 percent in 1985. Households possessing washing machines increased from 13 percent in 1974 to 37.2 percent in 1985. Households possessing television sets increased from 10 percent in 1972 to 66.1 percent in 1985. Households possessing gas or electric cooking ranges increased from 32.7 in 1974 to 84.6 percent in 1985.[12]

4. The nutritional value of food consumption in the West Bank is the highest among Arab countries. In 1979, the daily nutritional value was estimated at 2,833 calories compared to Jordan's 2,067 and Israel's 3,039. By 1986–87, the West Bank calorie value had increased to 2,931.[13]

5. The annual average increase in real agricultural production in the West Bank was 9.6 percent between 1968 and 1981. The value of production index [1968 = 100] reached 329.3 in 1981.[14]

6. As much as 30 percent of the labor hired in 1983 by Jewish settlements in the West Bank is Arab. In the small-scale labor-intensive firms of Kiryat Arba's industrial park, employment is approximately 50 percent Arab.[15]

Additional checklists enumerate, among other things, the gains made in education. There were six universities and twenty-four vocational schools in the West Bank and Gaza in 1985, where none existed in 1967. Others emphasize the contributions to the democratic process. For example, local elections and enfranchisement of women were introduced into the West Bank by Israel.[16]

Jacob Metzer's paper details the rates of growth in the West Bank over the longer period from 1922 to 1986.[17] His 1968 to 1986 data support the view that West Bank economic performance has been quite successful (see Table 8.5).

West Bank's 5.2 percent annual rate of growth from 1973 to 1986, sustained through the worldwide recession of the 1970s, is a solid accomplishment, bettering Israel's own 3.1 percent. A major contributor to the West Bank's high-growth profile was its exports to Israel. In 1970, Israel bought 65 percent of West Bank and Gaza exports. The percentage increased to 73 in 1984. In his paper, Metzer asserts, "We may therefore conclude that in so far as exports can be identified as a growth-generating factor in the Arab economy of Palestine and in the territories since 1967, one may consider the Jewish and the Israeli economy as this factor's main driving force."

His observation is supported by Ephraim Kleiman and Michael Mi-

Table 8.5
Average Annual Rates of Growth in GNP in Israel, West Bank, and West Bank and Gaza, 1968–1986

	Israel	West Bank	West Bank and Gaza
1968-72	11.1	20.1	20.0
1973-86	3.1	5.2	5.4
1968-86	4.8	7.9	8.0

Source: Jacob Metzer, "Arab Economic Growth in the Administered Territories and Mandatory Palestine: An Historical Perspective," 1988, p. 39.

chaeli who analyze the high profile of interregional exports and imports
in terms of relative gains. They conclude that the advantage going to
the West Bank and Gaza is consistent with international trade theory,
which shows the main beneficiary of a union between a large and a small
economy to be the latter.[18]

What is common knowledge to most economists is not very common
to others. For example, referring to essentially the same data, Meron
Benvenisti notes in *The West Bank Data Project*, "The benefits accrued
from interaction with the Israeli territories have been unevenly distrib-
uted. They flow to the economically stronger side at the expense of the
weaker."[19] His comment expresses resentment, fashionable among
Third World intellectuals, but lacking nonetheless in substance.

THE IDEOLOGY OF SHARED INTEREST

Likud feels confident arguing that its West Bank policy of rapidly
expanding Jewish settlements does not infringe upon the economic well-
being of its Arab Palestinian population. Relying on the ideas of con-
ventional economic theory and on the statistical data supporting them,
Likud pushes the economic argument further: that the integration of
the West Bank economy—both its Arab and Jewish sectors—with the
Israeli one strengthens each. It means also to Likud that its avowed
singular interest in the well-being of the Jewish people—after all, that
has always been its raison d'être—is not, in fact, prejudicial.

EVEN WITH THE INTIFADA

Whereas others see the intifada as instigating fundamental changes
in the political and social environments of Israel and the West Bank that
could undermine the economic life in both regions, Likud sees the intifada simply as the basic conflict exercised in yet another form. For
example, Likud tends to depreciate the short-run economic consequences of an unstable West Bank labor supply and a reduction in interregional exports caused, in part, by the intifada. Likud's horizons are
more long run.

According to Likud, in this longer run, the economic forces that have
shaped the development of the West Bank economy, as well as its links
to the Israeli economy, will continue to exercise their power. These forces
prevail with or without the intifada. The intifada cannot hope to be a
major decision maker in shaping the West Bank's economic life unless
it changes its role from politico-military "enforcer" disrupting economic
life in the region to a primary negotiating participant in it. But Likud
sees no evidence to suggest a change in Arab-Palestinian policy toward
Israel. To the contrary, it offers much counter evidence supporting the

view that the centrality of the conflict—the Arab refusal to tolerate a Jewish independent entity in the region, regardless of the physical space it occupies—is still the pervasive reality.

In this reality, Likud sees the intifada's unwillingness or inability to change its own political agenda as leading to heightened political instability within the West Bank population, creating ultimately—as it has before—even higher levels of migration. At the same time, the strong inducements of economic gain afforded to Arabs and Jews by exports, imports, and labor mobility will, in spite of intifada pressure, continue to favor interregional economic intercourse.

NOTES

1. Meron Benvenisti, *The West Bank Data Project: A Survey of Israel's Policies* (Washington, D.C.: American Enterprise Institute, 1984), 6. Hereafter cited as *WBDP, 1984*. In the 1986 and 1987 *West Bank Data Project Reports*, Benvenisti offers a different view. Citing population projections made by Israel's Central Bureau of Statistics, he revises his 1984 opinion on the issue. See Meron Benvenisti, *The West Bank Data Project, 1987* (Jerusalem: *The Jerusalem Post*, 1987), 5. Hereafter cited as *WBDP, 1987*.

2. *Statistical Abstract of Israel, 1988* (Jerusalem: Central Bureau of Statistics, 1988), 728. Hereafter cited as *SAI/88*. See also *WBDP, 1987*, 18.

3. *Annual Report, Bank of Israel*, Jerusalem, 1988, 84.

4. S. A. Gabriel and E. F. Sabatello, "Palestinian Migration from the West Bank and Gaza: Economic and Demographic Analysis," *Economic Development and Cultural Change* (January 1986): 251.

5. *MERIP Report*, May 1985, 13–15.

6. G. Feiler, "Oil Prices and Foreign Labour in the Middle East," *Middle East Focus* (Summer 1987): 13–17.

7. *SAI/88*, 705.

8. "The relatively large migration of the mid and late 1970's mainly drained young people of pre-parental or early parental ages (15–29)." *WBDP, 1987*, 3. Concerning the relationship between recent migration and political instability, Joel Brinkley of the *New York Times* quotes a U.S. official dealing with visa applications at the consulate in East Jerusalem: "At the beginning of the intifada, people were not despairing. But then starting last fall, we started seeing a steady increase, on average [of] 20 percent more each month than the year before. More and more of them are young men, 19 or younger." *Champaign-Urbana News Gazette*, September 1, 1989, A7.

9. See, for example, Kari Levitt, *Silent Surrender* (New York: St. Martin's Press, 1970). Levitt depreciates the gains Canada has enjoyed as a trading partner with the United States. Instead, she argues that the Canadian economy loses from its trade and close proximity to the United States. Her thesis represents the thinking of economists highly critical of neoclassical economics.

10. *SAI/88*, 179, 709. See also *WBDP, 1987*, 8–10.

11. *SAI/88*, 716; *SAI/88*, 711.

12. *SAI/88*, 719.

13. *SAI/88*, 717; *WBDP, 1984*, 13.

14. *WBDP, 1984*, 12. The value of the agricultural output reached $500 million in 1985–86. It equalled 25 percent of the value of Israeli agricultural goods, compared to 16 percent in 1984–85. *WBDP, 1987*, 18.

15. *WBDP, 1984*, 17.

16. Ibid., 10.

17. Jacob Metzer, "Arab Economic Growth in the Administered Territories and Mandatory Palestine: An Historical Perspective," 1988.

18. Ephraim Kleiman and Michael Michaeli, "The Economic Integration of Israel, the West Bank and the Gaza Strip," 1987.

19. *WBDP, 1984*, 15. See also *WBDP, 1987*, 24.

9

Achieving Peace Through Economic Development: The Case of the West Bank and Gaza

Marver H. Bernstein

From June 1967 until December 1987, when the intifada suddenly erupted in the Gaza Strip and the West Bank, remarkably little violence had accompanied the Israeli military occupation of the territories. Soon after the Israeli Military Government (IMG) was installed, a task force of Israeli specialists in economic development, land settlement, agriculture, and demography was appointed to study the economic status of the territories and to prepare proposals for their economic development. The government under Prime Minister Levi Eshkol received the report and recommendations, but it was totally unprepared to consider them. At no time since then did Israel craft a development strategy, and the gap has never been filled by Jordan, the PLO, the United States, or the Palestinians.

An early advocate of economic development of the West Bank was Moshe Dayan, then minister of defense. Immediately after the end of the Six-Day War, in his characteristically general and unsystematic way, he recognized a need to develop industries in the territories in order to promote stability and to improve living standards. For the next five years, he encouraged the nurturing of stronger links between Arabs and Jews. After two years of military occupation, in June 1969, he suggested a way for Israel to develop the economies of the West Bank and Gaza to provide necessary services locally and to utilize Israeli technology to create a modern economy. In general terms again, he proposed more intensive economic coordination, on Israeli terms, between Israel and the territories to enable Arabs and Jews to find ways to meet and work together.[1]

For twenty years under Israeli military rule, the residents of the territories experienced a vast improvement in their living standards. Little was done, however, by Israel, Egypt, Jordan, other Arab countries, the United Nations, or the United States to stimulate and finance capital investment. The experience of the Israeli occupation throws some light on the prospects and limitations of using economic development as a strategy to advance the movement toward reconciliation and peace in the Arab-Israeli conflict.

JORDANIAN RULE, 1950–1967

In the period of Jordanian rule of the West Bank from 1950 to 1967, the Palestinians were used primarily to serve the interests of the royal house. The West Bank was assigned a peripheral role in the economy of the East Bank, supplying resources in the form of capital and educated personnel for the development of the East Bank. Only Jordanian banks operated in the West Bank, and Jordan deliberately limited the economic and political development of the region.

In 1952 the West Bank contained 60 percent of the population of Jordan and contributed the same proportionate share of the gross national product. By 1967 the situation had been reversed. Only five factories employed more than 100 people—factories manufacturing cigarettes, furniture, chocolate, plastics, and shortening. While industrial products were barely 6 percent of the total West Bank production, Amman had become an urban center with large industrial and service sectors. From 1950 to 1967, Jordanian rule had succeeded mainly in moving the industrial center of the Hashemite Kingdom from the West Bank to the East Bank, while Egypt, which never formally annexed Gaza, practiced a policy of total neglect of the Gaza Strip.

ISRAELI MILITARY GOVERNMENT

When control passed to the Israelis in June 1967, the West Bank readily became dependent on Israel, as it had become dependent on Jordan earlier. But there was an important difference: The Palestinians had become a source of unskilled and semiskilled laborers for Israel. By 1970, about 40,000 were working in Israel; their numbers exceeded 100,000 in June 1987. Since 1967 long-term investment in the West Bank has been discouraged by Israel. Even West Bankers preferred to invest in the East Bank.

According to international convention, the occupied territories were administered by the military forces of Israel. Accordingly, Israel proceeded to establish a military government at the end of the Six-Day War. Although the minister of defense would be in charge, the government decided that other ministries would be engaged in administration in their special fields, such as police, interior, labor, welfare, health, and education. The basis for this decision was complex, but three factors were weighty. First, the army was not trained or equipped to deal with civilian matters of health, education, and welfare. Second, each cabinet minister wanted to have a hand in the military occupation. Third, Defense Minister "Dayan wanted to have maximum control over what was actually done but did not want to assume formal ministerial responsibility as the minister in charge of the territories."[2]

The ministries appointed civilians to serve as professional staff officers in the headquarters of the IMG in the West Bank and the Gaza Strip, under the direction of the military commanders. The West Bank is divided into seven districts, six of which are named after its main city: Hebron, Bethlehem, Tulkharm, Nablus, Ramallah, and Jenin. The seventh is the Jordan District, which stretches along the Jordan River from Jerico northward to the Beth-She'an Valley. In the headquarters of the military commander, administration is divided into three clusters of programs: public administration and services, economic affairs, and taxes and property. In 1981 the commander's title was changed to head of the civil administration. Under these arrangements, "the dominance of the Minister of Defense in the affairs of the territories is practically unchallenged by other members of the cabinet or even by the Prime Minister."[3]

The policy of the IMG with respect to economic affairs in the territories was never formally developed as an official statement. An article written by General Gazit, serving as coordinator of government operations in the territories, is the closest thing there is to an official IMG statement. Dayan's close aid, General Shlomo Gazit was thoroughly familiar with Dayan's thinking as minister of defense in charge of the territories. Israel, Gazit states, must see that the people in the territories have an adequate economic condition. For short-term interests, economic well-being and full employment were valued as the effective means to discourage terrorism.

Every resident of the territories is responsible first of all for his own home and family. The need to find a livelihood, the work which fills his day and would not leave free time for illegal activity, and a good economic situation for himself and his family enhance the chance of keeping the individual away from silly actions and will encourage him to continue his regular, calm way of life.[4]

For the longer term, Gazit noted:

Any political settlement which may be achieved would not be able to hold unless it be sustained by a large system of interests on both sides which will operate and maintain pressure for the continuation of the settlement. So this requires economic measures such as joint water plans, with one water source serving both Arab villages in the territories and villages in Israel, joint integrated health services, etc.[5]

Gazit added:

For those [in the territories] who yearn for independence, for sovereignty, for a flag, a national anthem, and all other paraphernalia of statehood, for those— we cannot offer any practical solution. However, as . . . to what extent the Israeli Military Government changes or affects the ordinary regular way of life of the Arab residents of the territories—here we can do a lot in order to dull the acuteness of the problem.[6]

Gazit emphasized three broad operating principles. First, the IMG should minimize the presence of Israeli rule as much as possible by reducing the visibility of military patrols and buildings, the Israeli flag, and other symbols of Israeli rule. Second, the Arabs should administer programs that meet local needs as much as possible, and the IMG should intervene only when local action in such matters as sanitation or economic activity may damage the Israeli economy. Third, bridges on the Jordan River should be open to enable Arab residents to move freely into and out of the West Bank and the Gaza Strip.

The first goal of minimizing the Israeli presence was, from the beginning, impossible to realize. The broad objective of benign occupation that would produce economic prosperity and wide acceptance of occupation by the occupied population had some success for two decades, but eventually, it gave way to the intifada, in December 1987. With respect to the second operating principle of nonintervention, the record of occupation has been mixed. As a general guide in operations, it did not prevent many forms of direct Israeli intervention.

In agriculture, Israeli instructors introduced modern technology and increased by three or four times the average yield per acre. In labor relations, the IMG issued a regulation requiring employers to insure their employees against accidents both at work and their way to and from. In auto insurance, mandatory coverage was raised to match the Israeli norms.[7]

In the early years of the occupation, a sense of temporariness pervaded Israeli thinking. When Israel assumed control of the territories, arbitrary rates of exchange were fixed, and stiff controls were imposed on trade and movement of goods. The initial objective seemed to be to keep the economies of Israel and the territories separated. Then consultative committees set to work to consider what policies should guide the Israeli administration. The initial arrangements for exchange rates and central control of trade proved to be unworkable. Large-scale public works, planned and financed by Israel, were initiated for the West Bank and Gaza; municipal, social, and other services were also resumed—financed by Israel. And the Israeli pound was made legal tender in the territories.

A special committee was created in this initial period of occupation to propose an overall economic policy. The committee concluded that "no alternative exists to economic integration of the occupied territories" and recommended "an immediate free flow of trade and capital" and selective subsidies to counteract the dislocation in production and marketing patterns which may be caused by economic integration.[8] The report underlined "the crucial importance of development projects both for restoring normal economic activity in the occupied territories, and for gradually moving them along the road to economic integration with Israel's established economy."[9] Public works were proposed to cope with the anticipated unemployment.

Other committees dealt with more detailed settlement plans. Given the political uncertainties about the situation and the lack of confidence of the Palestinians in Israeli control, the government of Israel was not prepared to deal in comprehensive fashion with the economic development of the territories.

After two years of occupation, the lives of one million people subject to the IMG appeared to be proceeding with less administrative intervention than under previous Arab regimes. According to one close observer:

By and large people are free to work, trade, travel, to go abroad—including the Arab states hostile to Israel—to cross into Israel inside the Green Line, to assemble, discuss, publish, protest, with no strings attached except what is considered necessary in order to maintain law and order.[10]

Israel had feared that its occupation would prove to be a severe drain on its economic resources, especially its foreign currency reserves. Many expected that cheap Arab labor would undermine Israeli trade unions and that Israeli farmers would not be able to compete with produce from the West Bank and Gaza. As it turned out, the trade balance was heavily in Israel's favor, and the territories became an extension of the home market. The markets for labor and farm produce were not upset, and the territories contributed substantially to the foreign currency balances. The official explanation was that the territories, instead of being "held and frozen in expectancy of an eventual peace agreement... [were] allowed to integrate with the Israeli economy, and to some extent—although rather feebly—even assisted in the process."[11] Manufacturing was spurred by orders from Israeli factories and customers. Traditional crops, such as melon and watermelons, were reduced, and new crops, such as tobacco, cotton, vegetables, and medicinal plants, were taken up and expanded. Exports to overseas markets were tied to Israeli export promotions and incentives.

The achievement of economic growth and the prosperity that accompanied it were dependent on the process of economic integration, which made changes in both the territories and Israel mutually complementary. To Arab nationalists, economic integration seemed to be an attempt to bribe the Palestinians to abandon the goal of Israel's destruction. Given the persistence of Arab terror bands coming overwhelmingly from the urban middle classes rather than from villagers and artisans, and the dislocation of traditional Arab society resulting from rapid economic and social change, the Israelis necessarily kept their eye on maintaining law and order in the territories.

In 1967, agriculture constituted about half of the economy of the West Bank. Since then, Israel's agricultural policy for the territories has developed in three stages. The first emphasis was to encourage a normal return to farming. The second stage focused on improving existing practices, including the use of fertilizers and better plant protection, especially as practiced by Arab farmers in Israel. The third stage featured development projects, mainly new seeds, irrigation, better cattle strains, and the use of price supports for some crops like tomatoes. Israel took steps to provide, for the first time on the West Bank, refrigerated stores and modern packing plants.

While Israel was already in 1969 self-sufficient in most crops, it did shift from foreign suppliers to the administered areas for the import of humus, sesame, and wheat. Israel was careful not to allow Arab competition with Israeli produce and to restrict Israeli food exports to the Arab market. One of the features of economic integration was the opening of Arab products to the European market through the ports of Ashdod and Haifa. Thousands of tons of winter crops from ordinary farms in the territories—eggplant, peppers, courgettes, tomatoes, watermelons, beans, and almonds—were exported. Israel's limited outlays for agriculture highlighted surveys and research to locate reserves of arable land and water resources to be tapped as a necessary preliminary step to development.[12]

Moshe Dayan dominated Israeli policy-making for the territories. According to one observer, his "decisions derive largely from intuition" which "is faster than his reasoning."[13] To describe the beginning of the open-bridges policy, James Feron, the *New York Times* reporter, tells a story that occurred during a routine visit by Dayan to Nablus in December 1967.

[The mayor of Nablus interjected], "You said you were going to give crossing permits [over the Jordan River] for Christmas, but this will involve only a few hundred Christians. Now we are on the eve of Id al Fitr [the festival that ends the sacred month of Ramadan]. Why not Moslems?" "Why not?" Dayan replied. It lasted three or four minutes, no more.... On the spot, he gave agreement in principle. The system guaranteeing that the pass-holders would not abuse the privilege by importing arms or explosives came later. In 1968 some 200,000 Arabs went across the bridges. Dayan had felt intuitively that it was a good idea. The details were completed later.[14]

Dayan's proposals for economic integration of the territories were strongly opposed by Pinhas Sapir, the minister of finance, and others, who feared that integration would lead to full integration or annexation and thus the end of the Jewish state. Sapir also effectively blocked Dayan's plans for establishing joint Arab-Israeli enterprises in the West Bank. Dayan believed that economic integration would draw the Arab population into the Israeli economy and lead first to coexistence and eventually peace. His short-term goal was

to make the people more dependent on Israel and less on Jordan.... If their electricity were linked to our power lines, they would think twice before sabotaging our pylons. I'm a realist and I would like to eliminate disturbances as much as possible. The question is how to do it. I think that the answer—it's not a guarantee—is the normalization of life. Let us permit them to live their own lives, let them elect their own mayors and municipal groups, but let us also integrate them into our economic life in such a way that, if they sabotage something, it will hurt them.[15]

For the long term, Dayan envisioned a confederacy:

I would...like to see a new kind of relation established between them and us. I think we have to have free access everywhere, and that they have to have free access here. And the kind of life on the West Bank will be different from what exists in all the other Arab countries.[16]

On the results of his policy on economic integration, Dayan claimed, "It's worked very well, you know. I have heard of no incident among the 15,000 Arabs [in June 1969] who come to work in Israel every day. I have not heard a single complaint, neither from them nor from the Israelis."[17]

A different version of the origin of the open-bridges policy is offered by Shabtai Teveth, a distinguished journalist and scholar.[18] He suggests that during the initial period of occupation the IMG was a triumph of improvisation, quick thinking, and on-the-spot decision making. He relates that Eitan Israeli, the Agriculture Ministry's representative at the IMG, in just a few hours, saved the West Bank's summer crop in the summer of 1967 by getting Dayan's consent to go along with local Arab initiatives to send their produce eastward across the Jordan River, thereby giving birth to the open-bridges policy. Both versions involve Dayan and both underline the importance of on-the-spot decision making.

While Dayan, as minister of defense, remained firmly in control of the IMG, he did not prevail in the deepening conflict with Sapir in 1968 and 1969 on the issue of opening the entire Israeli economy to the Palestinians. The cabinet under Eshkol sided most of the time with Sapir and limited the development of public services and investment in the territories. According to Teveth:

In Dayan's view, the two nations in the area formerly called Palestine could function within a single economy, even though they belonged to different cultures and sovereign states. The basic principle in his approach was neighborliness, or, in his phrase, "a joint way of life."[19]

Sapir's perspective emphasized the imperative of survival of the Jewish state. He believed that a million and a half Arabs would threaten the demographic status of the country's Jewish majority. By employing Palestinians in industry and manual labor, Israel, he feared, would change its image as a nation of workers. Sapir believed that marked differences between Israel and its Arab neighbors would guarantee the survival of Israel's Jewish identity.[20]

The inability of Eshkol's government to enunciate a guiding policy on this fundamental issue has been emulated by all succeeding Israeli governments. In Eshkol's case, the "war of attrition" with Egypt and increased Soviet penetration of the Middle East seemed to rule out a clearcut decision on economic development. But events in the territories nonetheless led to increasing economic integration. "Electric power, water, roads, transport, agricultural coordination, marketing of agricultural produce, control over plant and livestock diseases, preventive medicine, and particularly the exploitation of manpower were all shared with Israel."[21]

On August 19, 1971, Defense Minister Dayan, addressing a passing out ceremony of the Command and Staff College, made remarks that were interpreted widely as a suggestion that Israel formally annex all the administered territories. To clarify his remarks he stated:

In my opinion, the question of what should be done in areas should be occupying most of our attention. Not the question of collecting taxes, but of spending money there. The fact that we have now been in the areas for four years—and I assume that we will go on being there for a long time yet without any permanent arrangement, and that after an arrangement we will also remain in most of the areas: the Golan Heights, and the West Bank—this is no light matter.

Dayan then stressed the economic linkage of Arab and Jew:

It is very important to what extent the Arabs of the West Bank and the Gaza
Strip, as individuals, are linked to Israel. When they are working here, when
they are visiting here, when there will be economic partnerships, etc., it will be
easier to cut them off from the other side.

Dayan saw no immediate prospect for a peace settlement, but he insisted that Israel should radically improve the human status of the refugees, especially in the Gaza Strip,

first by seeing to it that they are gainfully employed instead of sitting around
in their pyjamas waiting for the oil and olive rations. When they are working
and earning a decent wage, their standard of living will rise. The style of their
housing has to be changed, so that they will live in quarters fit for human beings.[22]

Dayan repeated:

The key to a peace settlement . . . is agreement on boundaries. And I don't see
Syria agreeing to our sitting on the Golan, or Hussein agreeing to our sitting in
Jerusalem. . . . I don't think we ought to return to the previous boundaries, and
I hope that we won't.[23]

In conclusion, he stated:

If the struggle is a long one—then long it will be. For the time being, I don't
see any signs of weakness on our part, or of any inability to stand up to the
struggle.[24]

By 1971 Dayan conceived of economic development as an effective
strategy for a relatively benign military occupation that would become
increasingly accepted by the Palestinians as they experienced major improvements in the human quality of their lives—in gainful employment,
standards of living, housing, health services, and education. In fact, for
two decades, under Israeli control, production grew rapidly and standards of living improved continuously—until 1988. Several factors account for rapid economic growth, especially in the 1970s: the opening
of the Israeli labor market to the residents of the West Bank and Gaza;
the booming economy of Saudi Arabia and the Gulf States, which provided for private transfers of remittances to Palestinians; the removal
of barriers between Israel and the territories; and some improvements
in water, electricity, and roads, but without any central economic authority and with only low levels of capital formation.

In the first ten years under Israeli control, the economies of the West
Bank and Gaza expanded by about 13 percent a year, nearly double the

Israeli rate. The level fell after 1977, grinding down to nearly zero in the mid-1980s. In terms of income, education, health, and other factors, the standard of living under Israeli control improved dramatically. The moving force of economic growth has been about 90,000 to 100,000 Palestinians crossing the Green Line to jobs in Israel, equal to about 40 percent of the working population in the territories. Between 1972 and 1981, for example, the percentage of households with electricity rose from 35 to 82, and the percentage with television sets rose from 10 to 64. Agricultural production improved substantially, although industrial production was severely restricted by Israeli controls and a shortage of investment funds. The territories ran up a huge trade deficit with Israel that was largely funded by the earnings of Palestinian workers in Israel.

With the labor government in power from 1967 to 1977, investment and development continued to be discouraged. Israel sought prosperity and improved standards of living on the West Bank, but it would not risk the development of industries and a modern infrastructure that would provide the underpinnings for an independent Palestinian state. As it turned out, increased prosperity and modernization produced a greater political awareness in the territories but failed to generate a representative, territory-wide leadership. With hindsight, it appears that the policies of Jordan and Israel produced a political vacuum that was filled gradually by the Palestine diaspora, led by the PLO, which became the major unchallenged political force. Historically this was just the op-posite of the process within the Zionist movement and Israel, in which the territorial unit became the central political force and the diaspora became the peripheral supplier of resources. By discouraging the emer-gence of central political leaders and institutions in the territories, both Israel and Jordan encouraged the growth of the externally based PLO. This result is significant if only because the PLO, under nonresident control, has been able to avoid the type of accommodation that an in-ternally based political organization might have accepted, however re-luctantly. Thus even the PLO turned the West Bank into a peripheral region and came to dominate Palestinian organizations and institutions. The failures of the PLO from 1982 to 1987 then gave rise to the indig-enous leadership of the intifada.

In November 1981, the civil administration, which had been placed under military control from the beginning of the occupation, was sep-arated from the military administration, but it remained an organ of the military government.[25] Civil administration does not mean that the administration is operated by civilians; rather, it means an administration dealing with the affairs of civilians. The head of civil administration is appointed by the commander of the IDF in the area and is empowered to appoint local officials, enact subsidiary legislation, appoint staff offi-cers and government employees, and delegate authority to them. From the Israeli perspective, the division of functions between military and civilian officers suited the needs of the population and the policy objectives of the government more effectively. Meron Benvenisti argues that this change in the status of the civil administration intended to interpret the discussions in the autonomy talks with Egypt at Camp David in 1978 by providing for the transformation of the civilian administration *"from a temporary to a permanent system"* (italics in original).[26]

In his 1986 report on developments in the West Bank, Benvenisti cautions that statistics on economic activity in the Palestinian sector, excluding Jewish settlements, "can be accepted only as approximations, showing general trends, rather than as useful economic indicators."[27]

The Palestinian gross domestic product (GDP) for 1980 and 1983 remained at the same level—approximately $810 million. In 1984, the GDP dropped when a severe drought caused a decline in agricultural production of from 10 to 15 percent. Income from employment of Palestinians abroad declined from $308 million in 1983 to $268 million in 1984, or about one-fourth of gross disposable income.[28] The GDP in the Palestinian sector in 1983 comprised the following:

Industry, including quarrying	7%
Agriculture	27%
Construction	16%
Transport, communication, and private services	36%
Public services	14%
	100%

The share of the industrial contribution to the GDP was 9 percent in 1968, 8.2 percent in 1975, 6.5 percent in 1980, and 6.7 percent in 1983. Similarly the contribution of agriculture declined from almost 40 percent in 1980 to 27 percent in 1983.

In the mid-1980s, about 10,000 workers were employed in industrial plants on the West Bank. The average plant employed only 4 workers. Plants producing goods for local consumption—olive oil, soap, paper, cigarettes, food, and soft drinks—were less dependent on the Israeli economy and more profitable than plants producing for the export market.

In the 1980s Israel experienced an economic slowdown while the West Bank and Gaza economies continued to grow rapidly, a situation that is explained perhaps by the civil war in Lebanon; a growth spurt in Jordan; and large capital transfers from individuals and from Arab governments, international welfare organizations, and the Israeli government. But soon the economy began to sag, and unemployment, which had nearly disappeared in the late 1970s, rose. Increases in the GDP were barely 1 to 2 percent a year.

The conditions that prevented development are clear: political instability; a narrow industrial base that provides less than 10 percent of the GDP from industrial activity, no financial base, and no banking system for investment purposes; inadequate infrastructure in telecommunications and transportation; and Israeli control of exports and capital imports. The outcome of the forces was that only small-scale projects on a family basis were undertaken, for example, construction for residential purposes. Sources of employment for a growing, better educated labor force were slim. In Gaza, the situation seemed hopeless, without links to Jordan, with a monstrous density of population that leaves almost no land for development, and with grim prospects of domestic development.

The economic dependence of the West Bank and Gaza has been aggravated by the rapid rate of population growth. For example, between 1980 and 1986, the population increased by 19 percent—a rate faster than the rate of economic growth in the territories. Throughout the Middle East, at least 400,000 Palestinians—the ones who are most likely to seek to return to a Palestinian state—continue to live in refugee camps. They have the fewest skills and require the largest expenditure of welfare funds.

Beginning in 1983, some signs of economic entrenchment appeared. College graduates found it difficult to find jobs, and before inflation in Israel was brought under control in 1985–86, those earning wages and salaries in Israel lost their buying power. It was widely predicted in the Middle East that, when prosperity gave way to poverty, the revolutionary incentive would become stronger.

Up to 1988, trade patterns reflected rapidly developing ties with Israel. Ninety percent of imports into the territories came from or through Israel, and from 55 to 60 percent of the exports were to Israel. In 1984, 84 percent of the imports from Israel were Israeli-manufactured goods that enjoyed government protection and left West Bank products with little chance to compete with Israeli industry. Farmers were encouraged to grow crops that fitted into the Israeli economy. For example, funds were shifted from foods of high water content (melons) to leguminous crops. Palestinians turned more to crops with year-round cultivation periods—olive trees and grape vines. The West Bank became increasingly tied into Israel's road and utility infrastructure. Road building emphasized a network of roads above the Jordan Valley for military purposes and roads linking settlements with each other and with Israel. Electric power supply was contentious. Israel denied most applications to import generators, and some West Bank towns were tied into Israeli grids. This strategy of occupation met Israel's security needs and enabled Israel to keep its military forces at modest levels.

In the 1980s, twenty-five municipalities and eighty-two active village councils in the West Bank provided local services in electricity, street lighting, water, roads, sidewalks, sewage and sanitation, construction, markets, licensing of business, fire protection, slaughterhouses, and cemeteries. The Israeli civil administration collects property and business taxes and distributes 90 percent to local authorities. There are separate budgets for operations and for development. The development budget provided by the civil administration increased from 2.5 percent of total development funds in 1979 to 75 percent in 1984, underlining a growing dependence on Israeli financing of development projects. In 1985, the civil administration approved for development projects $1.9 million from Jordan and $6.5 million from international bodies.[29]

Until the intifada required large increases in military expenditures, Israel collected more in tax revenues in the West Bank and Gaza than it spent on programs to serve Palestinians. Before 1988 some economists estimated that Israel earned about $1 billion annually from the territories in cheap labor, captive export markets, taxes, and other items. Significant improvements in health care, roads, schools and education, and public facilities were made by the civil administration, sometimes with the assistance of voluntary agencies funded by U.S. aid. When Shimon Peres headed the National Unity Government from 1984 to 1986, there was more flexibility in approving economic projects that did not compete with Israeli industry, but the objective of maintaining dependence on the Israeli economy remained in place. This approach had been workable as long as employment opportunities provided by Israel, Jordan, and the Arab oil-producing states absorbed the labor that could not be sustained by local agriculture and small-scale commerce. Personal prosperity and the steady rise in standards of living seemed to take the edge off the adversities of military occupation for middle-class Palestinians.

Before Egypt and Israel signed a peace treaty in 1978, no Arab country was willing to make peace with Israel, and none has since then. No Arab country was prepared to consider resettling refugees. Jordan had in effect accepted and relied on Israel as its not-so-secret ally in combatting revolutionary forces in the PLO. With a state of war prevailing between Arab countries and Israel, the massive Soviet arming of Syria, Israel's need to strengthen its military position, and relative calm and prosperity in the territories, Israel's policies in the territories seemed to most Israelis to be sound and effective.

Prior to the onset of the intifada in December 1987, studies of economic development of the West Bank and the Gaza Strip stressed several key findings and conclusions:

1. The territories have progressed economically much more under Israeli rule than they did under the rule of Jordan and Egypt.

2. Israel has improved significantly the economic infrastructure of the territories; it has constructed a network of roads; and it has greatly improved the quality and availability of health care.

3. Israel has improved industry and manufacturing in the territories by developing vocational training, by making technology available, and by distributing new work to businesses in the territories.

4. Israel has been concerned to improve living conditions of Palestinians consistent with its primary obligations to safeguard its own security. From the beginning, however, its approach to the economic development of the West Bank and Gaza has been characterized as "a piecemeal and patchwork approach—simultaneously humanitarian, exploitative, responsive, and discriminatory."[30]

5. Investment in industry and manufacturing in the territories has been hampered by bureaucratic red tape, priorities accorded to security considerations and to protections to Israeli industry, and by high taxes, plant inspections, and other regulatory constraints. These factors have also severely hampered capital investment and the development of new business within Israel itself.[31]

6. While Israeli policies have increased individual prosperity for most Palestinians, they also—for purposes of national security—have discouraged the growth of an independent Palestinian economy. These included policies of preventing competition with Israeli enterprises, limiting credit and banking facilities, maintaining a low level of industrial infrastructure, and treating the Palestine economy mainly as auxiliary to the Israeli economy, principally to supply unskilled and low-skilled labor.

7. Because of its linkage to and dependence on the Israeli economy, economic life in the territories has been adversely affected by economic stagnation in Israel in recent years and especially during the severe agriculture crisis of the 1980s brought on by phenomenal productivity.

JORDAN: 1967–1988

When Israel captured the West Bank from Jordan in 1967, the Jordanian administration and bureaucracy remained in place. Until 1987 Jordan had done little to promote the West Bank economy and had totally ignored Gaza. Palestinian exports to Jordan accounted for only 2 to 3 percent of total exports from these areas. According to Benvenisti, beginning in June 1967, Jordan aimed to freeze the structure of industry in the West Bank as it had existed in 1966. Under the pretense of observing the Arab boycott of Israel, it permitted imports from the West Bank only from factories established before the occupation. Since 1979, it had not registered a single new company in the West Bank or Gaza.[32] It also made imports from the West Bank conditional upon the purchase of raw materials and machinery in or through Jordan. Such materials were then liable to Israeli custom duties in addition to higher costs of importing raw materials and machinery through Jordan. Very few firms on the West Bank exported goods to Jordan in part because "Jordan prohibits imports of textiles, stone and tiles, detergents, and pharmaceuticals, ostensibly to maintain the Arab boycott but in fact to protect infant Jordan industries."[33]

Following the Arab summit conference in Baghdad in 1978, Jordan and the PLO set up a joint committee to oppose the establishment of Jewish settlements in the territories and Anwar Sadat's efforts to reach a peace agreement with Israel. Arab sources contributed funds to various official and private groups in the territories, some of which were intended to develop an economic infrastructure to ward off Israeli steps toward annexation. In 1982, the Israeli military administration banned the use of these funds for development investment, but in 1984 this policy was reversed. As a result, the transfer of Arab funds to the territories increased. Banned or not, between 1980 and 1985, Jordan contributed about $435 million for economic development of the West Bank and the Gaza Strip.[34]

The Jordan-PLO agreement was renegotiated in February 1985, but the transfer of Arab funds for economic development was halted by the breakdown in relations between Yasir Arafat and King Hussein in 1986. The king then announced a five-year development plan for the West Bank and the Gaza Strip, and the U.S. Congress appropriated $5.5 million for fiscal year 1986 and $14 million for fiscal year 1987. The plan proposed to spend $1.3 billion for housing, construction projects, education, agriculture, social development, and industry. Only $63 million was allocated to industry, less than 5 percent of the total. Only the United States pledged more than token support. Early in 1987 Jordan budgeted $150 million to initiate the plan, but economic conditions in Jordan discouraged substantial funding of projects in the territories. In addition, many Palestinians were suspicious of King Hussein's motives and did not believe that the king's plan would advance their objective of establishing a Palestinian state. While funding lagged, some projects were started.

In late July 1988, before the development plan had any impact, King Hussein withdrew from the West Bank, cancelled the plan, and renounced his claims to sovereignty over the West Bank. By that time, Jordan had invested $7.8 million and the United States $5.5 million in development projects. Twenty-four projects were completed, and forty-nine municipal development projects were underway.[35] Prior to withdrawal, the king had occasionally provided direct aid to his supporters in the West Bank. Elias Freij, the long-time mayor of Bethlehem, frequently visited Amman whenever he was short of funds. The last such occasion was in July 1988, when he received $60,000 toward a $200,000 road project. The king's objective was to demonstrate the inability of the PLO to replace Jordan by funding and administering these projects in the territories. As the intifada persisted, other priorities preoccupied the PLO.

THE UNITED STATES AND VOLUNTARY AID

Beginning in 1975, U.S. Agency for International Development (AID) funds for were made available mainly to seven private voluntary organizations (PVOs) through grants and cooperative agreements to administer programs in the territories to improve the standard of living of Palestinians to meet their humanitarian and economic needs.[36] From 1975 through 1988, about $86 million was provided by AID, and $15 million was budgeted for 1989. Normally AID funds provided from one-half to two-thirds of the cost of each project, and the PVOs and the local population the balance. Beginning in the early 1980s, AID projects shifted in emphasis from humanitarian activities to development projects, mainly in poor, rural areas. In addition, the United States contributes funds to the United Nations Development Fund, which carries on development projects in the West Bank and Gaza. The United States also contributes substantially to the United Nations Relief and Works Agency (UNRWA), which works in the refugee camps.

AID projects have covered three areas: (1) agricultural and industrial, including land reclamation and modernization, dairy and food processing, marketing, and technical services; (2) health, community services, and education, including construction of buildings, self-help projects, scholarships, and vocational training; and (3) public works, including water, irrigation, sewage, roads, and electricity.

In 1989, seven PVOs had grants and cooperative agreements with AID.

1. American Near East Refugee AID (ANERA) has provided assistance to agricultural cooperatives in land reclamation, mechanization, and other activities.

2. American Mid-East and Training Services (AMIDEAST) has, since 1951, supported three universities by helping to develop faculties, providing scholarships, and purchasing equipment for laboratories.

3. Agricultural Cooperative Development International (ACDI) administers a cooperative development project to provide technical assistance and training for cooperatives to encourage self-sufficiency.

4. Catholic Relief Services (CRS) has been active especially in special education and rural development. It has instituted programs in health education, the care of physically handicapped persons, and the distribution of Public Law 480 surplus food.

5. Community Development Foundation/Save the Children Fund focuses on rural development projects, including water, sanitation, agriculture, social development, and loans to farmers.

6. International Executive Service Corps provided technical assistance and training for local businessmen in 1986 and 1987, until the intifada forced cancellation of the program.

7. Society for the Care of Handicapped Children operates in the Gaza Strip, where it provides basic training to physically and mentally handicapped children and plans to expand health services to other children.

The real policy decisions to approve or disallow specific projects are made by the Israeli military government. Prior to 1984, most projects required from six months to one year to obtain Israeli approval. The projects most likely to be approved were for drinking water, sewage, electricity, and health. In agriculture and industry, only 33 to 40 percent of the projects were approved. Those involving the purchase of tractors, bulldozers, and processing of agricultural produce were usually turned down. Overall, between 1979 and 1983, less than half of the projects designed for developing the economic structure of the territories were approved; half of all the approved projects were consumption oriented.

In 1984, Secretary George Shultz launched a policy of "improvement in the quality of life," which emphasized economic development and improved relations between the Israel administration and the Palestinians. With the secretary's encouragement, the criteria for approval were eased in 1985 and the proportion of projects that were approved increased. Approved projects reflected needs solicited by local residents. They did not emerge from a development strategy or a comprehensive approach to improvement of the economic condition of Palestinians. Faced with Israeli imperatives of national security and protection of Israeli economic interests, the U.S.–funded projects made only marginal contributions to the economic development of the territories.

In the spring of 1983, a group of prominent American Arab and American Jewish businessmen began to think about the idea of promoting private and civil development projects in the territories. These ideas dovetailed with those of the State Department, and the two groups kept in touch. In July 1984 a group of young Labor party activists in Israel, led by Yossi Beilin, who became secretary of the cabinet in the new National Unity Government under Shimon Peres, called for the relaxation of economic controls in the West Bank as a way to encourage Palestinian and Jordanian participation in the peace process. Stephen Cohen of the Graduate School of the City University of New York became advisor to a group of about forty business executives organized as the Business Group for Middle East Peace and Development.[37] In November 1984 among the first projects considered was the establishment of a quarry, a cement factory, a juice plant, and a pharmaceutical plant. Some of the Jewish members of the group were known for their opposition to Jewish settlement in the West Bank and their support for a territorial compromise. The participation of Najeeb Halaby, the father-in-law of King Hussein, suggested to some that the development plans had Jordanian approval. Hence the group's objectives were strongly resisted by hawkish constituencies in Israel.

Shultz and Peres discussed private development efforts late in 1984, but nothing of substance emerged. Israeli authorities informed the group that economically viable projects would be approved but that Israeli economic interests would be taken into account. Again, political and military concerns were paramount, and the group of successful business executives was dismissed as politically naive or dangerous to Israel's security or both. *The Jerusalem Post* quoted a leading Palestinian moderate interested in economic development with a mixture of regret and resentment: "We are not ready for Arab-Jew cooperation, especially with people like Squadron and Klutznick. After all, they are Zionists."[38] Opposed by radical Palestinians and by militant nationalists in Israel, the business consortium understood the odds against them and recognized that they would have to move slowly to gain credibility from both Palestinians and Israelis. A *New York Times* reporter stated that the group believes that "as businessmen, engrossed by the practical rather than the political, they may be able to avoid some of the difficulties that ensnare efforts to cooperate in the Middle East."[39] The obstacles, however, proved to be too great to overcome.

Another approach to the challenge of economic development has been the pursuit of integration of the economies of Israel, Jordan, and the West Bank and Gaza. Herbert Stein noted that the resources of the region are small. "Israel," he said, "is much better supplied with technology, entrepreneurship, and capital and less well supplied with labor and land." In 1983, he estimated that the gains from economic integration "would probably be greater than the gains from the economic integration of western Europe." But he also warned that peace itself does not automatically provide for a measure of free economic intercourse. "After all, something like peace has been established between Israel and Egypt, but economic relations are severely limited."[40]

Another approach has been to allow more competitive markets to flourish. In January 1988, after the intifada had begun, Edgar Harrell, who directed the Jordan mission of U.S. AID from 1978 to 1981, wrote that we continue to "overlook the one real potential force for stability and growth in . . . Israeli-occupied territories. This is the area's business people and farmers, who run several thousand mainly small and family-owned enterprises." He stressed that the highly restrictive business environment in the West Bank and Gaza stifles the entrepreneurial spirit.

"West Bank and Gaza businessmen and farmers putter along, no longer role models for children, who in turn look for alternatives, more radical means to express creativity and expend energy." He concluded that a few adjustments in administration and attitude by Israel and Jordan might bring about long-term political gains.[41]

Harrell's plea for giving a free market approach a chance was developed also by Joyce Starr, who urged the United States to push ahead with a serious program of economic aid for the Palestinians.[42] Starr believes that the future status of the West Bank and Gaza will be determined as much by economics as by politics, and she recommends that American efforts be directed toward developing a comprehensive marketing system and encouraging businessmen in the territories and elsewhere to take risks and start new ventures. Starr also calls for the United States to direct financial support to the West Bank and Gaza.

THE INTIFADA

The intifada has brutally disrupted the economic life of the territories. Throughout 1988 and much of 1989, negative effects predominated. Family income dropped from 40 to 50 percent below 1987 levels. Strikes limited the hours that shops could remain open. Some Palestinian workers responded to demands that they reject jobs in Israel. Some Jewish settlers in the West Bank reacted to violent attacks by emulating Arab attackers. Key agricultural exports such as olive oil, citrus, and tomatoes plummeted, while small-scale food production for local consumption increased. Jordanian funds were substantially withdrawn from the West Bank. Severe economic hardship spread throughout the territories. The recession in Israel further reduced the number of jobs available to Palestinians.

Nonetheless in 1989 the intifada began to reshape the structure of the Palestine economy, especially in separating it from the Israeli economy. A leading West Bank economist activist wrote: "The intifada is giving people an opportunity to cleanse themselves economically, to break connections with Israel. Before, some businessmen would have been against the creation of two states. Now, they have economic reasons as well as political reasons to support it."[43]

The Palestinian boycott of Israeli goods has stimulated shifts in business toward import substitution in food and light industry, many of which are inefficient and counterproductive. Yet Palestinian activists believe that may help at least to lay the groundwork for independence.

The psychological effect of economic disengagement may be more significant for Palestinian nation building than it is for economic development. According to Meron Benvenisti, "If they [the Palestinians] think they can cut themselves off from the Israeli economy and pursue independent development, it's premature and the whole approach is childish. This is not economic development, it is an economy mobilized for political aims."[44]

CONCLUSION

Starr concluded her study of development diplomacy with advice for American authorities: "Above all, the United States should recognize that the West Bank and Gaza systems . . . have stagnated in an environment of politically spawned underdevelopment for the last forty years under Israeli, Jordanian, or Egyptian administration."[45]

The record suggests a somewhat different conclusion. Given the priorities Israel had to assign to national security; a national administrative competence undermined by the realities of coalition government in a multiparty system based on an extreme form of proportional representation; the predominance of the public sector over the private sector in the Israeli economy; and the heavy burdens of immigrant absorption, welfare needs, and the development of human resources; the improvement in Palestinian living standards under military occupation is wholly remarkable. If, during the two decades from 1967 to 1987, some Palestinians in the West Bank or in the diaspora had held out territorial compromise as a basis for peace negotiations with Israel, Israel's policies as occupier might have accommodated greater efforts to develop a more viable Palestinian economy.

The unsurprising conclusion about economic development in the context of military occupation is that political and related military considerations have shaped the economic policies of the parties. In Israel's case, given its perception of the requirements of democratic survival in a hostile region of the globe, the overall impact of its policies on economic development has been about as satisfactory as circumstances permitted. Any serious approach to economic development of the West Bank and Gaza with the objective of strengthening the infrastructure of Palestinian statehood requires a stable and less threatening political environment and a substantial lessening of mutual distrust and hatred between Israelis and Arabs.

NOTES

1. A collection of Dayan's interviews and speeches can be found in *Mappa Hadasha, Yehassim Aherim* (A new map, different relations) (Tel Aviv: Ma'ariv Books and Shikmona Publishers, 1969).

2. Shlomo Gazit, *Ha-Makel ve Ha-Gezer* (The stick and the carrot) (Tel Aviv: Zmora, Bitan, 1985), 64. General Gazit was the coordinator of government operations in the territories from 1967 to 1974. Quoted in Menahem Milson,

"Israel's Policy in the West Bank and the Gaza Strip" (Colloquium paper, Wood-row Wilson International Center for Scholars, Washington, D.C., June 8, 1985), 11–12.

3. Milson, "Israel's Policy," 14.

4. Shlomo Gazit, "The Occupied Territories: Policy and Practice," *Ma'arachot* (monthly journal of the Israeli army), January 1970, quoted in Milson, "Israel's Policy," 18.

5. Ibid., 18.

6. Ibid., 19.

7. Ibid., 31.

8. Moshe Ater, ed., "Propping up the West Bank," *The Jerusalem Post*, Week-end Magazine, August 11, 1967, 7.

9. Ibid.

10. Moshe Ater, ed., *The Jerusalem Post Magazine–June War Anniversary*, June 6, 1969, 11.

11. Ibid.

12. For example, see David Krivine, "West Bank Farmers Go Mod," *The Je-rusalem Post Magazine*, March 28, 1969, 7.

13. James Feron, "Yigal Allon Has Supporters, Moshe Dayan Has Disciples," *The New York Times Magazine*, April 27, 1969, 92.

14. Ibid.

15. Moshe Dayan, "We Must Not Return to the Old Map," trans. Stanley Hochman, *The New York Times Magazine*, June 8, 1969, 32.

16. Ibid.

17. Ibid.

18. Shabtai Teveth, *The Cursed Blessing* (London: Schocken, 1969). See also Teveth, *Moshe Dayan: The Soldier, the Man, the Legend* (London: Weidenfeld and Nicolson, 1972), 341–59.

19. Teveth, *Moshe Dayan*, 350.

20. Ibid., 350–51.

21. Ibid., 351.

22. Moshe Dayan, "A Human Life for the Refugees," *The Jerusalem Post*, Au-gust 27, 1971, 4.

23. Ibid.

24. Ibid., 6.

25. For a full account of Order 947, "Israel Defense Forces Order Concerning the Establishment of a Civil Administration," see Joel Singer, "The Establishment of a Civil Administration in the Areas Administered by Israel," *Israel Yearbook on Human Rights*, vol. 12 (1982): 259–89.

26. Meron Benvenisti, *The West Bank Data Project: A Survey of Israel's Policies* (Washington, D.C.: American Enterprise Institute), 44.

27. Meron Benvenisti, *1986 Report: Demographic, Economic, Legal, Social and Political Developments in the West Bank* (Jerusalem: *The Jerusalem Post*, 1986), 5.

28. The data in this section are taken from Benvenisti, *1986 Report*, Chapter 2, 5–25.

29. A useful source of data and analysis on economic developments in the 1970s is Raphael Meron, *Economic Development in Judea, Samaria and the Gaza District: Economic Growth and Structural Change 1970–80* (Jerusalem: Bank of Israel

Research Department, May 1983). Similarly for 1981–82, see Dan Zakal, *Economic Developments in Judea-Samaria and the Gaza District, 1981–82* (Jerusalem: Bank of Israel Research Department, April 1985).

30. Joyce R. Starr, *Development Diplomacy: U.S. Economic Assistance to the West Bank and Gaza* (Washington, D.C.: The Washington Institute for Near East Policy, 1989), 31.

31. Edgar Harrell, "The West Bank's Potential Peacemakers," *The Wall Street Journal*, January 29, 1988, A10.

32. Ibid.

33. Benvenisti, *The West Bank Data Project*, 16.

34. Starr, *Development Diplomacy*, 19.

35. Ibid., 21.

36. These data come from Benvenisti, *1986 Report*, 19–20 and Starr, *Development Diplomacy*, 2–10, 44–46.

37. Its members included Philip Klutznick, Howard Squadron, Najeeb Halaby, William Baroody, Lester Crown, Jay Pritzker, Robert Arnow, Steven Shalom, Henry Kaufman, and other prominent executives.

38. *The Jerusalem Post*, November 10, 1984.

39. *The New York Times*, February 25, 1985.

40. Herbert Stein, "Economic Opportunities in Palestine." *The Wall Street Journal*, editorial page, September 20, 1983.

41. Harrell, "The West Bank's Potential Peacemakers."

42. Starr, *Development Diplomacy*.

43. Quoted in Jackson Diehl, "Boycott Spurs Palestinian Business," *The Washington Post*, September 8, 1989, 25–26.

44. Ibid., 26.

45. Starr, *Development Diplomacy*, 43.

Appendixes

A: Official Knesset Election Results, 1984 and 1988

Party	Votes Received		Seats	
	1984	1988	1984	1988
Likud	661,302	709,305	41	40
Labor Alignment	724,074	685,363	44	39
SHAS	63,605	107,709	4	6
Agudat Israel	36,079	102,714	2	5
Citizens Rights Movement	49,698	97,513	3	5
National Religious Party	73,530	89,720	4	5
Democratic Front for Peace		84,032		4
Tehiya	88,037	70,730	5	3
Mapam		56,345		3
Tzomet		45,849		2
Moledet		44,174		2
Shinui	54,747	39,538	3	2
Degel HaTorah		34,279		2
Progressive List for Peace	38,012	33,695	2	1
Arab Democratic Party		27,012		1
Rakah	69,815		4	
Yahad	46,302		3	
Morasha	33,287		2	
TAMI	31,103		1	
Kach	25,907		1	
Ometz	23,845		1	

B: Composition of the Twenty-Third Government of Israel, December 1988

Yitzhak Shamir	Prime Minister (Likud)
	Minister of Labor and Social Affairs
Shimon Peres	Vice-Premier (Labor)
	Minister of Finance
Yitzhak Navon	Deputy Prime Minister (Labor)
	Minister of Education and Culture
David Levy	Deputy Prime Minister (Likud)
	Minister of Construction and Housing
Moshe Arens	Minister of Foreign Affairs (Likud)
Haim Bar-Lev	Minister of Police (Labor)
Arye Deri	Minister of the Interior (SHAS)
Rafael Edri	Minister without Portfolio (Labor)
Mordechai Gur	Minister without Portfolio (Labor)
Zvulun Hammer	Minister of Religious Affairs (National Religious Party)
Moshe Katsav	Minister of Transport (Likud)
Avraham Katz-Oz	Minister of Agriculture (Labor)
Dan Meridor	Minister of Justice (Likud)
Ronnie Milo	Minister of the Environment (Likud)
Yitzhak Moda'i	Minister of Economics and Planning (Likud)
Moshe Nissim	Minister without Portfolio (Likud)
Ehud Olmert	Minister without Portfolio (Likud)
Gidon Patt	Minister of Tourism (Likud)
Yitzhak Haim Peretz	Minister of Immigrant Absorption (SHAS)
Yitzhak Rabin	Minister of Defense (Labor)
Moshe Shahal	Minister of Energy and Infrastructure (Labor)
Avner Hai Shaki	Minister without Portfolio (National Religious Party)
Ariel Sharon	Minister of Industry and Trade (Likud)
Yaakov Tsur	Minister of Health (Labor)
Ezer Weizman	Minister of Science and Development (Labor)
Gad Yaakobi	Minister of Communications (Labor)

C: Composition of the Twenty-Fourth Government of Israel, June 1990

Yitzhak Shamir	Prime Minister (Likud)
	Minister of Labor and Social Welfare*
	Minister of the Environment*
David Levy	Deputy Prime Minister (Likud)
	Minister of Foreign Affairs
Moshe Nissim	Deputy Prime Minister (Likud)
	Minister of Industry and Trade
Moshe Arens	Minister of Defense (Likud)
Arye Deri	Minister of the Interior (SHAS)
Rafael Eitan	Minister of Agriculture (Tzomet)
Zvulun Hammer	Minister of Education and Culture (National Religious Party)
Moshe Katsav	Minister of Transport (Likud)
David Magen	Minister of Economics and Planning (Likud)
Dan Meridor	Minister of Justice (Likud)
Ronnie Milo	Minister of Police (Likud)
Yitzhak Moda'i	Minister of Finance (Likud)
Yuval Ne'eman	Minister of Science and Development (Tehiya)
	Minister of Energy and Infrastructure
Ehud Olmert	Minister of Health (Likud)
Gidon Patt	Minister of Tourism (Likud)
Yitzhak Haim Peretz	Minister of Immigrant Absorption (SHAS)
Raphael Pinchasi	Minister of Communications (SHAS)
Avner Hai Shaki	Minister of Religious Affairs (National Religious Party)
Ariel Sharon	Minister of Construction and Housing (Likud)

*Temporarily held by the prime minister

D: Vote of Confidence, March 1990

Party	Yes	No
Likud	40	
Labor Alignment		39
SHAS	1	
Agudat Israel		5
Citizens Rights Movement		5
National Religious Party	5	
Democratic Front for Peace		4
Tehiya	3	
Mapam		3
Tzomet	2	
Moledet	2	
Shinui		2
Degel HaTorah	2	
Progressive List for Peace		1
Arab Democratic Party		1
Total	55	60

E: Votes for the Government Established June 1990

Party	Seats
Likud	40
SHAS	6
National Religious Party	5
Tehiya	3
Tzomet	2
Moledet	2
Degel HaTorah	2
Ephraim Gur	1
Eliezer Mizrachi (Agudat Israel)	1

F: Program of the Government of Israel, December 1988

At the center of the activity of the National Unity Government presented to the 12th Knesset are the following tasks:

1. (a) Recognition of the shared fate and common struggle of the Jewish people in the homeland and the diaspora;

   (b) A sustained effort to create the social, economic, and spiritual conditions to achieve the State of Israel's central objective—the return of the diaspora Jews to their homeland;

   (c) Boosting immigration from all countries, encouraging immigration from Western countries, and consistently striving to save persecuted Jews by bringing them to safety and realizing their right to immigrate to Israel.

2. The central political objectives during this period are: Continuing and extending the peace process in the region, consolidating the peace with Egypt, and ensuring the security of the northern settlements.

3. (a) The government will act to cultivate friendly relations and mutual ties between Israel and all peace-loving nations;

   (b) The government will continue to foster the deepening of ties of friendship and understanding between the United States and Israel;

   (c) The government will strive for a resumption of diplomatic relations with the Soviet Union and with the countries that have severed their ties with Israel.

4. Israel's foreign and defense policies will aim to ensure the nation's independence, to better its security, and to establish peace with its neighbors.

5. The government will strive to increase the strength, deterrent capability, and the endurance of the IDF against any military threat, and will take firm action against terror, regardless of its source. The IDF and other security forces will continue to act firmly to curtail the unrest, to prevent violence, to restore order, and to assure the safety of the inhabitants.

6. United Jerusalem, Israel's eternal capital, is one indivisible city under Israeli sovereignty; free access to their holy places and freedom of worship will continue to be guaranteed to members of all faiths.

7. The government will continue to place its desire for peace at the head of its concerns and will spare no effort to promote peace.

8. The government will work to promote and strengthen mutual ties with Egypt in accordance with the peace treaty. The government will call upon Egypt to fulfill its part of the peace treaty with Israel, and to give it substance and content in keeping with the spirit of the treaty and the intentions of its signatories.

9. The government will work to continue the peace process in keeping with the framework for peace in the Middle East agreed upon at Camp David, and to resume negotiations to give full autonomy to the Arab residents of Judea, Samaria, and the Gaza District.

10. Israel will call on Jordan to begin peace negotiations, in order to begin a new page in the region, for the sake of the region's development and prosperity. The Israeli government will consider proposals for negotiations.

11. The Arabs of Judea, Samaria, and the Gaza District will participate in determining their future, as stipulated in the Camp David accords. Israel will encourage representatives of the Arabs of Judea, Samaria, and Gaza to take part in the peace process.

12. Israel will oppose the establishment of an additional Palestinian state in the Gaza District, and in the area between Israel and Jordan.

13. Israel will not negotiate with the PLO.

14. During the term of the unity government, there will be no change in the sovereignty over Judea, Samaria, and the Gaza District except with the consent of the Alignment and the Likud.

15. (a) The existence and development of the settlements established by Israeli governments will be ensured (and the scope of their development will be decided on by the government); attached document "a" will specify various subjects on which there will be an agreement to implement them within this framework.

    (b) 3–8 settlements will be set up within one year (the names will be spelled out in attached document "b").

    (c) The settlements specified in attached document "c" will be set up in the following years on dates to be agreed on between the prime minister and the vice prime minister (Likud-Alignment) toward the end of the first year.

16. The government will do everything necessary to ensure peace for the Galilee.

17. The socioeconomic policy will work to:

    (a) Reduce the country's economic dependence by reducing the balance of payments deficit, increasing exports, and reducing imports;

    (b) Stabilize the economy by checking inflation;

    (c) Renew economic growth while maintaining full employment;

    (d) Change the structure of the economy by enlarging and strengthening the export and productive sectors, and reducing the proportion of public and administrative services and government involvement;

    (e) Encourage and extend the settlement areas and develop towns throughout the country; distribute the (economic) burden fairly among all sectors of the public; and adequately maintain the systems of education, health, and housing.

18. To achieve these goals, the government will work to:

    (a) Reduce public, civilian, and defense expenditure and consumption, and curb private consumption;

    (b) Reach a socioeconomic agreement with the Histadrut, the employers, and other factors in the economy.

    (c) Encourage various kinds of national saving;

(d) Promote and develop the capital market by gradually reducing the government's role therein;

(e) Reform the taxation system in order to encourage productivity, expand tax collection, and provide for just distribution of the tax burden.

(f) Provide support for the basic commodities so as to ensure regular supply, and as a means of agricultural planning while striving for a fixed rate of consumer price supports;

(g) Solve the grave condition of the retarded, children up to the age of 14 in boarding schools, and juvenile delinquents in jail.

19. The government will act to:

(a) Expand the infrastructure for technological services and render it more efficient; develop industries, increase investment, and establish high technology enterprises;

(b) Bolster agriculture and increase exports of agricultural produce;

(c) Encourage domestic and incoming tourism;

(d) Maintain housing policies designed to absorb new immigrants and provide housing for young couples and large families;

(e) Build rental apartments at reasonable rents, especially for young couples and large families;

(f) Expand and intensify Project Renewal;

(g) The government will act to implement an overall reform in civil service, placing a special emphasis on its duty to improve the services extended to citizens.

20. The government will help sectors with national-social priority, including the settlement sector (in the framework of a recovery program), and development towns population.

21. The government will act to prevent emigration and to bring back to their homeland those citizens who have left.

22. The government will act to continue the development of the Arab and Druse sectors, and to complete masterplans for the Arab and Druse settlements, in order to enable future construction in accordance with the masterplans.

23. Special efforts will be made to integrate educated minority group members into government service and into various public institutions, in order to advance their participation in state and public responsibility.

24. The government will look into the issue of the Moslem religious trusts.

25. The principle of national ownership of the land will be preserved. A ministerial committee will be established to deal with exceptional cases.

26. The government will decide concerning the sale of business assets owned by the state.

27. The socioeconomic policy will be based on a comprehensive program which will be brought to the knowledge of the Knesset and the public, and will be implemented in a coordinated and consistent manner to attain its goals.

28. The government will continue to act to guarantee full equality of rights to all inhabitants, regardless of race, creed, nationality, sex, or ethnic origin.

29. The government will act to implement a reform of local government.

30. (a) The government will act to eliminate crime and violence and to instill recognition of the primacy of the rule of law;

    (b) The police capability to fight crime in all its manifestations will be bolstered.

31. In order to bolster the state's democratic regime, and also to increase the government's ability to operate as a link between the electorate and the elected, the possibility of changing the government and election systems will be examined.

32. The unity of the nation and the proper functioning of society require the fostering of mutual tolerance and freedom of conscience and religion. The government will prevent all religious or antireligious coercion from any quarter; will guarantee public religious needs via the state; will maintain freedom of religion and conscience for all the non-Jewish communities; will supply their religious needs at public expense; and will assure a religious education for all children whose parents desire it.

33. The status quo in matters of religion in the state will be preserved.

34. Education will be founded on the eternal values of the Jewish people.

35. The government will carry out all the international commitments of the State of Israel.

G: Program of the Government of Israel, June 1990

The following is the agreed program of the proposed government's policies:

At the center of the activities of the national government being presented to the Knesset, will stand the following programs:

1. (a) In recognition of a shared fate and of the common struggle for the existence of the Jewish people in Eretz Yisrael and in the Diaspora, and in order to realize the central goal of the State of Israel—the ingathering of the Jewish people to its land—the government will place immigration and absorption foremost among its national objectives.

   (b) The government will act to accelerate immigration from all lands and will act to save persecuted Jews.

   (c) The government will act to create the social, economic, and spiritual conditions for the speedy and successful absorption of the immigrants in their homeland.

2. The eternal right of the Jewish people to Eretz Yisrael is not subject to question, and is intertwined with its right to security and peace.

3. The central political goals of the government in this period will be: ensuring the independence and sovereignty of the state, strengthening security, preventing war, and achieving peace with all its neighbors. To these ends, the government will act as follows:

   (a) The government will be vigilant in increasing the strength of the IDF, its power of deterrence and its fitness to withstand threats from the states of the region, including threats of unconventional missile weaponry.

   (b) The government will act forcefully against terrorism, from all sources. The IDF and other security forces will act emphatically and with perseverence to ensure peace for all residents, to uproot the phenomenon of violence and disturbances and to generate calm throughout the country.

   (c) The government will place the desire for peace at the top of its concerns and will not spare any effort in the advancement of peace.

   (d) The government will act for the continuation of the peace process along the lines of the framework for peace in the Middle East, agreed upon at Camp David, and of its peace initiative of May 5, 1989, in its entirety.

   (e) Israel will encourage representatives of the Arabs of Judea, Samaria, and Gaza to take part in the peace process.

   (f) Israel will oppose the establishment of another Palestinian state in the Gaza Strip and in the territory between Israel and the Jordan River.

   (g) Israel will not negotiate with the PLO, directly or indirectly.

   (h) Israel will call upon all the Arab states to enter into peace negotiations in order to turn over a new leaf in the region, so that it may prosper and flourish.

(i) The government will act for the futherance and strengthening of bilateral relations with Egypt in accordance with the peace treaty between the two states. The government will call upon Egypt to fulfill its obligations as set forth in the peace treaty with Israel, including its commitments laid out in the Camp David accords, and to bestow upon the peace treaty meaning and content as per its clauses, spirit, and the intentions of its signatories.

(j) (1) The government will act to foster relations of friendship and mutual ties between Israel and all countries which seek peace.

    (2) The government will continue to maintain the relations of friendship and understanding which exist between the United States and Israel and will seek to deepen them in all areas, including strategic cooperation.

    (3) The government will continue the movement of renewing diplomatic relations with the countries of Eastern Europe and other regions, especially with the Soviet Union, and will seek to establish diplomatic relations with China.

(k) United Jerusalem, Israel's eternal capital, is one indivisible under Israeli sovereignty; members of all faiths will always be ensured freedom of worship and access to their holy sites.

Jerusalem will not be included in the framework of autonomy which will be granted to the Arab residents of Judea, Samaria and the Gaza Strip, and its Arab residents will not participate, either as voters or as candidates, in elections for the establishment of representation of the residents of Judea, Samaria and the Gaza Strip.

4. Settlement in all parts of Eretz Yisrael is the right of our people and an integral part of national security; the government will act to strengthen settlement, to broaden and develop it.

5. In the wake of rising expressions of anti-Semitism in various countries of the world, the government will act, in concert with enlightened governments and with Jewish communities and other bodies in the continuing struggle against these phenomena.

6. In the area of socioeconomic policy, the government will act:

(a) To maintain the stability of the economy and further reduce inflation.

(b) For lasting economic expansion and a reduction of unemployment in order to achieve full employment.

(c) To lessen the economic dependence of the state by reducing the deficit in the balance of payments.

(d) To change the structure of the economy in order to build it on a competitive base and to lessen the role of the public sector and government involvement.

(e) To ensure private enterprise, equal opportunity, and the promotion and welfare of the individual while safeguarding his rights and freedoms.

(f) For the encouragement, strengthening, and advancement of the development towns and regions of the Galilee, Negev, Judea, Samaria, and the rest of Eretz Yisrael so that they may fulfill their important national role.

(g) For the just distribution of the [national] burden among the various sectors of the public, the improvement of the situation of the weaker classes, and the proper functioning of the education, health, housing, and other welfare services.

(h) For a solution to the severe plight of the mentally retarded, children under 14 in boarding institutions, and juvenile delinquents in jails.

7. In order to achieve these goals, the government will act:

(a) For cuts in public consumption while ensuring the required resources for the national program, most importantly immigrant absorption.

(b) To achieve socioeconomic agreement with the Histadrut, employers, and other factors in the economy.

(c) To encourage national saving in its various forms.

(d) To continue reform in the money market, for its advancement and development, while reducing the role of the government therein.

(e) To continue tax reform in order to encourage production, to intensify collection and the just distribution of the burden of taxation.

(f) To privatize government-owned corporations.

(g) To encourage the increase of efficiency and production.

8. The government will act:

(a) For the promotion of the education system and the development of basic and applied sciences and of international scientific cooperation.

(b) For the development and expansion of the road, communications, and technological infrastructures.

(c) For the establishment of a policy which will make adequate housing and appropriate employment possible for new immigrants, young couples, and families with many children.

(d) For the broadening and intensification of the program of Project Renewal.

(e) For the implementation of reform, including within the civil service, with special emphasis on the role of the public service in improving service to the citizen, in accordance with government decisions regarding the implementation of the Kovarsky Commission Report.

(f) For protection of the environment.

9. The government will act to avert the emigration of Jews from the country and to return them to their homeland.

10. The government will view the advancement of the status of women as a socioeconomic goal. The status of women vis-à-vis salaries and employment will be equated to that of men, and women will be integrated into the senior levels of the administration.

11. The government will continue to act to preserve full equal rights and obligations for all residents, regardless of religion, race, nationality, gender, or ethnic association.

12. The government will act to continue the development of Druze and Circasian villages, in accordance with government decision #373 of April 21, 1987, including providing the necessary resources.

13. The government will strive to continue the development of the Arab sector in all fields relating to the development of infrastructure, zoning and building plans, as well as the area of employment. The same will be done for their absorption in the various government ministries. The necessary resources will be provided for this purpose.

14. The government will act for the participation of all public bodies in the continuing and energetic struggle against road accidents.

15. The government will continue to battle the phenomenon of dangerous drugs, in all possible ways.

16. The government will act to implement reform in local government.

17. (a) The government will act to uproot crime and violence and to inculcate a recognition of the supremacy of the rule of law.

    (b) The ability of the police, the prosecutor, and the courts to fight crime in all its manifestations will be increased.

18. With a view toward strengthening democracy in the state, increasing both the capability of the government to act and the connection between the voter and his representative, the possibility of changing the system of government and the electoral system will be examined.

19. (a) The unity of the nation and proper social conditions require the fostering of mutual tolerance, the bringing together of the segments of the nation, and freedom of conscience and religion. The government will prevent all religious and antireligious coercion of all types; public religious needs will be guaranteed by the state and, on a basis of equality, religious education for all children whose parents so desire will be ensured.

    (b) Freedom of religion and conscience, including providing for religious needs, will be ensured for all ethnic groups.

20. The religious status quo in the state will be strictly preserved.

21. Education in Israel will be based on the eternal values of our nation: the Torah of Israel, love of the people Israel, and love of the homeland.

22. The government will foster an attitude of respect toward the heritage of Israel and will strengthen the ties between Israel and the diaspora.

23. The government will honor all the international commitments of the State of Israel.

Selected Bibliography

Noah L. Dropkin

BOOKS

Arian, Asher. *Politics in Israel: The Second Generation*. 2d ed. Chatham, N.J.: Chatham House, 1989.

Aronoff, Myron J. *Israeli Visions and Divisions*. New Brunswick, N.J.: Transaction Books, 1989.

Avineri, Shlomo. *The Making of Modern Zionism: Intellectual Origins of the Jewish State*. New York: Basic Books, 1981.

Badi, Joseph. *Religion in Israel Today: The Relationship Between State and Religion*. New York: Bookman, 1959.

Begin, Menachem. *The Revolt*. Rev. ed. New York: Nash, 1977.

Bell, J. Bowyer. *Terror out of Zion: IZL, Lechi, and the Palestine Underground, 1929–1949*. New York: St. Martin's Press, 1977.

Ben-Porath, Yoram, ed. *The Israeli Economy: Maturing Through Crises*. Cambridge, Mass.: Harvard University Press, 1986.

Ben-Raphael, Eliezer. *The Emergence of Ethnicity: Cultural Groups and Social Conflict in Israel*. Wesport, Conn.: Greenwood Press, 1982.

———. *Israel-Palestine: A Guerrilla Conflict in International Politics*. Westport, Conn.: Greenwood Press, 1987.

Caspi, Dan, Abraham Diskin, and Emmanuel Gutmann, eds. *The Roots of Begin's Success: The 1981 Israeli Elections*. New York: St. Martin's Press, 1984.

Drezon-Tepler, Marcia. *Interest Groups and Political Change in Israel*. Albany: State University of New York Press, 1990.

Efrat, Elisha, ed. *Geography and Politics in Israel since 1967*. London: Frank Cass, 1988.

Eisenstadt, S. N. *The Transformation of Israeli Society*. Boulder, Colo.: Westview Press, 1985.

Elazar, Daniel J. *Israel: Building a New Society*. Bloomington: Indiana University Press, 1986.

Elazar, Daniel J., and Chaim Kalchheim, eds. *Local Government in Israel*. Lanham, Md.: University Press of America, 1988.

Elazar, Daniel J., and Shmuel Sandler, eds. *Israel's Odd Couple: The Nineteen Eighty-Four Knesset Elections and the National Unity Government*. Detroit, Mich.: Wayne State University Press, 1990.

Freedman, Robert O. *Israel in the Begin Era*. New York: Praeger, 1982.

Friedlander, Dov, and Calvin Goldscheider. *The Population of Israel*. New York: Columbia University Press, 1979.

Friedman, Robert I. *The False Prophet: Rabbi Meir Kahane: From FBI Informant to Knesset Member*. Brooklyn, N.Y.: Lawrence Hill Books, 1990.

Gavron, Daniel. *Israel After Begin*. Boston: Houghton Mifflin, 1984.

Halevi, Nadav, and Ruth Klinov-Malul. *The Economic Development of Israel*. New York: Praeger, 1968.

Horowitz, Dan, and Moshe Lissak. *The Origins of the Israeli Polity*. Chicago: University of Chicago Press, 1978.

———. *Trouble in Utopia: The Overburdened Polity of Israel*. Albany: State University of New York Press, 1989.

Kieval, Gershon R. *Party Politics in Israel and the Occupied Territories*. Westport, Conn.: Greenwood Press, 1983.

Kimmerling, Baruch, ed. *The Israeli State and Society: Boundaries and Frontiers*. Albany: State University of New York Press, 1989.

Klieman, Aaron S. *Israel & the World after Forty Years*. Elmsford, N.Y.: Pergamon, 1989.

LeMay, Michael C., ed. *The Gatekeepers: Comparative Immigration Policy*. New York: Praeger, 1989.

Liebman, Charles S., and Eliezer Don-Yehiya. *Civil Religion in Israel: Traditional Judaism and Political Culture in the Jewish State*. Berkeley: University of California Press, 1983.

Luebbert, Gregory M. *Comparative Democracy: Policymaking and Governing Coalitions in Europe and Israel*. New York: Columbia University Press, 1986.

Mahler, Gregory S. *Israel: Government and Politics in a Maturing State*. New York: Harcourt Brace Jovanovich, 1989.

Medding, Peter Y. *Mapai in Israel: Political Organization and Government in a New Society*. Cambridge: Cambridge University Press, 1972.

———. *The Founding of Israeli Democracy, 1948–1967*. London: Oxford University Press, 1990.

Medding, Peter Y., ed. *Israel: State and Society, 1948–1988*. London: Oxford University Press, 1989.

Merhav, Peretz. *The Israeli Left*. New York: A. S. Barnes, 1980.

Newman, David. *Jewish Settlement in the West Bank: The Role of Gush Emunim*. Durham, England: University of Durham Press, 1982.

Newman, David. ed. *The Impact of Gush Emunim: Politics and Settlement in the West Bank*. London: Croom Helm and New York: St. Martin's Press, 1985.

Pack, Howard. *Structural Change and Economic Policy in Israel*. New Haven, Conn.: Yale University Press, 1971.

Patinkin, D. *The Israeli Economy: The First Decade.* Jerusalem: The Maurice Falk Institute for Economic Research in Israel, 1960.

Peleg, Ilan. *Begin's Foreign Policy, 1977–1983: Israel's Move to the Right.* Westport, Conn.: Greenwood Press, 1987.

Peleg, Ilan, and Ofira Seliktar, eds. *The Emergence of a Binational Israel: The Second Republic in the Making.* Boulder, Colo.: Westview Press, 1988.

Penniman, Howard R., and Daniel J. Elazar, eds. *Israel at the Polls, 1981: A Study of the Knesset Elections.* Washington, D.C.: American Enterprise Institute and Bloomington: Indiana University Press, 1986.

Peretz, Don. *The West Bank: History, Politics, Society and Economy.* Boulder, Colo.: Westview Press, 1986.

Peri, Yoram. *Between Battles and Ballots: Israeli Military in Politics.* New York: Cambridge University Press, 1984.

Perlmutter, Amos. *Military and Politics in Israel: Nation Building and Role Expansion.* New York: Praeger, 1969.

———. *Politics and Military in Israel, 1967–1977.* London: Frank Cass, 1978.

Raphael, Gideon. *Destination Peace: Three Decades of Israeli Foreign Policy.* New York: Stein and Day, 1981.

Reich, Bernard. *Israel: Land of Tradition and Conflict.* Boulder, Colo.: Westview Press, 1985.

Reich, Bernard, and Gershon R. Kieval, eds. *Israeli National Security Policy: Political Actors and Perspectives.* Westport, Conn.: Greenwood Press, 1988.

Reich, Bernard, and Gershon R. Kieval, eds. *Israel Faces the Future.* New York: Praeger, 1986.

Reiser, Stewart. *The Politics of Leverage: The National Religious Party of Israel and Its Influence on Foreign Policy.* Cambridge, Mass.: Center for Middle East Studies, Harvard University, 1984.

———. *The Israeli Arms Industry: Foreign Policy, Arms Transfers, and Military Doctrine of a Small State.* New York: Holmes & Meier, 1989.

Roberts, Samuel J. *Party and Policy in Israel: The Battle Between Hawks and Doves.* Boulder, Colo.: Westivew Press, 1990.

Roth, Stephen J., ed. *The Impact of the Six-Day War: A Twenty-Year Assessment.* New York: St. Martin's Press, 1988.

Rubner, Alex. *The Economy of Israel: A Critical Account of the First Ten Years.* New York: Praeger, 1960.

Safran, Nadav. *Israel: The Embattled Ally.* Cambridge, Mass.: Harvard University Press, 1978.

Sager, Samuel. *The Parliamentary System of Israel.* Syracuse, N.Y.: Syracuse University Press, 1985.

Sanbar, Moshe, ed. *Economic and Social Policy in Israel: The First Generation.* Lanham, Md.: University Press of America, 1990.

Schechtman, Joseph B. *Fighter and Prophet: The Vladimir Jabotinsky Story.* New York: Thomas Yoseloff, 1961.

Schechtman, Joseph B., and Yehuda Benari. *History of the Revisionist Movement.* Tel Aviv: Hadar, 1970.

Schiff, Gary S. *Tradition and Politics: The Religious Parties of Israel.* Detroit, Mich.: Wayne State University Press, 1977.

Schweitzer, Avraham. *Israel: The Changing National Agenda*. London: Croom Helm, 1986.

Seliktar, Ofira. *New Zionism and the Foreign Policy System of Israel*. London: Croom Helm, 1986.

Shalev, Michael. *Labour and the Political Economy in Israel*. London: Oxford University Press, 1989.

Sharkansky, Ira. *What Makes Israel Tick? How Domestic Policy-Makers Cope with Constraints*. Chicago: Nelson-Hall, 1985.

Shimshoni, Daniel. *Israeli Democracy: The Middle of a Journey*. New York: Free Press, 1982.

Shlaim, Avi. *The Politics of Partition: King Abdullah, the Zionists, and Partition, 1921– 1951*. New York: Columbia University Press, 1990.

Shokeid, Moshe, and Shlomo Deshen. *Distant Relations: Ethnicity and Politics among Arabs and North African Jews in Israel*. South Hadley, Mass.: J. F. Bergin Publishers, 1982.

Smooha, Sammy. *Israel: Pluralism and Conflict*. Berkeley: University of California Press, 1978.

Sprinzak, Ehud. *Gush Emunim: The Politics of Zionist Fundamentalism in Israel*. New York: American Jewish Committee, 1986.

Weingrod, Alex. *Studies in Israeli Ethnicity: After the Ingathering*. New York: Gordon and Breach, 1985.

Wolfsfeld, Gadi. *The Politics of Provocation: Participation and Protest in Israel*. Albany: State University of New York Press, 1988.

Yaacobi, Gad. *The Government of Israel*. New York: Praeger, 1982.

Yanai, Nathan. *Party Leadership in Israel*. Philadelphia: Turtledove Publishing, 1981.

Yaniv, Avner. *Dilemmas of Security: Politics, Strategy and the Israeli Experience in Lebanon*. London: Oxford University Press, 1987.

Zohar, David M. *Political Parties in Israel: The Evolution of Israeli Democracy*. New York: Praeger, 1974.

ARTICLES

Abramson, Paul R. "Generational Replacement, Ethnic Change, and Partisan Support in Israel." *Journal of Politics* 51 (August 1989): 545–74.

Arian, Asher. "Israeli Democracy 1984." *Journal of International Affairs* 38 (Winter 1985): 259–76.

Ben-Zadok, Efraim. "Incompatible Planning Goals: Evaluation of Israel's New Community Development in the West Bank." *American Planning Association Journal* 53 (Summer 1987): 337–47.

Brichta, Avraham, and Yair Zalmanovitch. "The Proposals for Presidential Government in Israel: A Case Study in the Possibility of Institutional Transference." *Comparative Politics* 19 (October 1986): 57–68.

Carmi, Shulamit, and Henry Rosenfeld. "The Emergence of Militaristic Nationalism in Israel." *International Journal of Politics, Culture, and Society* 3 (Fall 1989): 5–49.

Cohen, E. "Ethnicity and Legitimation in Contemporary Israel." *Jerusalem Quarterly* 28 (Summer 1983): 111–24.

Diskin, Abraham. "The Israeli General Election of 1988." *Electoral Studies* 8 (April 1989): 75–85.

Dowty, Alan. "The Use of Emergency Powers in Israel." *Middle East Review* 21 (Fall 1988): 34–46.

Eisenstadt, S. N. "Israeli Society Transformed." *Jerusalem Quarterly* 34 (Winter 1985): 50–58.

Freedman, Robert O. "Religion, Politics, and the Israeli Elections of 1988." *Middle East Journal* 43, no. 3 (Summer 1989): 406–22.

Friedlander, D., and C. Goldscheider. "Peace and the Demographic Future of Israel." *Journal of Conflict Resolution* 18 (Summer 1974): 486–501.

Galnoor, Itzhak. "The 1984 Elections in Israel: Political Results and Open Questions." *Middle East Review* 18 (Summer 1986): 51–58.

Hadar, Leon T. "The Decline and Fall of the Israeli Labor Party." *World and I* 5 (March 1990): 598–615.

Hertzberg, Arthur. "The Religious Right in the State of Israel." *Annals of the American Academy* 483 (January 1986): 84–92.

Inbar, Ephraim. "Attitudes Toward War in the Israeli Political Elite." *Middle East Journal* 44 (Summer 1990): 431–45.

Inbar, Michael, and Ephraim Yuchtman-Yaar. "The People's Image of Conflict Resolution: Israelis and Palestinians." *Journal of Conflict Resolution* 33 (March 1989): 37–66.

Lewis, Samuel W. "Israel: The Peres Era and Its Legacy." *Foreign Affairs* 65, no. 3 (1987): 582–610.

———. "Israeli Political Reality and the Search for Middle East Peace." *School of Advanced International Studies Review* 7 (Winter/Spring 1987): 67–80.

Lustick, Ian S. "Israel's Dangerous Fundamentalists." *Foreign Policy* (Fall 1987): 118–39.

Marcus, Jonathan. "The Politics of Israel's Security." *International Affairs* 65 (Spring 1989): 233–46.

Melman, Yossi. "Domestic Factors and Foreign Policy in the Arab-Israeli Conflict." *Washington Quarterly* 9 (Summer 1986): 33–42.

Newman, David. "Civilian and Military Presence as Strategies of Territorial Control: The Arab-Israel Conflict." *Political Geography Quarterly* 8 (July 1989): 215–27.

Oren, S. "Continuity and Change in Israel's Religious Parties." *Middle East Journal* 27 (Winter 1973): 36–54.

Peretz, Don, and Sammy Smooha. "Israel's Twelfth Knesset Election: An All-Loser Game." *Middle East Journal* 43, no. 3 (Summer 1989): 388–405.

Reich, Bernard. "Israel's Year of Transition." *Current History* 86 (February 1987): 69–72, 87–88.

———. "Israel at Forty." *Current History* 87 (February 1988): 65–68, 88–89.

Reshef, Yonatan. "Political Exchange in Israel: Histadrut-State Relations." *Industrial Relations* 25 (Fall 1986): 303–19.

Richman, Alvin. "American Attitudes Toward Israeli-Palestinian Relations in the Wake of the Uprising." *Public Opinion Quarterly* 53 (Fall 1989): 415–30.

Roumani, Maurice M. "The Sephardi Factor in Israeli Politics." *Middle East Journal* 42 (Summer 1988): 423–35.

Sanbar, Moshe. "The Political Economy of Israel, 1948–1987." *International Problems* 27 (Summer 1988): 63–78.

Sharkansky, Ira. "Who Gets What Amidst High Inflation: Winners and Losers in the Israeli Budget, 1978–84." *Public Budgeting and Finance* 5 (Winter 1985): 64–74.

Weissbrod, Doron, and Lilly Weissbrod. "Inflation in Israel: The Economic Cost of Political Legitimation." *Journal of Social Political and Economic Studies* 11 (Summer 1986): 201–26.

Will, Donald S. "The Impending Polarization of Israeli Society." *Arab Studies Quarterly* 8 (Summer 1986): 231–52.

Yanai, Nathan. "Critical Aspects of the 1984 Elections in Israel: The Crisis of Coalition-Forming Politics and the Government of National Unity." *Journal of International and Area Studies* 1 (Fall 1986): 151–74.

Index

World Jewry Solidarity Conference, 32–33
World Zionist Organization, 100

Yaacovson, Zvi, 82
Yahad, 53, 99
Yishuv, 1

Yom Kippur War (1973), 10–11, 59, 63
Yosef, Ovadia, 22, 81, 82, 83

Ze'evi, Rehavam, 19
Zionism, 96, 99, 111, 115
Zucker, Dedi, 90

About the Editors
and Contributors

ASHER ARIAN is Professor of Political Science at the Graduate School of the City University of New York. Among his many works are *Ideological Change in Israel* (1968) and *The Choosing People: Voting Behavior in Israel* (1973) as well as a series of edited books on Israeli elections.

MARVER H. BERNSTEIN served as Professor in the School of Foreign Service at Georgetown University in Washington, D.C., and as a former Dean of the Woodrow Wilson School of Public and International Affairs of Princeton University in Princeton, New Jersey, and President of Brandeis University in Waltham, Massachusetts. He is the author of numerous works including *The Politics of Israel* (1957).

NOAH L. DROPKIN is a Ph.D. candidate and a graduate teaching fellow in the Department of Political Science at the George Washington University, in Washington, D.C.

DANIEL J. ELAZAR is Professor of Political Science at Bar-Ilan University in Tel Aviv, Israel, Director of the Center for the Study of Federalism at Temple University, Philadelphia, Pennsylvania, and President of the Jerusalem Center for Public Affairs in Jerusalem, Israel. His numerous books include *The Jewish Polity* (1985).

CALVIN GOLDSCHEIDER is Professor of Judaic Studies and Sociology and a Faculty Associate of the Population Studies and Training Center at Brown University in Providence, Rhode Island. Among his most recent books are: *The Population of Israel* (1979), *The Transformation of the Jews* (1984), and *Jewish Continuity and Change: Emerging Patterns in America* (1986). He is completing a book on *Israel's Changing Society: Population, Ethnicity and Development*.

FRED GOTTHEIL teaches in the Department of Economics at the University of Illinois in Urbana.

GERSHON R. KIEVAL is Adjunct Professor in the Department of Political Science at George Washington University in Washington, D.C. He is the author of *Party Politics in Israel and the Occupied Territories* (1983), co-author of *Israel Faces the Future* (1986), and co-editor of *Israeli National Security Policy: Political Actors and Perspectives* (1988).

BERNARD REICH is Professor of Political Science and International Affairs at George Washington University in Washington, D.C. He is the author of *Quest for Peace: United States–Israel Relations and the Arab-Israeli Conflict* (1977), *The United States and Israel: Influence in the Special Relationship* (1984), and *Israel: Land of Tradition and Conflict* (1985), as well as co-author of *Israel Faces the Future* (1986) and co-editor of *Israeli National Security Policy* (1988), among other works.

STEWART REISER is a faculty associate at the Center for Middle Eastern Studies and Committee on Degrees in Social Studies at Harvard University, Cambridge, Massachusetts. He is the author of *The Politics of Leverage: The National Religious Party of Israel and Its Influence on Foreign Policy* (1984), *The Israeli Arms Industry: Foreign Policy, Arms Transfers and Military Doctrine of a Small State* (1989), and various articles on Middle Eastern politics.

IRA SHARKANSKY is Professor of Political Science and Public Administration at The Hebrew University of Jerusalem.

CHAIM I. WAXMAN, Professor of Sociology at Rutgers University, New Brunswick, New Jersey, has written widely in the areas of political sociology and the sociology of religion and ethnicity, with particular emphasis on the sociology of American Jews and Israeli society and culture.